Acadian to Cajun

Louisiana in 1866. Courtesy of *Harper's Weekly*, 3 February 1866.

ACADIAN TO CAJUN

Transformation of a People, 1803–1877

CARL A. BRASSEAUX

UNIVERSITY PRESS OF MISSISSIPPI
Jackson & London

Copyright © 1992 by the University Press of Mississippi
All rights reserved
Manufactured in the United States of America

95 94 93 92   4 3 2 1

The paper in this book meets the guidelines for permanence and durability
of the Committee on Production Guidelines for Book Longevity of the
Council on Library Resources.

Library of Congress Cataloging-in-Publication Data

Brasseaux, Carl A.
    Acadian to Cajun : transformation of a people, 1803–1877 / Carl A.
Brasseaux.
       p.   cm.
    Includes index.
    ISBN 0-87805-582-7 (cloth).—ISBN 0-87805-583-5 (paper)
    1. Cajuns—History—19th century.   2. Louisiana—History—
1803–1865.   I. Title.
F380.A2B7   1992
976.3'0041—dc20   92-17759
                                                            CIP

British Library Cataloging-in-Publication data available

TO

PERCY JOHNSON, SR.

AND THE LATE

NITA DIES JOHNSON

OF CHURCH POINT

Un peuple sans passé est un peuple sans futur.
—Antoine Bourque, acceptance speech, induction into the
Ordre des Palmes Académiques, July 1991

Contents

INTRODUCTION   xi

1. *Emergence of Classes in the Antebellum Period*   3

2. *Acadian Folk Life in the Nineteenth Century*   20

3. *Acadians and Politics, 1803–1860*   45

4. *Secession Crisis and the Civil War*   58

5. *Declining Economic Fortunes in Postbellum Louisiana*   74

6. *Cultural Integration, Transformation, and Regeneration*   89

7. *Politics and Violence in the Reconstruction Era*   112

CONCLUSION   150

APPENDIX   155

NOTES   185

BIBLIOGRAPHY   225

INDEX   243

Introduction

Because of the lingering influence of Henry Wadsworth Longfellow's *Evangeline,* students of Acadian history have been aware of the dispersal of Nova Scotia's Acadian population in 1755, the group's subsequent wanderings, and the reestablishment of one group of exiles in Louisiana's bayou country. The transformation of the exiles' transplanted culture in this new and radically different subtropical environment, however, has been largely overlooked by scholars of Acadiana. This work is the first to examine comprehensively the demographic growth, cultural evolution, and political involvement of Louisiana's large Acadian community during the nineteenth century.

The product of twelve years of intensive effort, this book was spawned by an interest in the Acadian involvement in the Civil War. It soon became apparent, however, that the Acadians' wartime experiences could be understood only from the vantage point of a much broader chronological perspective. The present study thus examines the evolution of three generations of Acadian society. Beginning with the Louisiana Purchase in 1803, when the transplanted culture began to take on a decidedly Louisiana character, the investigation extends to 1877, the end of Reconstruction in Louisiana, by which time ascriptive distinctions between Acadians and neighboring groups had become blurred, giving rise to the creation of a new people—the Cajuns.

The latter development serves as a major watershed in the society's metamorphosis from an imported culture into the distinctly local and modern cultural synthesis now called Cajun. Tracing the course of the Acadian community's cultural and social peregrinations is difficult because of the dearth of traditional primary source materials. Only a handful of contemporary south Louisiana newspapers exist, and the literate Cajun minority of the early and mid-nineteenth century left little personal correspondence and virtually no diaries. As a result, Acadian/Cajun historians must seek alternative resources.

Perhaps the most abundant materials are the civil records housed in south Louisiana's parish courthouses. Consisting primarily of conveyance, mortgage, probate, and judicial registers, these civil instruments amply document the material culture and the commonplace business dealings of persons of all walks of life and social status. In addition, they shed considerable light on Acadian/Cajun real estate holdings, movable property holdings, involvement in agribusiness, use of credit, and indebtedness to the state's then primitive banking system. Finally, the civil records help to verify the socioeconomic standing of individuals listed in the decennial federal census reports, records of occasionally dubious accuracy.

The population, slave, and agricultural schedules of Louisiana's nineteenth-century census reports must be approached warily because local census takers, often political hacks, were notoriously careless. Individuals residing some distance from the main roads were routinely ignored. The amount of information about households also varied from parish to parish. These perennial problems were compounded by the open hostility of many whites toward Republicans named to compile the 1870 census of south Louisiana. Enrollment of farmers in the agricultural census reports was also occasionally haphazard. These factors, coupled with periodic rural resistance to census takers, make the accuracy of the compilations a matter of considerable scholarly debate.

Despite their manifold problems, decennial federal census reports afford researchers the most comprehensive available view of nineteenth-century Acadian/Cajun society. The population schedules, which list only the free population in the antebellum period, generally provide data regarding settlement patterns, socioeconomic status, real wealth, movable property, and literacy. Slave schedules help to identify the nature of the movable property indicated in the population schedules. Finally the agricultural schedules of 1850–70 provide the best available insight into the land development, land usage, agricultural pursuits, and ranching practices of contemporary Acadian/Cajun farmers. Together, the component schedules of the decennial census reports provide many crucial pieces of the fragmentary documentary mosaic.

Decennial census reports and the civil records are complemented by south Louisiana's ecclesiastical records. Unlike many contemporary Protestant records of the Deep South, south Louisiana's Catholic birth, marriage, and burial registers provide a wealth of genealogical information, allowing historical researchers to determine patterns of intermarriage and, to a limited extent, the role of mothers as transmitters of culture and religion. The registers also permit historians to gauge the religiosity of the Cajuns by tracking their seasonal pilgrimages to local churches and chapels.

Acts of Louisiana's general assembly and the parish police juries shed considerable light on Acadian/Cajun business activities and the growing regional concerns regarding the "peculiar institution." The acts of the state legislature occasionally identify the chief stockholders in Louisiana's major businesses and banks chartered before the Civil War. These charters usually name not only the businesses' chief stockholders but their local and regional agents as well. Legislation passed in the wake of slave uprisings and police jury ordinances establishing slave patrols and restrictions on slave movements speak volumes about race relations in the Cajun parishes on the eve of the War Between the States.

Finally, ward and parish electoral returns, when used in conjunction with decennial census returns, provide considerable evidence not only regarding Acadian/Cajun participation in the political process but also their attitudes regarding the major issues of the day. Police jury minutes, census reports, local newspapers, the journals of Louisiana's general assembly, and the biographical directories of Congress provide abundant evidence regarding Acadian/Cajun officeholding at the local, parish, state, and national levels.

When taken individually, these varied documentary resources provide a shallow, one-dimensional view of nineteenth-century Acadian/Cajun society. Taken together, however, they afford a broad view of a largely nonliterate people whose contemporary oral traditions are now all but forgotten. Indeed, despite problems, the civil records and the census reports remain the most important extant resources for the study of nineteenth-century Acadian demographic, social, and economic history.

Surnames provide the most effective guide to Acadian materials in the documentary collections, but, by 1877, surnames were no longer an accurate cultural guidepost for Acadians of all economic strata. By that time, many members of the upperclass no longer considered themselves Acadian, with more than a little justification. Aside from their biological ties to the Acadian community, these upwardly mobile individuals experienced little contact with their mother culture, which they consciously avoided while doing everything possible to become full participants in the Anglo-American mainstream.

Outsiders quickly came to identify downwardly mobile elements of other local white ethnic groups with the dominant ethnic group in their humble socioeconomic niche—the Cajuns. Through intermarriage, these newcomers were rapidly drawn into the Cajun community. But the numerous cross-cultural marriages, particularly in the early postbellum era, influenced the Cajun community as much as they did the smaller groups that were absorbed. The cultural interchanges born of these unions transformed the Cajun community, producing, in the process, a new people. This new community would create a cultural synthesis based on traditional Acadian values but including numerous cultural, culinary, linguistic, and musical elements of the group's adopted members.

The focus of any study tracing the course of sociocultural evolution is ultimately determined by the fragmentary documentary record. I have attempted to examine as many facets of the culture's development as the historical evidence will permit. In studying these historical materials, I have attempted to answer many riddles that have been ignored by scholars who have too long viewed Louisiana's Acadian/Cajuns as a monolithic people. Such simplistic views have distorted outsiders' perceptions of the Cajuns. Members of the community, however, have long been acutely aware of the internal class and cultural cleavages as well as the fierce independence of individual members that have fragmented the group. These differences have repeatedly prevented Cajuns from mobilizing collectively on behalf of the group at large, frequently to the community's detriment.

Acadian to Cajun

ONE

Emergence of Classes in the Antebellum Period

Outsiders have consistently viewed the Acadians as a monolithic group of honest but ignorant and desperately poor fishermen and trappers, clinging tenaciously to an ancient way of life in the isolation of Louisiana's swamps and coastal marshes. Indeed, some writers have suggested that Acadiana has remained relatively unchanged since the time of the Acadian migration to Louisiana. Dudley J. LeBlanc, perhaps the most widely read of these, summarily dismisses the entire nineteenth century in his two classic works on the Acadians as though it did not exist, ostensibly because nothing significant changed in Acadian society. Recent scholarship, however, refutes this view.[1]

Indeed, it would appear that the foundation of the highly diversified Acadian society of the modern era was laid in the antebellum period, when its acceptance of materialism served as a catalyst for sociological transformation. In predispersal Acadia and in the early years of settlement in Louisiana, the Acadians were not materialistic in the modern sense. They aspired only to a comfortable existence, and though they consistently produced small agricultural surpluses for sale to acquire commodities they could not themselves produce, they did not labor to produce cash surpluses for the sake of possessing specific material goods, particularly the trappings of high social status. Thus, though significant economic differences existed among individuals, the poorest predispersal Acadian considered himself no less worthy than his wealthiest neighbor.[2]

This worldview was carried to Louisiana by the twenty-five hundred to three thousand Acadian exiles who carved a new homeland in the Mississippi Valley between 1764 and 1803. Yet during the late eighteenth century, when the exiles labored feverishly to recreate life as they had known it in Canada, the seeds of a new society were planted. This new society was nurtured by the social and economic systems in which it took root. Frontier egalitarianism was comparatively easy to maintain in Acadia, where slavery was unknown and indentured servitude was a distant and unpleasant memory. In lower Louisiana, however, Negro slavery was a well-established institution at the time of the Acadian migrations, and though most of the exiles demonstrated little interest in the peculiar institution, their children and grandchildren exhibited no such apathy. Beginning in the 1780's, significant numbers of Acadians began to acquire slaves, first as wet nurses and later as field hands. By 1810, a majority of the Acadians residing in the alluvial lands along the Mississippi River and bayous Teche and Lafourche owned slaves.[3]

Automatically elevated in social status through the acquisition of their human chattel, these Acadian slaveholders soon aspired to the rarefied social position of Creole planters, which necessitated their adoption of the materialistic values and life-style of their slaveholding neighbors. (Creole society, like its Acadian counterpart, was not monolithic, and upwardly mobile Acadians wished to emulate only those Creoles of higher social status than their own.) The Creole planters, descendants of European settlers in Louisiana, generally sought to recreate in Louisiana a romanticized vision of feudalistic France, with themselves as the New World aristocracy. Inspired by the French nobility's belief that a person was only as rich or powerful as he appeared to be, ambitious Creoles mimicked the Old World aristocracy and sustained their social pretensions by building grand homes and by purchasing carriages, fine furnishings, and domestics.[4]

Upwardly mobile Acadians who aspired to the planter caste embraced their wealthy neighbors' proclivity for conspicuous consumption; this, in turn, increased their need for money, which ultimately meant expansion of both their real property holdings and their slave labor force. Many Acadians, however, rejected this materialistic mentality and sought to perpetuate their traditional life-style in the relative isolation of the lower Lafourche Basin and in the vast prairies of southwestern Louisiana. Between these polar extremes lay a majority of the descendants of the Acadian exiles, who found themselves torn increasingly between the self-sufficiency of the past and the materialism of the present.

The fragmentation of the once extremely cohesive Acadian community appears to have taken place between 1790 and 1810, when second- and third-generation Acadians embraced both slavery and the plantation system. Slavery had been anathema to many of the original Acadian immigrants, for the refugees from the Middle Atlantic colonies—particularly Maryland—had often worked alongside blacks during their long residence in the region's tobacco-producing areas. Yet some Acadian exiles began to acquire slaves in the late 1770s. These slaves were usually females, who apparently were used as wet nurses, for records consistently list them in households with infant children. But by the 1780s, a few Acadians along the Mississippi and the south Louisiana bayous had begun to purchase male field hands to assist in clearing their densely wooded *habitations*. The number of Acadian slaveholders continued to grow throughout the late eighteenth century, despite an abortive slave insurrection in the predominantly Acadian Lafourche District (present-day Assumption and Lafourche parishes) in 1785, which demonstrated all too clearly the ever-present threat of violence posed by the servile population. Indeed, the Acadians' increasing dependence on slavery persisted throughout the late 1780s and 1790s, despite the exiles' rejection of Spanish efforts to engage them in more labor-intensive staple crop production.[5]

Acadians' growing acceptance of slavery gradually transformed their transplanted culture, particularly in the water bottoms, where staple crop production slowly began to take root. Though slaveholders still constituted a minority of the total Acadian population in the early 1800s, a majority of those residing along the Mississippi River and Bayou Teche owned human chattel by 1810, and they produced large surpluses of cotton for sale to the New Orleans commercial establishment.[6]

The development of the plantation system in Acadian settlement areas was temporarily arrested by the British blockade of Louisiana during the War of 1812, the resulting local economic depression, and a simultaneous armyworm invasion, which virtually destroyed the cotton industry along the lower Mississippi River, near New Orleans, and along Bayou Teche. These setbacks, however, proved only temporary. Sugar production in Louisiana surged dramatically in the mid-1820s, as die-hard south Louisiana cotton planters turned to sugar as a result of repeated crop failures caused by the "rot." By 1830, plantations were flourishing in most of the original eighteenth-century Acadian settlement sites.[7]

The rejuvenation of the economies in the Acadian parishes resulted directly from the introduction of sugar cultivation. The 1828 crop in particular helped economic regeneration. Impressed by the substantial profit margin which the sugar industry then afforded planters, a small number of Acadian farmers began to cultivate sugar in the mid-1820s. Pierre A. Delegos's report on sugar production indicates that, in 1829, ninety-two Acadian farmers—constituting approximately 0.5 percent of the state's Acadian heads of households—produced sugar commercially. Fifty-six farmers produced at least twelve hogsheads (one thousand pounds) of sugar in the river parishes (St. James, Ascension, Iberville, and West Baton Rouge), and fifteen Acadian households manufactured an average of fourteen hogsheads in Assumption and Lafourche parishes. West of the Atchafalaya River, thirteen St. Martin and Lafayette parish Acadians boasted a median output of 31.6 hogsheads per farm.[8]

From these modest beginnings, the Acadian sugar growers quickly emerged as a significant force in the Louisiana sugar industry. By 1849, 304 Acadian sugar growers were scattered widely among south Louisiana's parishes: West Baton Rough, 29; East Baton Rouge, 1; Iberville, 62; Ascension, 23; St. James, 17; Assumption, 59; Lafourche, 23; Terrebonne, 7; St. Mary, 12; St. Martin, 38; Lafayette, 23; St. Landry, 6; Vermillion, 3; and Calcasieu, 1. The uneven geographic distribution of sugar growers matched their varying degrees of commitment to the industry. Along the Mississippi, for example, only a small circle of wealthy planters in St. James and Ascension parishes participated in the sugar industry, but the wealth generated by the industry attracted more and more farmers. In neighboring Iberville and West Baton Rouge parishes, at least 650 and 262 Acadian farmers respectively became sugar growers by 1850. The number of Acadian sugar growers in Assumption and Lafourche parishes tripled between 1829 and 1850.[9]

At the same time, production increased significantly. In 1829, for example, only five Acadian sugar planters produced 100 hogsheads or more of sugar in the river parishes, while those in the Vermilion, Teche, and Lafourche Valleys produced less. Only two of the fifteen Lafourche area sugar growers produced more than 25 hogsheads, and the largest output was 42. During the 1830s and the 1840s, capital investment in the industry rose dramatically as production levels increased. The growing Acadian commitment to the sugar industry produced a corresponding rise in local sugar production, from 2,820 hogsheads in 1829 to 16,590 hogsheads in 1850; profit margins increased proportionally as cane growers began to employ economies of scale.[10]

The transformation of Acadian society in the mid-nineteenth century is perhaps best reflected in the sudden and dramatic growth in the number of slaves on Acadian plantations. In 1810, only one Acadian owned more than fifty slaves, the minimum required for classification as a large slaveholder according to Karl Joseph Menn; by 1860 forty-nine did so. Scores of Acadians counted themselves among the region's planter aristocracy by the Civil War, having acquired at least $10,000 in real estate and more than twenty slaves. Yet the wealthy remained a relatively small segment of the total Acadian population. With the exception of Iberville Parish, where slightly over 30 percent of all Acadian households were headed by planters, they constituted between 8 and 15 percent of all Acadian households in the parishes along the Mississippi River. Planters formed a significantly smaller segment of the Acadian population along bayous Lafourche and Terrebonne—5.4, 2, and 1 percent respectively in Assumption, Lafourche, and Terrebonne parishes. They were equally rare west of the Atchafalaya River, except in St. Martin Parish, where they were found in 20 percent of all Acadian households. Along bayous Teche and Vermilion planters constituted 8, 3, and 2 percent respectively of the Acadian households in St. Mary, Lafayette, and St. Landry parishes.[11]

Prosperous farmers, less affluent but aspiring to become members of the planter caste, constituted the more numerous antebellum Acadian upper middle class. The decennial federal census reports of the late antebellum period indicate that a large plurality of the sugar growers along the Mississippi River as well as bayous Lafourche and Teche were either farmers with small slaveholdings or planters of moderate means. The 1860 census, for example, indicates that 34 percent of all Acadian sugar growers in Ascension, Assumption, Iberville, and West Baton Rouge parishes failed to meet the financial criteria used here for identification of the planter class—ownership of at least $10,000 in real estate and twenty slaves. But even the Acadian planters were only moderately wealthy by Southern standards; 48 percent owned between $10,000 and $20,000 in real estate. Acadian sugar planters, particularly those along the river, owned less than 30 percent of the total property holdings in their respective parishes. For example, in Iberville Parish, where sugar planters owned 80 percent of all real wealth and 60 percent of all personal property, Acadian sugar planters owned 14 and 11.7 percent of each category respectively. Moreover, in Ascension Parish, where sugar planters possessed 91 percent of all wealth, Acadian sugar planters owned 28 percent of all real property and 19 percent of all personal wealth. In Assumption and Lafayette parishes, Acadian sugar growers owned 12.5 and 19.4 percent of all local property respectively.[12]

Though the economic gap between the small planter and the typical farmer was frequently small, the groups were separated by an ever-widening cultural gap. Having risen to the upper economic class either through their own or, more commonly, their parents' labors, Acadian sugar planters rapidly assumed the culture of their new economic class and its attendant social caste. Nouveau riche Acadians bent upon divesting themselves of their cultural baggage initially looked to the local Creole elite for role models. By the late antebellum period, however, Acadian planters had begun to remake themselves in the image of south Louisiana's new economic kingpins—Anglo-Americans transplanted from the eastern seaboard. Thus in the early nineteenth century, Acadian planters' homes, furnishings, and cultivated tastes for liquors were often slavish imitations of those of their Creole counterparts, particularly along the Mississippi River. In addition, many Acadian planters on both sides of the Atchafalaya—especially those with political aspirations—had begun to identify themselves as Creoles, having come to consider the term *Acadian,* or *Cajun*—its nineteenth-century incarnation—as degrading. Emulating the new economic pacesetters later in the antebellum period, the Acadian elite followed their Anglo-American role models to popular Gulf Coast watering holes. began rising Kentucky thoroughbreds, and built elegant Greek Revival homes resembling those introduced by the Anglos.[13]

Perhaps even more indicative of their cultural transformation are the numerous late antebellum business ventures initiated by Acadian planters. Many diversified their business interests, following the lead of the Anglo-American transplants, organizing sugar-refining corporations—some with capital in excess of $100,000—and taking active roles in the organization of banks, steam navigation companies, and railroads.[14]

To maintain the life-style expected of their caste, antebellum Acadian planters demanded ever-increasing output from their agricultural operations. The resulting surplus in disposable income was employed not only for conspicuous consumption but also to pay the tuition for their sons, who were sent to the finest schools in the Midwest, along the East Coast, and in New England, and their daughters, who were sent to in-state Catholic finishing schools. Upon completion of their educational careers, these scholars frequently applied their talents to management of their fathers' plantations or to the legal, medical, and educational professions, the latter group forming the nucleus of an Acadian bourgeoisie, centered in the local parish seats.[15]

Like the planter class, the Acadian bourgeoisie was confined geographically to the fertile water-bottom parishes bordering the Mississippi River and bayous Lafourche, Teche, and Vermilion. Though the managerial, medical, educational, and legal professions were the exclusive domain of the wellborn, many trades were filled by Acadian artisans from the lower economic strata. The 1860 census lists seventeen categories of Acadian tradesmen in Lafourche Parish. Particularly prominent among the craftsmen who constituted 20.8 percent of Lafourche's Acadian work force were carpenters, brick masons, and coopers, the latter indispensable to the local sugar economy. By 1860, theses trades had become so institutionalized that Acadian artisans' households—particularly those of brick masons and carpenters—frequently included resident apprentices.[16]

By 1860, wealth in the Acadian community was concentrated in the planter class and bourgeoisie. In Assumption Parish, for example, the planter class, which constituted only 5.4 percent of the Acadian households, controlled 54 percent of real and personal (i.e., movable) property. In the river parishes, the planter caste was an even greater economic force; 15.85 percent of households there owned 77 percent of the real property and 71.88 percent of the movable property. The trend toward concentration of wealth among the planter class in the sugar-producing parishes was not confined to the Acadian community. The 1860 census of Ascension Parish, for example, reveals that Acadian, Creole, and Anglo-American sugar planters possessed over 91 percent of all personal property within the region, but Acadians owned only 19 percent of this total and only 28 percent of the parish's real estate. Moreover, though Acadians were wealthier than their Creole neighbors, who controlled only 12.9 percent of all local real estate and 10.5 percent of movable property, the Anglo-Americans were the economic leaders in Ascension Parish. Nineteen Anglo-American households possessed 50.3 percent of local real estate and 62 percent of the personal wealth.[17]

The rapid accumulation of wealth by the local elite, however, did not smother the more tradition-bound Acadian yeomanry. Living in the shadow of the planter aristocracy, many Acadians maintained the mores of their late colonial era forebears, continuing to produce small agricultural surpluses with the assistance of their sons and two or three slaves. In 1860, nearly 60 percent of Louisiana's Acadian population, a majority of whom were small farmers, resided on sugar plantations east of the Atchafalaya River.[18]

The coexisting cultures were not entirely compatible. American sugar planters generally viewed the Acadian small farmers and the far less numerous *petits habitants* (subsistence farmers possessing no slaves) as nuisances who "demoralized" their slaves. Not only did the small farmers' comfortable existence persuade blacks "that it was not necessary for men to work so hard as they themselves were obliged to," but the Acadians frequently hired slaves to do odd jobs, paying them with "luxuries" their masters did not wish them to have. To rid themselves of the problems, planters—particularly American planters—often tried to buy out their less affluent neighbors at prices two to three times their properties' actual value.[19]

Contrary to the findings of some writers of the late 1970s, however, the pressures did not result in a massive, involuntary exodus of Acadians from their second homeland, the so-called Second Expulsion. The *petits habitants* were generally not intimidated by the planters' expropriation efforts, and most remained on their farms, except in the river parishes. Most Acadians abhorred indebtedness, and many river parish debtors—probably unlucky gamblers—found the planters' generous offers all too appealing. Other Acadian farmers lacked either the means or the willingness to comply with the flurry of police jury ordinances enacted after the great flood of 1828 mandating the construction and maintenance of levees and public roads on waterfront properties and thus gladly accepted the planters' offers. Moreover, several Acadian families, whose efforts in the eighteenth century to join relatives at Attakapas and Opelousas had been thwarted by restrictive Spanish settlement policies, sold their property at the first opportunity under the American regime and moved to the prairie parishes west of the Atchafalaya. Other settlers, burdened with large families, sought unoccupied lands along the lower Lafourche and in Terrebonne Parish, for acquisition of riverfront property at inflated prices with their modest financial resources was difficult, if not impossible.[20]

Louisiana's forced heirship laws, which required equitable division of estates among all children, made further land division impractical on many small landholdings by the 1830s. As early as 1807, 87 percent of all Acadian river parish landholdings included less than seven arpents frontage on the Mississippi River, while 55 percent encompassed four arpents or less. The typical migrant Acadian family in Terrebonne Parish contained seven persons. Thus with five or more heirs in the average family, young migrants from the river parishes faced the bleak prospect of inheriting only a small portion of the family farm, which had already been reduced to one or two arpents in width. Finally, some *petits habitants* were undoubtedly dissatisfied with the changes wrought in their community by the emergence of the plantation system and sought to relocate in more isolated regions, where more traditional Acadian values still held sway.[21]

The displaced Acadians followed two migratory patterns. Residents of the river parishes found new homes in the lower Lafourche Valley and, to a far lesser extent, in St. Landry Parish, while settlers from the upper Lafourche Valley established themselves in northern Terrebonne Parish, the Pierre Part region of Assumption Parish, and along Bayou Black in western Terrebonne and southeastern St. Mary parishes. The extent of these migrations is best reflected in the 1830 census of Terrebonne Parish, which indicates that 44 percent of Terrebonne's Acadian community had resided in either Assumption Parish or the river parishes in 1810. The Acadian influx continued after 1830, though on a much smaller scale. Nevertheless, immigration, coupled with the established settlers' propensity for large families, contributed to the Terrebonne Acadian community's remarkable growth rate—452 percent—between 1830 and 1860, a rate 1.65 times greater than that of Louisiana's Acadian population as a whole.[22]

Not all river Acadians were displaced by the emerging plantation system. A plurality of the male Acadian residents of the eastern sugar parishes were yeomen farmers. In 1860, for example, these farmers, who produced small agricultural surpluses, usually with the aid of a handful of slaves, constituted 34 percent of all Assumption Parish Acadian men whose occupations were identified in the federal census reports. They also formed 41 percent of the Acadian work force in Ascension Parish, 47 percent in St. James, 38 percent in Lafourche, and 34 percent in Terrebonne. Unlike the Acadian planters, who engaged in extensive staple crop production, the yeoman farmer tilled four to twenty acres—depending on the size of the family and the number of sons in the family labor pool—and produced small quantities of cotton, sugar, peas, beans, sweet potatoes, and corn. Each of these products, with the exception of corn (which in Ascension Parish was produced in quantity for sale to planters), was grown strictly for home consumption. The diet of bayou Acadians—indeed of Acadians throughout antebellum Louisiana—was little different from that of poor whites throughout the South. Similarly, small numbers of horses, milk cattle, hogs, and work oxen provided meat, milk, leather, and transportation.[23]

This diversified agriculture made the typical small farm essentially self-sufficient. Nevertheless, the presence of waterborne peddlers offering items such as calico and iron cookware apparently satisfied the demand for manufactured goods that could not be made at home, and many Acadian freeholders in the upper Lafourche Valley supplemented their income by working as day laborers on sugar plantations, cutting cane for $1.25 per day. In 1860 Acadian day laborers made up 19.5 percent of the population in Ascension, 27 percent in Assumption, 28 percent in Lafourche, and 49 percent in Terrebonne.[24]

Acadian day laborers were far more common in Terrebonne Parish, where the standard of living was much lower than in the upper Lafourche area and the river parishes. Fifty-one percent of Terrebonne's Acadian residents—primarily displaced river parish residents and their children, who in 1860 constituted 44 percent of the local Acadian population—owned no real estate in 1860. Most of these landless immigrants, 49 percent of all gainfully employed Terrebonne Acadians in 1860, worked as day laborers, apparently to acquire funds for land purchases and perhaps for home and land rental charges.[25]

The lot of Terrebonne's freeholders was little better than that of their landless neighbors. Families were larger in Terrebonne than in other south Louisiana parishes. The typical mature Acadian family in antebellum Terrebonne Parish was composed of eight to twelve individuals, although the median family size in 1860 was reduced by bachelors, newlyweds, and aged couples and thus included only 7.10 persons. Median family sizes for other Acadian parishes, based on the 1860 census, are as follows: Assumption, 5.53; Ascension, 5.04; Lafourche, 5.00; Iberville, 5.15; West Baton Rouge, 4.44; St. James, 5.62; St. Mary, 5.20; St. Martin, 5.69; Lafayette, 4.97; St. Landry, 3.49; Vermillion, 3.49; and Calcasieu, 5.32. Yet the terrain of the Bayou Terrebonne country made it difficult to support large numbers of dependents by traditional means. Acadian settlers who congregated along the low-lying banks of bayous Terrebonne, Little Terrebonne, Black, Little Caillou, Caillou, Du Large, and Blue were able to clear only 11 percent (an average of 13.35 acres) of their natural levee landholdings, only 28 percent as much property as their counterparts in Lafourche Parish. The Terrebonne Acadians thus raised only a few head of livestock, grew small quantities of corn and sweet potatoes, and adopted rice, a crop better suited to the swamp environment. By 1850, rice cultivation was so well established that Acadian yeomen produced small surpluses, probably for sale to local Anglo-American and Creole sugar planters. Because the Terrebonne Parish Acadians could devote less land to herding than their Lafourche Valley neighbors, they were more dependent on hunting to augment the protein in their diet.[26]

The Terrebonne Acadians as well as their swampland cousins in the

Pierre Part region of Assumption Parish did not completely sever their ties to the land. The residents of the ribbons of dry land along the eastern fringe of the Atchafalaya Basin were generally subsistence farmers, occasionally producing small cotton surpluses. But none of the Pierre Part residents engaged in swamp-oriented pursuits such as cypress lumbering, fishing, and moss gathering. In 1860, only two Acadians east of the Atchafalaya were designated as "hunter-fowlers," and only one, an Iberville Parish resident, was listed as a "swamper." This swamper, however, owned $10,000 in real estate and $1,000 in personal property.[27]

Subregional socioeconomic differences among swamp, bayou, and river Acadians also characterized the population west of the Atchafalaya River. As in the east, staple crop production served as a catalyst, transforming the once classless society into a highly stratified agrarian community. At the pinnacle of the new socioeconomic order were sugar planters who abandoned cotton production in the 1820s for small-scale sugar cultivation. In 1829, six Lafayette Parish and fourteen St. Martin Parish Acadian sugar growers produced an average of 29.8 hogsheads. Though the number of sugar growers was initially small, and, concomitantly, production levels were low at the outset, the Acadian sugar industry grew gradually during the 1830s and 1840s. In 1850, though sugar growers constituted only 6.6 percent of the Acadian households listed in the federal agricultural census of predominantly prairie Lafayette Parish, 27 percent of St. Martin Parish's Acadian farms produced sugar—15 percent more than in 1829. Production levels also increased. Median sugar production of individual farmers in Lafayette Parish more than doubled between 1829 and 1850, rising from 29.8 to 72.48 hogsheads.[28]

Residents of Lafayette and St. Martin parishes dominated the Acadian sugar industry west of the Atchafalaya River, but small numbers of Acadian farmers cultivated sugarcane in St. Landry and St. Mary parishes. Despite the ravages of the armyworm in the mid-1840s, which prompted many Anglo-American and Creole cotton farmers to turn to sugar cultivation, only three Acadian farmers in St. Landry Parish switched to this labor-intensive agricultural industry in 1850. St. Mary Parish's small Acadian community, however, engaged in sugar production, particularly in the extreme northwestern portion of the parish, where several transplanted St. Martin Parish residents congregated. In 1850, six of St. Mary's twelve Acadian farmers produced an average of 77.33 hogsheads of sugar.[29]

The scarcity of Acadian sugar growers on the upper and lower Teche vividly reflects the concentration of the industry in the central Teche Valley, particularly in the areas surrounding present-day Cecilia and Loreauville. Although restricted to a small geographic area, characterized by modest production levels and confined to a small percentage of the western Acadian population, these sugar growers played an important role in the economic development of the southwestern parishes. Led by such influential men as Alexandre Mouton, pioneer sugar growers amassed small fortunes in the 1830s and 1840s.[30]

Many of the Acadian small farmers in the upper Teche and Vermilion valleys adopted staple crop production in imitation of the sugar planters, growing increased quantities of cotton, which not only was better suited to prairie soils but required a small labor supply. Nevertheless, commercial cotton production depended on slave labor, and Acadian slaveholdings in the western cotton belt—eastern Vermilion Parish; southeastern St. Landry Parish; the Breaux Bridge, Grand Pointe, Anse Charpentier, and Petite Anse areas of St. Martin Parish; and Lafayette Parish—grew more commonplace and progressively larger. By 1850, 61.2 percent of St. Landry's Acadian farms produced an average of 9.95 bales of cotton, while 50 percent of St. Martin Parish's Acadian farms, particularly those in the Breaux Bridge and Parks areas, produced cotton commercially, harvesting an average of 6.82 bales annually. Finally, in Lafayette Parish, 55.4 percent of all Acadian farms engaged in commercial cotton production.[31]

Lafayette Parish was the hub of the cotton belt's emerging commercial agricultural system. In 1860, 75 percent of the region's large slaveholders were of Acadian parentage. Slaveholding was prevalent in all segments of local Acadian society. In 1850, 61 percent of the area's Acadian farmers produced staple crops, particularly cotton and sugar; in 1860, 83 percent of Acadian households possessed black slaves.[32]

Lafayette Parish was at an agricultural crossroads, located on the fringes of the central Louisiana cotton belt, the south Louisiana sugar bowl, and the southwest Louisiana cattle country. Plantations reflected the region's diverse economic pursuits. In 1850, for example, the Alexandre Guidry plantation produced 113 hogsheads of sugar, 4,520 barrels of molasses, 15 bales of cotton, 240 bushels of sweet potatoes, and nearly 1,300 head of livestock. With the exception of sugar and molasses, the same pattern of production existed on small slaveholders' farms, which constituted the backbone of the Acadian cotton belt economy. This stability permitted large and small Lafayette Parish farmers to experiment with new staple crops during the last decade of the antebellum period. Rice was the most successful of these experimental crops, with local production increasing from less than 2,000 pounds in 1850 to nearly 380,000 pounds in 1860, the third highest total in the state.[33]

On the prairies west of Lafayette Parish, "providence rice" was sown haphazardly in low areas and watered only by rainfall. The benign neglect exhibited by rice growers there pervaded all aspects of agriculture in the Acadian prairies. Commercial agriculture and the slaveholdings it necessitated consequently were practically unknown on the southwestern prairies. Unlike the fertile Lafayette, St. Martin, and southern St. Landry Parish water bottoms, the prairies possessed thick sod and a very shallow clay pan, which militated against agriculture, particularly with the wooden implements traditionally used by the prairie Acadians. It is hardly surprising, therefore, that the overwhelming majority of these people depended on cattle production for their livelihood.

The ease with which cattle could be raised on the open prairies as well as the availability of unclaimed land had drawn Acadians away from the region's principal watercourses since the 1770s. The number of Acadians in the remote areas west of Bayou Vermilion and north of Bayou Queue Tortue, however, remained small until the late antebellum period, when hundreds of nonslaveholders migrated to western Vermilion, St. Landry, and Calcasieu parishes.

As in the river parishes, the exodus of small farmers was apparently prompted by the emergence of the plantation system, the steady reduction of family landholdings through forced heirship, and the availability of cheap government lands in the southwestern prairie area. The Acadian migration to the unsettled prairie is clearly reflected in the 1830 census of St. Landry Parish, where Lafayette and St. Martin Parish immigrants constituted 28 percent of all households. In the remote areas of present-day Acadia Parish, such as the Mermentau River valley, however, immigrants constituted an overwhelming majority—73 percent—of the region's Acadian households.[34]

The transplanted bayou Acadians soon developed a life-style far different from that of their eastern neighbors, one much more compatible with their ancestors' nonmaterialistic values. The Acadians frequently squatted on government land, particularly along the narrow gullies punctuating the treeless plains. In 1860, for example, 49 percent of all Acadian households in St. Landry Parish owned no real estate. The prairie Acadians perpetuated the self-reliant spirit of their forebears, engaging in subsistence agriculture and ranching without the assistance of slaves. The 1860 slave census reported that in the Acadian communities of Calcasieu and Vermilion parishes 16 and 22 percent respectively of households owned slaves. Relying on family labor, the average prairie Acadian household cultivated eight to ten acres of corn—the staple of the antebellum Acadian diet—and only one acre of providence rice. These crops were grown on real estate holdings which in Vermilion and Calcasieu parishes averaged only $529.67 in value. In St. Landry Parish, the average Acadian family cultivated only one or two acres of cotton for home consumption. The typical prairie farmer raised twenty-five to one hundred cattle and twenty to forty hogs.[35]

Although subsistence agriculture predominated among the prairie dwellers, many western Acadians produced livestock commercially during the antebellum period, apparently for the money to acquire land. The growth of livestock production was prompted by the rapid proliferation of herds requiring minimal management on the verdant prairies as well as consistently high beef prices, which, as early as 1811, ranged from $15 to $20 per head at New Orleans. Attracted by such favorable market conditions, some Acadian cattlemen regularly drove their herds to Crescent City markets, using the trails blazed by their ancestors. Proceeds of these sales were invested in cheap government lands, and, over the years, these acquisitions were consolidated into large *vacheries* (ranches). By 1850, St. Landry, Vermilion, and Calcasieu parishes boasted twenty 500-acre ranches and one *vacherie* containing 5,000 acres.[36]

The growth of the Acadian *vacheries*, a barometer of the region's growing prosperity, reflects the corresponding increase in livestock production. In 1850, fully one-fourth of Calcasieu Parish's Acadian ranches contained over five hundred head of beef cattle. Moreover, thirteen southwestern Louisiana *vacheries*—seven of which were in Calcasieu Parish—contained over one thousand head. Cattle, however, were not the only measure of wealth on the Acadian prairies. Small, sturdy Creole ponies abounded on the grasslands; of the 233 Acadian households enumerated in the 1850 agricultural census of southwestern Louisiana, only two lacked horses. Moreover, 31 percent of these residences contained at least twenty horses, and 11 percent, most of them in Calcasieu Parish, boasted at least fifty mounts.[37]

Despite the evident prosperity and increasing concentration of wealth among the emerging Acadian cattle barons, life changed very little on the prairie frontier. Unlike their counterparts in the cotton and sugar belts, wealthy ranchers did not engage in conspicuous consumption. The typical rancher lived in a two- or three-room cypress and *bousillage*[38] house, differing only in its proportions from its more modest one-room predecessor than continued to shelter less affluent prairie cattlemen. Ranchers' homes were sparsely furnished with cypress furniture, a striking contrast to the elegantly appointed homes of the Acadian planter class. Unlike the planter class, the nouveau riche ranchers generally shared their poor neighbors' disdain for formal education, preferring instead that their numerous progeny be trained in agriculture and the domestic arts.[39]

The cattle barons' life-style was little different from that of their employees. Indeed, the 1860 census indicated that a significant minority of prairie Acadians, most of whom were small landholders, worked as day laborers, probably herdsmen and drovers employed by the large ranches. In Calcasieu and Vermilion parishes, adult laborers constituted 33.5 and 22.5 percent respectively of all gainfully employed Acadian adults. These laborers evidently sought temporary employment to finance the acquisition of public lands or to expand existing herds, for fully 80 percent of the Vermilion Parish laborers owned real estate and cattle. The laborers' median property holdings ($161 in real estate; $423 in personal property) constituted only 20.5 percent of the parochial average of $535 in real estate and $2,303 in personal property.

The social stratification on the Acadian prairies typifies the regional socioeconomic and cultural differences that emerged in Louisiana's

Acadian community in the antebellum period. Originally composed of an economically homogeneous group of subsistence farmers and ranchers, Acadian society was transformed by changing economic conditions, particularly the rise of staple crop production in the water-bottom areas and the adoption of commercial agriculture. Rapid accumulation of wealth and slaves between 1830 and 1860, particularly by the sugar growers, resulted in rigid social stratification.

TWO

Acadian Folk Life
in the Nineteenth Century

The development of Acadian society in the nineteenth century has been almost completely neglected by historians. What little is known is based primarily on travelogues written by outsiders who were generally interested only in the more exotic aspects of local life. Almost without exception, these observers failed to comprehend the complexity of Acadian society and therefore totally ignored all but the most impoverished strata of the community. Such ample attention must be regarded as a mixed blessing by historians, for, though it generated a wealth of primary source material regarding the *petits habitants*, the comments recorded by outsiders were frequently shallow and impressionistic, revealing more about the reporter than about the topic. Yet these pieces are often the only record of the folkways of the largely illiterate nineteenth-century Acadian population.

Despite the emergence of distinctive socioeconomic groups within the antebellum Acadian community, members of the lower social strata, particularly yeoman farmers and *petits habitants*, shared a lifestyle, language, and values little different from those of their more egalitarian forebears. The survival of traditional Acadian culture was a direct result of the society's social institutions and agricultural practices, which promoted economic self-sufficiency and group solidarity.

This is not to say that the Acadians were hostile to strangers. Early nineteenth-century travelers who visited Acadian homes consistently praised the hospitality they were accorded. But though outsiders were welcome, their materialistic values, strange customs, competitiveness, and preoccupation with business were not, at least among the poorer classes. Indeed, most Acadia yeomen and *petits habitants* rejected American ideals, preferring instead their fathers' precapitalistic values and folkways.[1]

This value system is vividly reflected in all aspects of traditional Acadian life. In agriculture, for example, Alcée Fortier, distinguished turn-of-the-century Louisiana historian, linguist, and folklorist, noted that postbellum Acadians were "laborious, but they appear to be satisfied, if by cultivating their patch of ground with their sons, they manage to live with a little comfort.[2] The 1850 agricultural census indicates that although the typical yeoman was capable of tilling fifteen acres of land, most farmers cultivated only four to twelve acres, depending on the needs of their families and the number of sons in the family labor pool. Indeed, of the ninety Acadian farms listed in the 1850 agricultural census of Terrebonne Parish, only twenty-three boasted more than fifteen cultivated acres.

Such small-scale farming obligated the Acadian farmer to engage in seasonal occupations to support his family. Plowing, planting, hoeing, mending fences, branding calves, and seasonal relocation of his herd, which usually grazed on public land throughout the cooler portion of the year, to summer pasturage, filled the farmer's spring and early summer days. The comparatively inactive summer and the early fall growing season provided the *petit habitant* with the opportunity to undertake extended hunting and fishing expeditions. The prairies and woodlands of south-central Louisiana abounded with game—unidentified varieties of migratory ducks, as well as woodcock, partridges, prairie chickens, snipes, wild geese, canvasbacks, mallards, black and teal ducks, brants, robins, ricebirds, opposums, raccoons, rabbits, deer, squirrels, wild turkeys, papabotes,[3] reed birds, *grosbecs*, and black bears—and all edible varieties were killed indiscriminately by hunters. Seasonal hunting forays, which occasionally ranged as far as the central Atchafalaya Basin and the Gulf Coast and lasted as long as two weeks, furnished Acadian families with a steady supply of fresh meat. The killing of wild game minimized the need to slaughter domesticated livestock, which in the prairie parishes ranged without supervision on unclaimed land in the spring and sultry summer months.[4]

Cool weather signaled the herd's return to winter pasturage, usually in wooded areas, as well as the beginning of the harvest season. The harvest on the Acadian frontier was a communal undertaking in which all members of the household, as well as "large numbers" of male and female *ramasseurs* (harvesters) participated. The fruits of each field were gathered in turn, and workers frequently labored "by moonlight" to "pick . . . every boll of cotton." Despite the long hours, the *ramasserie,* or communal harvest, took on a festive atmosphere. One observer noted that the workers, who were provided large quantities of *gateaux de syrop* (syrup cake, a local delicacy made with cane syrup), coffee, and whiskey by the host family, punctuated the monotony of cotton picking with "shouts of joy, songs, and animated talk."[5]

The *ramasserie* was nevertheless a serious undertaking requiring long workdays, for the corn, Irish potatoes, sweet potatoes, peas, beans, pumpkins, okra, and rice produced on the small farms constituted the farmers' main source of sustenance in the upcoming year. Products of the family farm were supplemented by wild game, domestic livestock, and home-grown fruit. During the antebellum period, for example, *petits habitants* east of the Atchafalaya reportedly produced "the peach, in great variety; the fig, the orange, prunes, raisins, grapes, pecans, and quinces." Pork production in the bayou and river parishes, as well as beef production in the prairie parishes, served as the *petits habitants'* principal source of meat. Travelers' accounts, however, indicate that fresh beef and pork, as well as old and unproductive hens and roosters, were served far less frequently than eggs, salt pork, and wild game.[6]

Blessed with such a broad variety of foods, the Acadian cook had little need for store-bought products. In fact, with the exception of small quantities of flour, which could not be produced locally, cooks relied exclusively on home-grown vegetables. The dishes which they prepared (which would now be called "soul food") were remarkably similar to those consumed by poor whites throughout the Deep

South. Frederick Law Olmsted, the famous New York landscape ar-
chitect who toured Louisiana twice in the 1850s, recalled in his travelogues meals served to him by an Acadian family in St. Landry Parish:
"Upon the supper-table, we found two washbowls, one filled with
milk, the other for molasses. We asked for water, which was given us
in a battered tin cup. The dishes, besides the bacon and bread, were
fried eggs and sweet potatoes. The bowl of molasses stood in the cen-
tre of the table, and we were pressed to partake of it, as the family
did, by dipping in it bits of bread. But how it was expected to be used
at breakfast, when we had bacon and potatoes, with spoons, but no
bread, I cannot imagine."[7] The recollections of typical antebellum
Acadian fare by an anonymous Teche Valley resident closely parallel
Olmsted's account: "boiled papabotes, fresh milk, chicken and ome-
lettes, peaches and cream for dessert, and coffee to wind up with."[8]

Though milk and wheat bread were delicacies reserved for celebrations and special guests, meals were, as Olmsted and the anonymous
writer suggest, rather mundane gastronomical experiences, noteworthy only for their monotonous lack of variety. Corn bread, boiled
Irish potatoes, baked sweet potatoes, fresh peas or beans, and meat
(fresh in summer, salted during winter) or wild game were the main-
stays of the nineteenth-century Acadian diet. The meat of semiwild,
grass-fed longhorn cattle, wild game, and old chickens was invariably
tough and thus required lengthy cooking for tenderization. Salted
meats required extensive boiling to take out the salt, followed by
steaming or a second round of boiling, usually with Irish potatoes.[9]

The extensive use of boiling in the preparation of foods, a legacy
of colonial Acadian cuisine, reflects the adaptation of traditional Acadian dishes to Louisiana products, hence the appearance of roux-
based stews, gumbos, and gravies. Boiling water was also used in the
preparation of small quantities of home-grown providence rice; for
jambalaya; for corn soup, a dish similar to traditional Acadian *fricot;*
and for crawfish, which were harvested in *maraises* (swampy or flood-
prone areas) on meatless Lenten days. Also boiled, usually in gumbos,
were saltwater shellfish caught during coastal hunting and fishing forays by Acadian farmers from the lower prairies and the Lafourche
area. Finally, although not mentioned in antebellum travel accounts,
boudin (sausage containing meat and rice) and hogshead cheese undoubtedly were part of traditional Acadian cuisine and were probably

produced only during winter *boucheries* (rural butcheries). Like other products of the early Acadian kitchen, these delicacies were cooked in boiling water.[10]

Boiling techniques were dictated not only by the toughness of locally produced meats, agricultural produce, and game but by extant cooking technology as well. Lacking funds for acquisition of Dutch ovens, the overwhelming majority of Acadian cooks prepared meals in kettles suspended above the hearth. Frying pans were scarce in mid-nineteenth-century Acadian homes and, in the Acadian areas west of the Atchafalaya, they appear to have been used primarily to cook *couche-couche* (fried cornmeal) and to bake corn bread. Acadians east of the Atachafalaya had much greater access to wheat flour, and consequently wheat bread was a far more important component of their diet. River and Lafourche Basin Acadians baked their loaves in dome-shaped outdoor ovens.[11]

Acadian adaptability and reliance on locally produced materials were also evidenced in clothing production. In the early nineteenth century, south Louisiana merchants in riverfront communities began to import surprising quantities of European-manufactured fabric. Much of this cloth apparently was purchased by middle-and upper-class Acadian women, causing a corresponding decline in the number of looms and spinning wheels in their households. But in lower-class households women continued to produce cotton cloth for domestically produced clothing until the end of the nineteenth century. On both sides of the Atchafalaya, Acadian women and children went into the fields to gather yellow cotton, produced in small quantities on the family farm. Following the harvest, cotton seeds were removed from the lint either by hand cards or with primitive cotton gins, resembling the wringer mechanisms on early washing machines. Women, assisted by their daughters, then spun cotton fibers into threads, which were ultimately woven into cottonade on the family loom. In some areas, particularly in the prairie region, small quantities of cotton fiber were carded and combined with wool for the manufacture of a heavy-weight winter cloth called *jeture de laine*. Summer and winter fabrics were then dyed blue, white, red, brown, and black with natural dyes either produced on the family *habitation* or gathered in the neighboring woods and then fashioned into clothing.[12]

Clothing styles remained remarkably static among *petits habitants* throughout the nineteenth century. At the dawn of the century, the typical man's outfit consisted of knee-length pants, called *braguettes,* cottonade shirts with jackets, and *capots,* heavy outer coats with long tails worn for formal occasions. Headgear consisted of hand-woven palmetto hats in the early nineteenth century and "broad-brimmed felt hats" by the 1890s. With the exception of men's pants, which became ankle-length garments by the 1830s, this outfit served as the basic male costume throughout the antebellum and Civil War years. Styles in facial hair also changed after the Civil War. Antebellum Acadian men were generally clean shaven; after the war, most Acadian men—like their contemporaries throughout the nation—wore beards. The beards of prairie dwellers, however, were notoriously "long and untrimmed."[13]

Women's fashions, at least among the lower classes, followed the evolutionary trends of their male counterparts. The female costume changed little during the early nineteenth century. This distinctive mode of dress is described in great detail in the "Anonymous Breaux Manuscript" (attributed to Chief Justice Joseph A. Breaux): "The women used to be dressed in very bright materials, with varied and often clashing hues. The skirts were made of woolen cloth with red, yellow, violet, and green stripes; woolen or cotton stockings were grey or white. A corset [the upper portion of the dress] was made with material different from that of the skirt. This garment allowed the real corset, which was usually dyed red, to be seen above the belt." This outfit was complemented by either wide-striped and brilliantly colored kerchiefs or, more commonly, *garde-soleil,* cotton sunbonnets with a *barbe,* or shoulder-length sunshade. In addition to their own clothes, Acadian women produced clothing for their children. Before the Civil War, "children of both sexes wore a dress with a catch at the back. Boys wore neither breeches nor trousers before six or seven years." Children were not permitted to wear moccasins or *cantiers* until the age of "ten or twelve." The materials used in the domestic manufacture of clothing, except for small quantities of calico, were the product of home industries. Acadian home manufactures, however, were not confined to clothing. Acadian women also produced fine mosquito netting, cotton sheets, cotton blankets, cotton and wool quilts, and cotton bed shirts.[14]

Footwear was also produced at home with domestically grown materials. Along Bayou Lafourche, Acadians wore *sabots* (wooden shoes) until the Civil War. River and prairie Acadian women wore cowhide and deerskin moccasins, while men wore *cantiers,* moccasins with knee-length leather leggings. Use of this footwear persisted among poorer Acadians until the late nineteenth century. In more affluent circles, Acadian women used revenues from the sale of eggs and other barnyard products to purchase "shoes brought from the East or imported from England and France." Shoes were a luxury and, except for church services and formal occasions such as weddings and funerals, Acadians went barefoot. According to Alfred Duperier, Acadian "girls going to church, or to a ball, would often carry their shoes in hand, to be worn only when they reached their destination. At home the shoes were carefully hung from the ceiling." The reverence with which Acadian women cared for their shoes also extended to their best dress. According to Alexandre Barde, Acadian women kept in the family armoire a special hand-made dress, mantilla, gloves, and cheap jewelry for social gatherings, particularly *bals de maison* (house dances).[15]

Construction of implements, wagons, furniture, and homes was men's work. Throughout the antebellum period, Acadian farmers relied exclusively on home-made agricultural implements, particularly ox-drawn wooden plows and harrows. *Petits habitants* also made ox-carts for the transportation of hay, corn, and cotton. Though Acadian men traveled on horseback, the women rode in horse-drawn *caleches,* gigs whose frames, body, wheels, axles, leather harness, tracings, and shock absorbers, even the feather cushions, were all produced by hand on Acadian *habitations.*[16]

Home-grown products were also used in the construction of Acadian homes, barns, furniture, and fences. In the dry fall months, Acadian farmers in water-bottom areas would fell cypress trees along their swampy back property lines and haul the timber to building sites with teams of oxen. The logs were split and fashioned into building timbers. Assisted by friends and neighbors, the builder then erected a frame of peg and mortise construction on cypress log pillars. The makeshift carpenters then manufactured natural insulation for the wall, called *bousillage:* "Into the studding were placed pins, extending from one to the other, horizontally, and about ten inches apart. The long grey moss of the country was then gathered and thrown by layers into a pit dug for the purpose, with the soil until the pit was full, when water was added in sufficient quantities to wet the moss through; this done, all who are assisting in construction of the house—men, women, boys and girls—jump in on it, and continue to tramp until mud and moss are completely intermingled . . . when it is gathered together and made into rolls about two feet long." The rolls of *bousillage* were then laid over the pins, beginning with the lowest, and on completion of the task, the facade and interior walls were smoothed by hand or shovel and allowed to dry. The cypress shingle roof and weatherboards were then installed to protect the waddle from the elements. Only under the ubiquitous front gallery was the *bousillage* exposed to view; a protective coating of whitewash was applied to the facade.[17]

Though the overall shape of the Acadian house remained constant throughout the nineteenth century, the size of the structure varied according to the means of the builder. Upon completion, the typical *petit habitant* house was a small, one-room, rectangular, raised structure, with a *garconnière,* a finished portion of the attic where adolescent boys slept. More affluent Acadians extended this basic house plan horizontally, creating double- or triple-wide versions. All of the antebellum Acadian homes at Acadian Village—the largest collection of historical Acadian structures in Louisiana—are of the latter type and were built by prosperous farmers and small planters.[18]

The furnishings of Acadian homes were equally varied. The typical *petit habitant*'s one-room house was modestly furnished with handmade cypress furniture. Though the walls were profusely decorated with religious pictures and commercial advertisements (to keep the wind from blowing through cracks between the boards), the structure itself usually contained only one buffet, one table, four to six chairs, one armoire, one permanent bed, and several small roll-away beds. More affluent homes were often equally spartan, but the slightly more plentiful furnishings were far more elegant. By 1810, the homes of many upwardly mobile Acadian farmers contained mahogany, walnut, and cherry armoires, chests of drawers, tables, and chairs, as well as silver flatware.[19]

Whatever of its size and furnishings, the typical Acadian house was surrounded by a double *pieux*, or cypress post, fence. An outer fence enclosed both a barnyard and a small (10′ x 10′ to 15′ x 15′) square *magasin* (shed) of *poteaux-en-terre* (post-in-ground) construction, which served the small farmer as a barn. A second cypress picket fence surrounded the house, preventing hens from nesting beneath the structure.[20]

The tremendous amount of labor required to build, insulate, furnish, and enclose an antebellum Acadian house required the cooperation of neighboring households. On the Acadian frontier, such assistance was readily given without expectation of financial recompense. Participation in a house-raising party, however, was not without compensation. One observer indicates that "copious refreshments and a heavy meal cooked on the spot by the womenfolk are the reward for their service."[21]

The group cohesiveness manifested in Acadian house raisings extended to other social institutions such as *boucheries* and *bals de maison*. By bringing together isolated frontier residents for practical purposes, social events reinforced sociocultural bonds between members of the Acadian community. Such reinforcement was necessary because flights and feuds all too frequently punctuated the tranquility of the south Louisiana frontier. It is thus significant that rural settlers regularly participated in neighborhood folk dances sponsored on a rotating basis. Numerous nineteenth-century observers noted that *bals de maison* were held every Saturday night. By all accounts, Acadians regarded these weekly house dances as a welcome respite from their difficult and monotonous existence; hence Acadian farm families needed no encouragement to attend.[22]

The high level of Acadian participation in the weekly house dances is especially important because invitations were not issued on an individual basis. In the prairie parishes "a youth on his pony would take a small wand, and tie to its top end a red or white flag, and ride up and down the bayou, from the house where the ball was intended, for two or three miles; returning, tied the wand . . . above the gate informing all—'*This is the place.*'" Assumption Parish planter W. W. Pugh suggests that the dance summons was somewhat different along the Lafourche: "No cards of invitation to these parties were sent out . . . but the messengers were sent forth, who fired a gun before the door of each dwelling to attract attention, and announced in a loud voice, *bal ce soir chez* [a dance tonight at], and this was enough to secure a large attendance of both old and young." Whatever the mode of invitation, all neighbors were welcome, and attendance was inevitably heavy.[23]

Participants made their way to the dance by whatever means of transportation was readily available. Upon approaching an Acadian house dance in the prairies near Jeanerette, Alcée Fortier observed "vehicles of all sorts, but three-mule carts were most numerous." Balls were generally held "on galleries," "in bedrooms," and, according to oral tradition, in the front yards of *petit habitant* farmsteads. No admission was charged, and "any white person decently dressed" was admitted. Upon entering, parents deposited their small children in bedrooms adjoining the room designated as the dance floor, then dispersed into groups organized by age, sex, and marital status. Matrons, according to Fortier, spent the "whole evening assembled together in one corner of the hall . . . watching over their daughters." Older men organized friendly card games. (Serious gamblers were banished to the host's barn.) Only nonalcoholic beverages (usually black coffee) were dispensed by the hosts. (Some hosts apparently charged their guests for "refreshments.") Persons desiring alcohol had to leave the hall. Gumbo—in the prairie areas, chicken gumbo with rice—was served at midnight.[24]

Dancing resumed after the repast, with participants "generally [performing] cotillions & round dances." Nineteenth-century Acadians—at least most Acadians of the lower classes—were passionately fond of dancing. Observers of all backgrounds universally agreed that Acadian dancers exhibited remarkable dexterity and grace on the dance floor. Music was ordinarily provided by two, or less frequently, three fiddlers, who performed until four or five o'clock in the morning, when, in the prairie areas, they brought the gathering to a dramatic close. One observer was told by an authoritative source that "when the dance was over the musicians would rise, and going out in the yard would fire several pistol shots in the air, crying out at the same time: *le bal est fini* [the dance is over]."[25]

In the early nineteenth century, these gatherings were, according to eyewitness accounts, exceptionally peaceful and enjoyable, but, reflecting the rising tide of violence in rural Louisiana during the late antebellum, Civil War, and postbellum periods, relations between participants grew less and less harmonious. Outlanders who observed Acadians before the 1840s consistently indicated that the participants, clad in their finest attire, always maintained their best behavior, and even Acadian detractors conceded that "nothing boisterous was ever known" at early antebellum Acadian house dances. But according to George Washington Cable, by the late 1870s house dances often degenerated into fistfights between male participants outside the hosts' houses. By the 1880s, Cajun combatants routinely used handguns against their adversaries.[26]

Fights also occasionally marred other forms of entertainment, particularly during and after the Civil War. Violence sometimes resulted from disputes over unpaid gambling debts, usually owed by non-Acadians. One such dispute during the Civil War ended in a shootout between an Acadian and his parish priest in front of St. Mary Magdalen Catholic church in Abbeville, Louisiana. Such violent confrontations over disputed gambling debts were by no means an everyday occurrence, but they helped to confirm the widely held belief that by contemporary Anglo-American standards the Acadians were inveterate gamblers.[27]

This belief was reinforced by the Acadian fondness for horse racing. Throughout the nineteenth century, horse races featuring blooded stock attracted hundreds of Acadian observers. Most races, however, were private affairs matching Creole ponies or even draft animals after the Civil War. One observer maintained that "all the Acadians are great riders and they and their little ponies never seem to be tired. They often have exciting races."[28]

The primary function of horse races, card games, and *bals de maison* was, of course, entertainment, but dances also served as a means of regularly using, and thus preserving, the Acadians' traditional music, cuisine, dances, and language. Like the *bal de maison,* the *boucherie* served a dual role within Acadian society; as with the rural dances, sponsorship of the butchery was on a rotating basis, and all members of the Acadian community within a small geographic area participated. Though *boucheries* provided the participants with a continuous supply of fresh meat in an age without refrigeration, the regular meetings gave neighbors the opportunity to renew acquaintances and to exchange views, thereby periodically reinforcing the sense of group identity.[29]

Acadian community spirit was also undergirded by frequent nocturnal visits, or *veillées.* In these visits, which were usually held in the idle winter months after the evening meal, hosts and visitors divided into groups by sex and age. While men carved "wooden utensils, repaired their farm tools and made baskets," women manufactured thread, repaired torn clothing, and cared for the children who clustered around them. Though the conversation was inevitably dominated by males, the usual topic of conversation was not politics or agriculture but folktales. As the fire in the fireplace cast flickering shadows across the one-room *caban*, fathers recounted miraculous cures by local *traiteurs* (folk healers) or personal encounters with mythical *sabbats* (apparitions) and *feux-follets* (will-o'-the-wisps).[30]

Though intended to relieve the monotony of frontier life during the idle and dreary winter months, which were punctuated only by festive Christmas, New Year's Day, and Mardi Gras celebrations, *veillées* also preserved Acadian folk beliefs. Folkways and superstitions were not only a conspicuous part of Acadian oral tradition; they constituted an integral part of everyday life. Poor crops or livestock epidemics were typically attributed to a sorcerer's spell. Omens also foretold good or ill fortune, phases of the moon dictated the proper time for cutting hair, and religious feast days signaled the onset of the planting season. Finally, most *petits habitants* firmly believed in faith healing.[31]

The dominant institutions in Acadian folk theology were *traiteurs* and sorcerers. Combining elements of mysticism and Catholic dogma, *traiteurs* and sorcerers practiced a unique brand of folk medicine. In rural areas, particularly in the southwestern Louisiana parishes, medical doctors were unavailable. Therefore, settlers stricken with illness turned out of necessity, as well as by choice, to the folk physician. Like their modern college-trained counterparts in the health care field, *traiteurs* specialized in various human and animal diseases, ranging in severity from warts to *charbon* (anthrax). The most commonly treated maladies, however, were warts, toothache, earache, rheumatism, inflammations, tumors, and bleeding. *Traiteurs* also treated *rezipère*, a disease causing swelling in the extremities, as well as erysipelas, angina, dislocations, and whitlow. In most instances, patients traveled to *traiteurs'* homes for treatment, but bedridden persons were treated either by proxy at the homes of the "most powerful" *traiteurs* or, more commonly, through house calls.[32]

In treating an ill patient, the attending *traiteur* usually administered "holy water, wax and signs of the cross, mixed with secret prayers." These prayers, which invoked the power of *Notre Père* (God the Father) or *la Sainte Vièrge* (the Holy Virgin), were the most powerful weapons in the *traiteurs'* medical arsenal, and, as the "divine gift of healing" was considered a sacred trust, the incantations were closely guarded secrets. Moreover, most *traiteurs* neither sought nor accepted payment or verbal *remerciements* (thanks) from their patients. Though *traiteurs* frequently instructed their children in Acadian folk medicine, the intricacies of the extrareligious healing services were usually passed on to young men, both black and white, who sought private instruction in folk medicine; the apprentice *traiteurs* were strictly enjoined to maintain a veil of secrecy around their mystical rituals. Treatments for ailments such as burns, warts, toothache, eczema, and *rezipère* were communicated only to immediate family members of the opposite sex, whereas treatments for childhood diseases and female disorders were transmitted exclusively to female family members.[33]

Like *traiteurs,* sorcerers invoked divine providence to relieve the pain of "severe arthritis, internal sickness, and sickness of the members." Unlike *traiteurs,* sorcerers mixed Catholic sacramental and religious trappings, such as holy water, with medieval black magic. According to the "Anonymous Breaux Manuscript," these "wizards," after "arresting" the disease with magical incantations, prescribed novenas and plasters made with mysterious elements, such as May dew drops, which, though medically ineffective, frequently evoked psychosomatic benefits. Once the patient's physical discomfort abated, Acadian sorcerers prepared a *sachet* or amulet containing spiders and frog and snake bones to be placed around the patient's neck for nine days to dislodge the evil spirit responsible for the illness.[34]

Reliance on folk healers and black magic did not diminish Acadian devotion to the Catholic church. *Traiteurs* and sorcerers consistently were (and remain) devout Catholics and regular churchgoers. The devotion of Acadians to their Catholic faith remained unshakable throughout the nineteenth century. Writing at the turn of the century, Alcée Fortier maintained that the rural Acadians with whom he had recently come into contact were "deeply religious." The relationship between Acadian Catholic communities and their respective pastors, however, was far less harmonious. Religious disputes were not confined to any economic class or geographic region.[35]

Acadians from all walks of life, but usually from the lower rungs of the economic ladder, resented the encroachment of ecclesiastical authority when the Catholic church experienced explosive growth between 1815 and 1850. This was particularly true of the Teche Valley and prairie parishes, where contact between the western Acadians and local missionaries remained minimal into the antebellum period. Numerous churches were established specifically for these long-neglected Catholics, however, between 1819 and 1847: St. Charles Church, Grand Coteau, 1819; St. John the Evangelist Church, Vermilionville, 1821; St. Peter's Church, New Iberia, 1838; Our Lady of the Sacred Heart Church, Church Point, 1840; St. Mary Magdalen Church, Abbeville, 1845; and St. Bernard Church, Breaux Bridge, 1847. Sporadic but intense disputes broke out between priest and parishioners when clerics attempted to regiment their religiously lax and often unruly flocks. Priests were particularly alarmed by the "spirit of indifference in so many sections, especially among the men . . . who shied with steady determination at approaching the Sacraments and at attending Mass, or participating in Church activities." "Repeated inquiries [by priests] among old residents and aged members of the oldest families brought with monotonous regularity the same story: Men folks were completely indifferent to religion; they left that to the women and the children. Yet they insisted that they were Catholics and wanted to die and be buried as such." To overcome such resistance, missionaries to long-neglected areas and pastors of the new churches used their influence over their female parishioners to pressure men to attend mass. In addition, priests established special catechism programs for young boys as a means of tying Acadian men to the church. Acadian parishioners, particularly males, resented the priests' emendatory ambitions, demanding instead that the missionaries provide sacramental services only on request, with no strings attached.[36]

Such conflicting attitudes were not easily reconciled, and problems were inevitable. In late August 1834, for example, Father Ange-Marie-Felix Jan of St. Martin de Tours Catholic Church at St. Martinville refused, for unspecified reasons, to preside over the funeral of Acadian Jean Robichaud, and the priest was consequently forcibly expelled from the La Pointe (present-day Breaux Bridge) area by his predominantly Acadian parishioners and was publicly warned never to return.[37]

Despite such episodes, priests and missionaries gradually succeeded in luring to church a "nuclei of Catholic men on whom the pastor could depend." But this nuclei often proved far less tractable than their pastors would have hoped. Many of these lay church leaders—particularly those of Acadian descent—were Freemasons in open defiance of the church's ban against membership in such secret societies. Drawn usually from the gentry class, these Catholic men staffed the councils of *marguilliers*, or churchwardens, that ran south Louisiana's ecclesiastical parishes for much of the early nineteenth century when the Catholic church owned no real property. Under American law, "the Catholic church was not recognized as a legal entity[;] hence [it] could not acquire and hold any real property. In order to give the individual parishes of the diocese a legal entity, a corporation was formed, composed of laymen as trustees [*marguilliers*] chosen by the parishioners." Acadian churchwardens feuded almost constantly with clerics over the administration of local ecclesiastical affairs (both secular and temporal) throughout most of the antebellum period. Churchwardens for St. John the Baptist Catholic Church at Brusly, in West Baton Rouge Parish, bought and sold church property without consulting ecclesiastical authorities and also disbanded the Society of the Ladies of Benevolence, which evidently functioned as a social outreach adjunct of the church. When the local pastor objected, the council officially informed him that "hereafter he will not meddle in this matter since it is a temporal affair."[39]

Such incidents were commonplace in rural south Louisiana church parishes. The most serious clash between local ecclesiastical and secular authority, however, occurred in Vermilionville (present-day Lafayette). The troubles at St. John the Evangelist Catholic Church of Vermilionville began in 1825 with the arrival of its first resident pastor, Father Lawrence Peyretti, an Italian missionary who would serve the parish until 1841. By 1828, Peyretti had managed to alienate the St. John churchwardens, whom he evidently told the bishop were "not the most pious or exemplary Catholics by far"; the churchwardens, in turn, withheld $200 from Peyretti's salary, demanding that the pastor contribute to repayment of St. John's existing debt. Peyretti appealed the matter to the bishop, but he was unable to intercede because the churchwardens legally controlled the local church corporation. Peyretti was subsequently replaced, apparently because of his deteriorating relationship with the parish trustees, but relations between the St. John pastors and the churchwardens remained acrimonious. In later years, Fathers Joseph Billon and Francis P. Beauprez decried the impudence of their parishioners, who publicly complained about and occasionally insulted their priests.[39]

The local crisis of ecclesiastical authority reached its climax in 1842, when Father Antoine D. Megret was assigned to St. John the Evangelist Church. A highly controversial figure who had been expelled from Europe by the Vatican for his caustic contributions to *L'Avenir*, a French publication, Megret would brook no challenge to his authority as curé, and his short but stormy career in southwestern Louisiana (1842–53) was marred by almost unceasing feuding with secular officials and lay ecclesiastical authorities. He first ran afoul of the Vermilionville churchwardens in early 1843, when he attempted to proselytize the local slave population despite the vocal opposition of the president of the church council. The outraged churchwardens considered motions to suspend Megret's salary and to invalidate his appointment as pastor because of his refusal to renounce his French citizenship. Megret responded with a verbal assault on the lay council, whose motions he contemptuously labeled as "audacious." Not content to confront his opponents in the chambers of the church council, Megret established a short-lived weekly newspaper, *L'Union*, and filled it with ringing denunciations of the "rights of the *marguilliers*." Denying any obeisance to the churchwardens, the flamboyant Frenchman declared himself subject only to the bishop. The inevitable result was turmoil that disrupted the religious life in St. John parish, and in March 1843, Megret notified the bishop that "hell seems to be let loose."[40]

Megret's actions elicited an equally forceful response from the St. John curchwardens, who notified the Frenchman that he was free to leave if he could not abide the parish's administrative status quo. Not to be outdone, the curé replied that he fully intended to leave and that he would establish a second Catholic parish in Vermilionville in competition with St. John the Evangelist. Megret's impudence proved more than some of his parishioners could bear; after mass one day, apparently in the spring of 1843, Megret was insulted and assaulted by an irate Vermilionville Catholic in full view of numerous prominent townspeople, including the sheriff, who reportedly encouraged the assailant.[41]

Unintimidated by the attack, Megret refused to say mass in the St. John's church, and when his reports to the bishop failed to generate any response, he embarked on an abortive attempt to carry his case to the episcopal see. While Megret was detained by Catholic authorities at St. Martinville, the St. John churchwardens met and declared their intent to have no priest rather than submit to the ecclesiastical authority of the Diocese of New Orleans. The resulting impasse continued until June 1844, when the Louisiana Supreme Court, in a decision regarding a suit arising from similar circumstances in New Orleans, declared that the bishop of the Diocese of New Orleans had exclusive authority to regulate the public affairs and clergy of the church parishes in his jurisdiction. Capitalizing on the sudden reversal of the churchwardens' fortunes, Megret, in mid-1844, orchestrated the election of more pliant members of St. John's parish to a new church council by placing the polls in the church and manning the boxes with his own supporters. At the bidding of the curé, the new churchwardens began the task of dismantling secular control of the local Catholic church and, in 1846, transferred title to the facility to Bishop Antoine Blanc of New Orleans.[42]

Coinciding with, and contributing to, the vicious internecine struggle within the St. John the Evangelist parish was an effort by the local church to stamp out Freemasonry in the ranks of the Catholic community. Between the 1790s and the Civil War, Louisiana's Freemason lodges were dominated by Catholics, and Catholic Freemasons were often not only the leaders of the secular business and political communities but also members of the parish church councils. Freemasonry flourished in predominantly Catholic Louisiana despite the sometimes vocal opposition of church leaders. Though Freemasonry was not officially banned by the church until the first Vatican Council of the 1860s, the secret society had been the subject of periodic persecution by Catholic prelates since 1738. Because Louisiana was, for all practical purposes, a Catholic missionary diocese serviced by European missionaries throughout the nineteenth century, the hostility of many Continental Catholics toward Freemasonry was carried across the Atlantic. Freemasonry nevertheless continued to flourish in Louisiana, and its pervasiveness is perhaps best reflected in the membership of Bishop Louis-Guillaume-Valentin Dubourg's brother in the New Orleans lodge.[43]

Freemasonry flourished in Vermilionville long before Hope Lodge 145 chartered on February 10, 1857. Acadian planters and professionals were particularly prominent in the lodge. Four of the seven members of the parish council during the body's long-running feud with a succession of St. John pastors were reputedly Freemasons. Though the anti-Masonic wing of Vermilionville's Catholic community gained control of the parish council in 1844, French-speaking Catholics continued to dominate Hope Lodge until at least the Civil War era, in defiance of their pastors.[44]

The expulsion of the Freemasons and the restoration of the St. John church to episcopal control had profound ramifications for the evolution of Catholicism in the Acadian parishes. First, pastors increasingly dominated the ecclesiastical communities to which they ministered. These assertive curés also claimed and, in the absence of effective secular opposition, exercised exclusive jurisdiction over parish finances. The result was often unbridled spending in the form of massive capital improvement programs that left ecclesiastical parishes perpetually in debt.[45]

Rural Acadians were largely unaffected by controversies surrounding the urban church parishes. The principal point of contact with the Catholic church for most of them remained the major sacramentals. They seldom attended mass, and religious instruction was, and would remain, largely the province of Acadian females. Ron Bodin, the most recent student of Acadian Catholicism, has determined that

> there appears to have been little male involvement—aside from the priest's—in the church's saving mission. . . . Women preserved the Catholic faith in Louisiana. They substituted the home-based religious instruction they provided their children for formal educational opportunities not widely provided in the area until well into the 1920s. Since there were so few churches in the area, religious practices in the home were likewise substituted for church services and for the traditional Catholic sacramental practices traditionally provided by a church parish. Women taught their children to pray the rosary. . . . In the prairies women served as unofficial "deacons" of the sacraments. . . . Infants who could not be baptized by a priest were unofficially baptized by women in a ceremony referred to as an "andoyée." . . . Sometimes a priest was not able to visit remote rural areas for years, and this unofficial ceremony "held" until the child was officially baptized by a priest and was especially valued when an infant's life was in danger before it had been [officially] baptized. . . . Since few [rural Acadians] were able to attend church . . . the "white Mass" led by laymen, often "officiated" at by women who knew their prayers and acts, emerged for some as a

substitute for the church's eucharistic celebration. Practiced in private homes, but never widespread, [women explained] . . . the Mass to the assembled—even handing out communion as a practice to those being readied to receive the sacrament at the hands of a priest. With the passage of time, these instructional services became increasingly seen as an alternative to the real thing—the Mass. . . . The practice quickly died out when churches were established.[46]

Such informal practices were clearly seen as stopgap measures requiring validation by a priest. But as in the colonial period, baptisms and marriages were scheduled around hiatuses imposed by the ecclesiastical calendar (marriages could not take place during Advent and Lent) and the seasonal demands of the agricultural life. Yet the sacraments marking the three major milestones in life—birth, marriage, and death—were, and would remain, the three most important events in Acadian religious life.[47]

The birth of a child, announced by gunshots—three for a son, two for a daughter—brought the local women to the new mother's house. Though such mutual aid programs were significant social institutions, they were overshadowed by the selection of godparents for the child's christening, a practice that formally allied families. Godparents and godchildren formed bonds that endured a lifetime, and these bonds not only solidified ties between families but also reinforced group identity.[48]

Marriages, like baptisms, bound Acadian families dispersed along the frontier. Intercultural marriages, a means of social advancement for upwardly mobile Acadians such as Alexandre Mouton, also served to assimilate large numbers of poor Creoles, Anglo-Americans, Irishmen, and French immigrants into the lower strata of Acadian society. Unlike Acadian men of the lower economic strata, who usually married within the group, *Acadiennes,* who outnumbered their male counterparts, often married Creole and Anglo-American men. Over 40 percent of all Acadian women who married in Lafourche and Terrebonne parishes during the pre–Civil War era selected husbands from the lower economic strata of the aforementioned groups: 33.4 percent of Acadian brides took Creole spouses and 6.8 percent married Anglo-Americans. Though in a few instances these brides, particularly young, landed widows with small families, married above their station, most women selected husbands from the same social stratum. In exogenous unions, Acadians demonstrated a marked preference for French-speaking Creoles over Anglo-Americans, with Acadian-Creole marriages in prairie parishes outnumbering Acadian-American unions by three to one. In Lafourche and Terrebonne parishes, Acadian brides in exogenous marriages frequently took as husbands scions of Gallicized German Creole families. Originally from the German Coast (St. John and St. Charles parishes along the Mississippi River), these Germans, now French-speaking, had migrated into the Lafourche and Terrebonne regions at the time of the Acadian influx into these areas in the late eighteenth century. Children born of such exogenous marriages were reared as Acadians by their mothers, and within a generation, families such as the Quatrevingts, Hymels, Haydels, Verrets, Hulins, Begnauds, Domengeauxs, Burleighs, and many others were absorbed into Acadian society.[49]

The significance of interfamilial and intercultural alliances is best reflected in the severe scrutiny to which suitors were subjected. In the antebellum period, marriageable-age boys and girls were permitted to meet socially only at *bals de maison,* which were chaperoned by their parents. At such meetings "preferences developed and the young man who wanted to marry made his choice." Having selected a potential bride, the suitor selected a member of his clan to "negotiate" with the girl's parents. The representative called on the girl's family—always on a Saturday afternoon—and laid out the "good qualities and wealth of his *protégé,* while the girl's parents countered with eulogies of their daughter, her virtue and agreeable qualities." Though nothing was decided in the initial meeting, a warm reception by the girl's parents inevitably resulted in a dinner party for the couple and their parents, in whose presence a proposal was formally suggested. Acceptance of the proposal did not end the suitor's trials, for not only did the girl's parents "maintain a strict surveillance that was anything but agreeable," but the young man was compelled by custom to "obtain the permission of the numerous relatives of the bride-elect, even to the cousins." Having weathered this ordeal, the beau "hastened the wedding-day." On the appointed morning, the groom, accompanied by his parents and neighbors, traveled to the bride-elect's home, where the couple received her father's blessing. The wedding party then proceeded to the church, and after a brief wedding ceremony, the couple and their families returned to the bride's former home for a gala reception and a *bal de maison.*[50]

The Acadian love of ritual and the importance of the extended family, as manifested in weddings, was also highly visible at funerals. Upon the death of an Acadian, black cloths were draped over the pictures, mirrors, clocks, and beehives at the deceased's former residence. Straw was then removed from the deathbed and burned "near the house." The corpse, which had been bathed and enshrouded by persons who were not family members, was laid out in the largest available room and blessed by relatives with holy water. The bereaved family maintained an all-night vigil to permit distant relatives to view the body before interment. During the wake, mourners "prayed" and "sang Catholic hymns." On the following morning, large numbers of neighbors and friends gathered along the funeral route "to view the burial procession conveniently" and to accompany the improvised, ox-drawn hearse to the parish church, where, following a requiem mass, the body was buried.[51]

The deceased's memory was kept alive by the Acadian extended family, in keeping with the Catholic concept of the communion of saints. Acadian families regularly visited graves of relatives and friends, praying for the repose of their souls. The memory of the deceased was also kept alive by family gatherings where relatives reminisced about their lost loved one.[52]

The practice of preserving the memory of deceased family members illustrates the strength of familial ties within the Acadian community. Firmly bound together by cultural and blood ties, extended families constituted clans, centered on the original family property and dominated by the oldest surviving member, or patriarch. Interactions between clans were formal. Negotiations were conducted by clan representatives, and interfamilial marriages were viewed as formal alliances.[53]

Group identity transcended familial boundaries. *Petits habitants* east and west of the Atchafalaya River shared a common heritage, language, life-style, and life goals. Their culture was distinct from that of their more affluent Creole and Anglo-American neighbors. These cultural differences served to heighten the class tensions between the yeomen and their more affluent neighbors. *Petits habitants* resented the self-proclaimed superiority and sanctimony of their social "betters," while members of the social aristocracy were chagrined by Acadian "stubbornness" and "impudence." Poor Acadians were thus not only unwilling but unable to share to any great extent the materialism, social institutions, and improved technology that their neighbors so readily embraced.

The gulf between the *petits habitants* and Anglo-American planters, merchants, and professionals was especially wide, as is demonstrated in the reminiscences of J. B. Lawton, a veteran newspaperman who had solicited a subscription from a St. Martin Parish Acadian shortly before the Civil War: "He flatly told us he had no use for newspapers or books. He insisted that education made rascals of men and ruined women, unfitting them for positions as mothers and wives. He named . . . a number of persons in his own and neighboring parishes who were reputed to be smart men and said they were the biggest rascals in the country. 'No, no,' said he, 'I want my boys to be honest men and my girls good mothers and chaste wives, and if I educate them I will ruin them, and have only myself to blame for it.'"[54]

Self-imposed Acadian insularity was undergirded by economic self-sufficiency. The typical antebellum Acadian farm's garden provided adequate amounts of corn, potatoes, and vegetables, while home-grown cattle and hogs, as well as game killed during hunting expeditions, furnished the *petits habitants* a protein-rich diet. Aided by their children, Acadian men cultivated and harvested cotton and, in the prairie parishes, gathered wool for home consumption. Indeed, 51 percent of Vermilion Parish's Acadian ranches raised sheep, and nearly 40 percent of the *vacheries* in Lafayette, St. Landry, and Calcasieu parishes produced wool. Acadian livestock producers also often engaged in leather production. Leather, used in the manufacture of moccasins, boots, and furniture, was "softened and made easy to work by soaking it in a mixture of the cow's brain . . . and the marrow of the animal. It is then smoked, washed, and soaked again in hot water over a medium fire, and stretched and rubbed until dry, then scraped with a curved knife."[55]

Agriculture, herding, and hunting were male activities according to the Acadians' clearly defined sex roles. Men, however, contributed more to the household's support than food gathering and leather and fiber production. Antebellum probate records indicate that Acadian males were usually skilled carpenters and blacksmiths as well. A jack-of-all-trades, the typical *petit habitant* was capable of building his own wooden implements, furniture, carts, fences, and *sabots*, wooden shoes that were worn in the Lafourche Valley until the Civil War.[56]

The male's role as provider was shared by his spouse. Acadian women traditionally cared for the farm's barnyard animals, particularly milk cows, pigs, and hens. In the river and eastern bayou parishes, women sold surplus eggs to "market-boats from the city" (always meaning New Orleans), to generate funds for the acquisition of "a little flour, powder and shot," as well as pig iron, guns, and other manufactured items that could not be produced on the farm.[57] Acadian women spun and wove yellow cotton that was grown in small quantities on the *habitation,* producing Acadian cottonade, known throughout the state for its fine quality. The cottonade was dyed blue, red, brown, or black and then fashioned into clothing for family members. In the water-bottom areas, wives also constructed hats from palmetto fronds.[58]

Women's vital contribution to the Acadian family life included their role as transmitters of cultural values. Rearing of children was almost exclusively the domain of women, and, although teenagers were given a practical education at the hands of their respective role models, they received their cultural values as children from their mothers. Women's dominance over domestic affairs, always restricted by the husband's ultimate authority over family matters, became absolute on the death of the head of the household.[59]

Unlike fathers, who, as antebellum census reports and church records indicate, encountered little difficulty in remarrying, women burdened with children met with little success in securing a new spouse. Nor did many widowed matrons wish to remarry, for it meant loss of economic independence. Many widows successfully managed Acadian households and their attendant farming, ranching, and plantation operations. The 1830 census of St. James Parish, for example, indicates that 17.5 percent of all Acadian homes were headed by widowed mothers, and by the end of the antebellum period, widows had become a significant socioeconomic element in the affluent river parishes. Their importance is perhaps exemplified best by the fact that thirty-four of the ninety-one Acadian slaveholders in Ascension Parish were widows.[60]

Widows relied on their children or, in the river and bayou parishes, slaves to cultivate and harvest their crops, as well as tend the livestock. When such alternative labor sources were unavailable, widows, particularly in the prairie parishes, were forced to rely on the domestic arts—sewing, weaving, and spinning—to generate an income. Widows too old to support themselves by these means became professional midwives. For example, the 1860 census indicates that each of Calcasieu Parish's eight professional midwives was widowed, the head of a household, and between fifty and seventy years of age. Not all widows, particularly elderly ones, were obliged to support themselves. Married children usually cared for their aging parents, who, in turn, contributed baby-sitting services, thereby transmitting Acadian history and folklore to their grandchildren.[61]

Although charity began at home, it was not confined to intrafamilial relationships. Indeed, institutionalized mutual assistance programs were hallmarks of Acadian society. The group solidarity manifested in spontaneous gatherings of neighbors to assist needy friends was evidenced in traditions surrounding the three milestones of life: birth, marriage, and death. Upon the birth of an Acadian child, matrons from the local countryside would congregate at the new mother's home to assist her with child care, to cook for her family, and to care for her other children. Weddings were also an occasion for social gatherings. On the appointed morning, friends and relatives joined the bridal party for the wedding procession as well s the joyous reception that followed. Like the joys of life, the sorrow of death was shared by the Acadian community, which gathered for wakes and funeral processions.

Social bonds among Acadians were reinforced by agricultural institutions. The harvest, or *ramasserie*, was a communal undertaking, with men and women gathering individual crops on a rotating basis. Workers were paid only with generous amounts of food and drink, but the undertaking took on a festive atmosphere, characterized by "shouts of joy, songs, and animated talk." *Boucheries*, communal butcheries also sponsored by individual families on a rotating basis, not only provided Acadians with a continuous supply of fresh meat, but the gathering also helped to maintain community cohesiveness.

But antebellum Acadian society was not completely closed. Intercultural marriages provided the means of rapidly assimilating large numbers of poor Creoles, nineteenth-century French immigrants, and Anglo-Americans into the Acadian community. The identity of the core of Acadian society, the yeoman class, remained intact because existing ethnic and class cleavages, which usually coincided, remained well defined throughout the antebellum period and because relations between Acadian subsistence farmers and the Anglo-American and Creole planters were consistently poor. The resulting siege mentality among the *petits habitants* contributed greatly to Acadian social detachment and facilitated the preservation of traditional cultural institutions, as well as the equalitarian principles of their forefathers. Once absorbed into Acadian society through intermarriage, rival cultures could not survive.

THREE

Acadians and Politics, 1803–1860

The transformation of the antebellum Acadian community from a classless society to a highly stratified and diversified group profoundly influenced Acadian participation in the developing American political process. Nouveau riche sugar and cotton growers, small farmers, and *petits habitants* rallied around the political standards that purported to represent their individual and often conflicting interests. Hence by the end of the antebellum period, prominent members of the Acadian community's major economic groups emerged as leaders of rival political camps.

The high level of Acadian participation in Louisiana politics in the decade before the Civil War belies the group's initial reluctance to enter the political arena. Acadians were slow to participate in state politics but not because they were unfamiliar with democratic processes. In the eighteenth century, Acadians had elected delegates to deal with their English, French, and Spanish administrators. In addition, under the Spanish regime they had periodically elected *sindics* (eighteenth-century counterparts of modern police jurors) to supervise local public works projects and Acadians sporadically served as *sindics* throughout the south Louisiana districts in the late eighteenth

45

century. But the commandants, gubernatorial appointees who were the real political power brokers on the local level, routinely opposed Acadian interests when they conflicted with those of the Creole elite. The resulting political alienation of the Acadian population was reinforced by both the poor relationship between Louisiana's short-lived French regime and the Acadians and by the sense of uncertainty spawned by the colony's chronic political instability at the dawn of the nineteenth century. The Acadians were thus careful to maintain their distance from any government regime, maintaining a low profile as the colony passed from Spanish to French and ultimately to American hands in late 1803. American rule quickly proved as unacceptable as French domination, and Acadians shunned politics until the 1840s, when popular political parties and issues first emerged in rural south Louisiana.[1]

Acadian rejection of the American political system also stemmed from the group's frontier experience in that government positions were invariably occupied by the local non-Acadian minority that represented the interests of a distant and unsympathetic foreign power. Such had been the case in Acadia and Nova Scotia and later in Spanish Louisiana, and this pattern of foreign domination would continue in the early nineteenth century. Louisiana Acadians thus greeted the announcement in 1803 of the retrocession of Louisiana from Spain to France without enthusiasm. Acadian Francophobia stemmed directly from the 1785 immigrants' long, miserable sojourn in the motherland. A significant minority of Acadians in the river and Lafourche Valley parishes had participated in the 1785 migration, and their unpleasant memories of long years of exile remained vivid. Respect for the French colonial regime was further undermined by reports in November 1803, when Prefect Pierre-Clément Laussat assumed the reins of Louisiana's government, of the colony's sale to the United States. No longer facing the prospect of a stable, long-term French administration, the Acadians took no pains to conceal their antipathy toward Laussat and his new government.[2]

The exiles' reaction to the retrocession was, nevertheless, typically low-key. Upon his arrival at New Orleans, Laussat received messages of homage and support from residents of New Orleans and the German Coast (present-day St. John the Baptist and St. Charles parishes), but conspicuously absent were communiqués from the Acadian Coast, the Acadian settlements along Bayou Lafourche, and the Attakapas

District. The icy reception afforded the Frenchman by the Acadians contrasts sharply with their expressions of regret at the announcement of the Spanish evacuation, when several prominent Lafourche Acadians signed a memorandum deploring the Spanish withdrawal.[3]

Alienation of the Acadians from Louisiana's government was short-lived, for on December 20, 1803, William Charles Cole Claiborne took possession of Louisiana for the United States. Operating under presidential orders to draw French-speaking Louisianians into the embryonic American territorial government so as to broaden its base of support, Claiborne courted the Acadian Coast area in 1804 by appointing Ascension planter Joseph Landry as commandant of the Lafourche District on the basis of his government experience, bilingualism, and "profound attachment to the United States." In 1805, the chief executive named five Acadians as justices of the peace in the river parishes and ten influential river Acadians as officers in the Sixth Militia Regiment. Acadian support for the American regime thus seemed assured when, in September 1805, Joseph Landry, Felix Bernard, and Isaac Hébert were elected to Louisiana's first territorial legislature.[4]

Hopes for an Acadian-American political alliance were shattered in May 1806, when the Acadian representatives joined seven Creole legislators in condemning Claiborne's efforts to introduce English common law into Louisiana, as well as his excessive use of the executive veto. Acadian displeasure with the Claiborne administration became so intense that in 1806 Joseph Landry resigned from the legislative council in disgust.[5]

Landry's resignation apparently triggered a wave of popular rejection of American politics in the river parishes, and only one Acadian representative was elected to the first state constitutional convention in 1812. Louisiana's largest poor white element lacked a strong voice in the assembly, and its interests were ignored. The planter-dominated convention drafted a very undemocratic document reflecting the concerns of the state's emerging economic elite. Indeed, the state's first charter reserved the franchise for property holders, and state officeholding was effectively restricted to planters by high property qualifications: representative, $500 in property holdings; senator, $1,000; and governor, $5,000. Property qualifications for governor were especially significant, for the state's chief executive enjoyed extensive appointive powers and thus influence.[6]

The 1812 constitution profoundly affected politics in the Acadian

parishes for, although propertied Acadian males along the Mississippi, Lafourche, and Teche were generally unaffected, landless settlers in the southwestern prairies, the lower Lafourche Valley, and the
Terrebonne Parish area were disfranchised. As late as 1860, for example, 51.4 percent of all Acadians in Terrebonne Parish owned no
real estate. Since the state charter provided for rule by the social aristocracy, early political campaigns were essentially personality contests, and most Acadians expressed little interest in politics, except
in the river parishes, where ten prosperous Acadian farmers were
elected to the general assembly between 1812 and 1824. Acadian participation in national and gubernatorial elections was consistently
light until 1824, except in the river parishes of Iberville, St. James,
Ascension, and West Baton Rouge, where the gubernatorial campaign of Jacques Villeré, a French-speaking Creole sugar planter
from the neighboring German Coast, generated some fleeting interest. But aside from their electoral support for locally popular political
personalities, river Acadians initially demonstrated a marked reluctance to become full-fledged participants in the electoral process.
Only one river Acadian, Joseph Landry, appears to have run for the
state senate between 1812 and 1823. (Henry Schuyler Thibodaux,
founder of the town that bears his name, served in the Louisiana senate and as acting governor of Louisiana in 1824. But Thibodaux, born
of Acadian parents in Canada, was orphaned as a young child and
was raised by General Philip Schuyler, father-in-law of Alexander
Hamilton. Reared as an Anglo-American in New England and educated in Scotland, Thibodaux was hardly representative of the Louisiana Acadian community.)[7]

The political activity of the river Acadians, limited though it was,
contrasts sharply with the political paralysis of Acadians elsewhere.
The small voter turnout in the hinterlands is perhaps best exemplified by the 1816 gubernatorial returns for Lafourche Interior Parish, in that only eighty-nine of the area's approximately five hundred
potential voters participated. Of the eighty-nine Lafourche Interior
ballots, only eight were cast for Jacques Villeré, the only French-
speaking candidate, suggesting that many politically apathetic Acadians shunned the polls, permitting their more interested and aggressive, though less numerous, Anglo-American neighbors to carry the
election.[8]

Andrew Jackson's populist presidential campaigns of 1824 and 1828 attracted the interest of Acadians, particularly those at the lower end of the economic spectrum, who hovered dangerously close to disfranchisement under the 1812 state constitution. Jackson's populist image, his promise to expand suffrage, and his heroism at the Battle of New Orleans (1815), in which several hundred Acadians saw action, attracted many poor and moderately wealthy Acadians to Old Hickory's standard, particularly in the upper river and prairie parishes. Prairie Acadians were especially active in Jackson's campaigns, sponsoring barbecues and political rallies, and a leading Democrat, Alexandre Mouton, was elected as a Jackson presidential elector.[9]

The emergence of a populist element in Louisiana politics polarized budding Acadian politicians and voters along ideological lines that transcended class boundaries. In the 1828, 1832, 1836, and 1840 presidential elections, Acadian sugar growers in West Baton Rouge, Iberville, and Ascension parishes joined Lafayette Parish's less affluent Acadian ranchers in the Democratic camp. while the predominantly plantation parishes of St. James, Assumption, St. Landry, and St. Martin were solidly Whig. Factional cleavages among Acadians were most visible in the Teche Valley and in the parishes east of the Atchafalaya River. In the 1844 state senatorial election, Whig candidate Alexandre DeClouet carried the cotton-producing, predominantly Acadian precincts above St. Martinville, while A. E. Mouton, the Democratic candidate, carried all of the rural Acadian prairie precincts in Lafayette and Vermilion parishes. Only Fausse Pointe, an Acadian sugar-growing region in St. Martin Parish, broke the usually rigid bayou-prairie pattern, apparently drawn out of the Whig fold by Mouton's Acadian background.[10]

Acadian voters in Lafourche and Terrebonne parishes, particularly recent river parish immigrants, were politically inactive, having been disfranchised by the 1812 state constitution's property qualifications for voting. As late as 1860, 51 percent of all Terrebonne Parish's free households owned no real property. Hence the lower Lafourche and Bayou Terrebonne areas became bastions of Anglo-American Whiggery by default.[11]

Acadians in both political camps represented a broad range of socioeconomic groups, and only among the poorest Acadians was there a universal affinity to one party—the south Louisiana Democracy.

The diversity of the parties' adherents was also reflected in the Acadian leadership element in the Locofoco and Whig camps. Upwardly mobile Acadian river parish and upper Lafourche Valley sugar planters such as André LeBlanc and Aristide Landry were frequently staunch supporters of the Whig party, whose internal improvements and protective sugar tariff policies served their interests. As plantations displaced *petits habitants* in the late 1820s and 1830s, Acadian Whigs scored notable political victories in the eastern sugar parishes. At least twelve Acadian state representatives, one state senator, and one congressman were elected from the river and Lafourche Valley parishes under the Whig standard.[12]

Although eastern sugar parish planters occupied the most prominent positions in Louisiana's Whig party, less affluent Acadians held positions of importance in the local party machinery, particularly in the Teche Valley parishes. In St. Landry Parish, many large farmers and small planters, scions of long-established Acadian families, identified with the local Creole element and thus, not surprisingly, were staunch supporters of the Creole-dominated local Whig party. These Acadian Whigs often held prominent positions in the local party organization, serving on parish nominating committees, as delegates to partisan parochial assemblies, as parish representatives to state Whig conventions, and as members of Whig "vigilance committees," which roused the local electorate and supervised the polls on election day. Long years of service in the lower echelons of the local party organization were ultimately rewarded by nomination at the parish political caucuses as the party's standard-bearer in parochial elections; several Acadian Whigs were thus elected to police juries throughout south Louisiana.[13]

Though many prosperous and politically ambitious Acadians embraced the Whig party's tenets, particularly regarding internal improvements and protective tariffs, they realized that small farmers constituted a large plurality of voters in their home parishes. In 1860, for example, small farmers constituted 34 percent of all gainfully employed Acadians in Assumption Parish, 41 percent in Ascension, 47 percent in St. James, 38 percent in Lafourche, and 30 percent in Terrebonne. Because the small farmers looked upon the Whig party as an elitist and unsympathetic organization, it was expedient for aspiring planter-politicians to represent the views of their less affluent neighbors, who were roused from their political apathy by the equalitarian rhetoric of the Jacksonian Democrats. It is most significant that five of the six most highly placed antebellum Acadian officials—one U.S. senator, two governors, and two lieutenant governors—were elected on anti-Whig tickets.[14]

The leader of the Acadian anti-Whig forces was Alexandre Mouton, a third-generation Louisiana Acadian, who served as a Jacksonian Democrat in the U.S. Senate from 1837 to 1842. Upon returning to Louisiana in 1842, the Lafayette Parish planter attacked incumbent governor Isaac Johnson as a perpetual officeholder, denounced the state constitution of 1812 as an undemocratic document, and announced his candidacy for governor, advocating abolition of property qualifications for voting and direct election of all state officials. Johnson, an author of the 1812 constitution, futilely attempted to steal Mouton's thunder by advocating "a constitutional convention and the extension of the suffrage to every free white male without a property qualification."[15]

The significance of Mouton's successful linkage of the constitutional reform issue with his candidacy is best reflected in the 1842 returns in the Teche Valley and prairie parishes. The Democratic candidate garnered 60.45 percent of the votes cast in Lafayette, Calcasieu, St. Martin, and St. Landry parishes, while in the Teche Valley parishes, traditional bastions of political conservatives, three-fourths of the voters called for a constitutional convention in a local referendum. A closer examination of the constitutional referendum on the precinct level indicates that in St. Landry Parish, 90 percent of the ballots in the predominantly Acadian Grand Coteau and Plaquemine Brulée areas supported the call for a new state charter. Thus viewing Mouton as the champion of constitutional reform, Acadians as well as poor whites in north Louisiana and New Orleans rallied around the Democratic standard, propelling the former U.S. senator into office.[16]

Once installed as chief executive, Mouton launched a campaign to implement his political platform. His efforts to convene a constitutional convention to expand the suffrage initially were blocked by Whig legislators, who constituted a majority in the general assembly and who maintained that "the cry of conferring political power on laboring classes, and the assertion in the Declaration of Independence 'that all men are born free and equal,' was palpable fallacies." The general election for state legislators in 1843 proved to be a public mandate for the constitutional convention, and the necessary enabling act was approved by the legislature in 1844. Before the convention met in 1845, Mouton attempted to force the delegates' hand by sponsoring legislation designated to institute universal white male suffrage by substituting a nominal poll tax for constitutionally required property ownership. The general assembly deferred action on the bill, but the constitutional convention, honoring the recent mandate for electoral reform, extended suffrage to all white males over twenty-one years of age.[17]

The 1845 constitution received a resounding vote of approval by the state electorate in a November referendum. Support was nowhere greater than in the Acadian parishes, where 76 percent of the electorate approved the document. In the parishes where Acadians constituted a majority of the white population, the 1845 constitution enjoyed even greater popular support. In Ascension, Lafourche, and Lafayette parishes, it was approved by margins of 93, 85, and 99 percent respectively. Only in Terrebonne Parish, where most Acadian adult males were disfranchised by existing property requirements, was the constitution defeated, by a six-to-four margin.[18]

Three months after the constitution was approved, Mouton delivered his farewell address, expressing his wish to retire from public life. Although the former governor sought no office in the following decade, he maintained a very high profile in south Louisiana politics—as he had earlier during the 1842 and 1844 congressional and presidential elections—in an apparent effort to combat the effective use of Whiggish "demagoguery" in the Teche and prairie parishes. Because his crusade for universal white manhood suffrage had earned him "enormous power and influence among the masses . . . particularly in remote places," Mouton profoundly affected the course of politics in the western Acadian parishes during the twilight years of the antebellum period. Prairie parish political rallies featuring the former governor drew hundreds of spectators, and Mouton's fiery pro-Democratic and pro–Southern rights addresses fell on attentive ears. In elections in St. Landry Parish, Louisiana's most populous rural parish, between 1854 and 1860, for example, predominantly Acadian precincts gave Democratic candidates median majorities of 77.4 percent.[19]

This voting trend was not confined to the prairie and Teche Valley parishes. The Acadian planter-dominated precincts in Iberville and Ascension parishes, long bastions of the Louisiana Democracy, continued to provide Democratic candidates with large majorities throughout the 1850s. Similarly, Acadian small farmers and planters consistently provided Democrats with small margins of victory in the region's hotly contested local and state elections, and the propertyless Acadians in Lafourche and Terrebonne parishes, enfranchised by the 1845 constitution, transformed these areas from Whig strongholds in the 1840s to bitterly disputed political battlegrounds in the 1850s. Acadian Democratic voting strength was further augmented by the influx of many Acadian Whigs after the elitist party's demise in 1854 and the emergence of its anti-Catholic Know-Nothing successor in 1856. Although several of these political apostates supported the Know-Nothing party in 1856, most former Whigs remained in the Democratic camp, rising to positions of prominence in the local party organizations by 1860. In 1860, for example, former Whig and Know-Nothing Alexis O. Guidry campaigned in St. Landry Parish as a prosecessionist candidate sponsored by the Southern rights faction of the local Democratic party.[20]

Buoyed by this significant bloc vote, Democratic Acadian planters conducted successful campaigns for the state's highest offices. Sugar planter Paul Octave Hébert of Iberville Parish successfully campaigned for governor in 1852, and Trasimond Landry of Ascension Parish and Charles Homer Mouton of Lafayette Parish were elected lieutenant governor in 1845 and 1856 respectively.[21]

The impact of the growing Acadian participation in the political process was even more striking on the local level. In Ascension Parish, the proportion of Acadian members on the local twelve-member police jury rose from 25 percent in 1842 to 42 percent in 1855. Acadian political power, however, was nowhere more evident than in Lafourche Parish, where, in 1860, Acadians of modest means served as sheriff, assessor, ward constable, police jurors, and justices of the peace.[22]

Prairie Acadians were equally active in local politics. Though only two individuals attained such lofty positions as sheriff and district attorney, Acadians were well represented on the Lafayette, Vermilion, St. Martin, and St. Landry parish police juries. In St. Landry Parish, where Acadians constituted only 20 percent of the free population, they held, in 1856, the prestigious offices of police jury clerk and treasurer. Prairie Acadians also elected disproportionate numbers of delegates to Democratic parish conventions, a tribute to their political acumen, their unshakable loyalty to the local Democracy, and their willingness to sponsor and to participate in local political rallies. Indeed, on the prairies, Acadian residences were the usual sites of Democratic assemblies, and the hosts presided over the meetings in keeping with contemporary decorum.[23]

Because of the political opportunities afforded by the Democratic party as well as its tradition of populist reforms, Acadians remained the backbone of that political organization in south Louisiana, although after 1852 slavery and Southern rights replaced constitutional change as the major issues in local politics. In the late 1850s, at political rallies Acadian voters were subjected to progressively larger doses of Southern rights propaganda by leading Louisiana Democrats, including Alexandre Mouton, Charles Homer Mouton, Trasimond Landry, and Adolphe Dupuy. Because of their stature in the Democratic party and their high visibility in the Acadian community, these Democrats exercised tremendous influence over the Acadian electorate.[24]

The influence of the party leaders alone would not have been sufficient to maintain poor and modestly wealthy Acadians in the Democratic fold as the state Democracy grew increasingly radical in the 1850s. Most Acadian farmers and planters remained in the party, despite its changing ideology, because Louisiana's Democratic leaders articulated their views on slavery. Although antebellum Acadians of all major economic strata professed belief in the equality of all whites, most Acadians, particularly those in the sugar bowl parishes, displayed an equally fervent belief in the innate inferiority of blacks. A slaveowning mentality had appeared in the river and Lafourche Valley parishes by the late 1780s, and by 1810, small numbers of slaves were commonplace on Acadian river, Lafourche, and Teche Valley farms. The tremendous growth of the slave population in these areas after the emergence of a sugar-based plantation economy in the mid-1820s, as well as near hysteria generated throughout the sugar parishes by reports of Nat Turner's rebellion in Virginia in 1831, interacted to create a climate of paranoia among Acadian slaveholders in the 1830s. Acadian fears of slave uprisings prompted immediate action by the local governing authorities. In 1830, the Lafayette Parish police jury adopted an ordinance establishing heavy fines for free persons (potential abolitionists) found in slave quarters without the master's permission and for masters allowing the assembly of slaves from neighboring plantations. Later in the decade, the parish police jury adopted increasingly repressive slave regulations. Because of such oppression, the Lafayette Acadians' fear of slave revolts became a self-fulfilling prophecy, resulting in an abortive servile uprising in 1840. Fear of slave rebellions and the repressive local legislation they inevitably produced were not confined to Lafayette parish. St. Martin and the river parishes faced similar traumatic experiences, with identical results: abortive servile insurrections in the early 1840s.[25]

As the threat of black revolts loomed increasingly large on the horizon and Northern abolitionists intensified their humanitarian crusade, Acadian slaveholders joined the ranks of the Louisiana Democratic party, which in the late 1840s and early 1850s began to defend slavery as a positive influence on Negroes and Southern society. It is thus hardly surprising that the wealthy Acadian sugar planters of Iberville, Ascension, and West Baton Rouge parishes were among the Democracy's staunchest supporters.[26]

Prairie Acadians were equally loyal to the Democratic party even though most of the western ranchers and small farmers were not slaveholders. A slave mentality was noticeably absent on the prairies, and observers remarked that the few western slaveholders treated their chattel as humble members of the family. The ranchers' affinity to the Democratic party was based only secondarily on the party's stand on slavery. Far more important to the western Acadians was the leadership provided by Democrats in the local war against frontier brigandage.[27]

In the late 1850s, large numbers of rustlers began to prey on the prairie Acadians' large, unattended herds, and because of the absence of effective law enforcement, Acadian ranchers, like late antebellum farmers throughout the South and Midwest, felt compelled to police the prairies with extralegal vigilante groups. The first Acadian vigilante committee was organized at Côte Gelée (present-day Broussard), in Lafayette Parish, in January 1859. Neighboring communities soon followed suit, and by August 1859, at least sixteen committees operated in the prairie parishes. These quasi-military and judicial units combed the prairies at night for reputed criminals—particularly individuals recently acquitted of violent crimes—who, when apprehended, were either banished, flogged, or hanged. Sentences, determined in advance by fifteen-member vigilante judicial councils, were initially administered indiscriminately, and members of each major local ethnic group—blacks, Anglo-Americans, French and German immigrants, Creoles, and Acadians (even vigilantes' relatives)—tasted the vigilante lash.[28]

Although flogging was accompanied by an admonition to leave the state under penalty of death, many vigilante victims instead congregated in southwestern St. Landry Parish, near present-day Mire, and organized themselves into antivigilante groups, in emulation of their persecutors. The inevitable result was armed conflict. In early September 1859, south-central Louisiana's vigilante groups assembled to crush the growing antivigilante threat. Led by West Point graduate Jean-Jacques Alexandre Alfred Mouton and supported by a makeshift brass cannon, several hundred vigilantes formed a battle line in front of Emilien Lagrange's fortified home, where many antivigilantes and numerous, albeit reluctant, antivigilante conscripts—reportedly totaling approximately two hundred persons—had gathered. Although many antivigilantes dispersed immediately after the attackers' opening shots and many others surrendered peacefully, the victors dealt harshly with their captives, beating several to death and shooting an undetermined number of others who either resisted flogging or attempted to escape into the open prairie. The provigilante *Opelousas Courier* suggested that an additional eighty captives were transported to Lafayette Parish, near present-day Scott, Louisiana, where they were "tried by Judge Lynch" (that is, lynched).[29]

Though sympathetic local newspapers attempted to minimize the death toll at the so-called Battle of Bayou Queue de Tortue, this apparent bloodbath did not escape the notice of the state government. Antivigilante forces called for immediate and forceful action, but state authorities were slow to react. The government's reluctance to intervene was mistakenly interpreted by the vigilantes as tacit support. But their unabated activities eventually forced Governor Robert C. Wickliffe's hand, and the vigilance committees reluctantly disbanded when Wickliffe threatened to use the state militia against them in late September 1859. Prairie newspapers, however, suggest that the disbanding was only temporary. The *Opelousas Courier,* for example, reported on April 21, 1860, that "the vigilant[e]s are in motion! From Faquetaique, Plaquemine Brulée, Bois Mallet, Gros Chevreuil, even to Washington, the cry is they are marching calmly, quietly, but determinedly to the accomplishment of their purposes."[30]

Throughout the vigilance committees' reign of terror in 1859, they were shielded from Wickliffe's increasingly vocal opposition to their extralegal activities by prominent prairie parish Democrats. Foremost among the vigilantes' supporters was former governor Mouton, the president of the Vermilionville vigilance committee, whose unassailable reputation lent respectability to the paramilitary organizations. Mouton also personally interceded with Governor Wickliffe on the vigilantes' behalf. Because of his position as *"parrain* [godfather] of the men who raised the revolutionary standard of the vigilantes" as well as his position as elder statesman in southwestern Louisiana, Mouton emerged by 1860 as the undisputed political kingpen of the western Acadian parishes.[31]

The former governor's role in late antebellum prairie parish politics indicates that by 1860 the Democratic party had become, to paraphrase St. Paul, all things to all Acadians, In the twilight years of the antebellum period, western Acadians viewed local Democratic leaders as champions of law and order on the increasingly lawless frontier. Teche Valley Acadian sugar growers, as well as their more affluent counterparts in West Baton Rouge, Iberville, and Ascension parishes, viewed local Democratic leaders such as Trasimond Landry, Alexandre Mouton, Charles Homer Mouton, C. O. Hébert, Camille Landry, V. J. Dupuy, and Adolphe Dupuy as staunch defenders of the South's peculiar institution and thus their not inconsiderable investment in black chattel. The *petits habitants* and the propertyless Acadian migrants in Lafourche and Terrebonne parishes viewed the south Louisiana Democracy as the defender of the common man and the author of the Jacksonian constitution of 1845, which had enfranchised the state's poor whites. Because Acadian voters throughout southern Louisiana looked to the planter-dominated Democratic hierarchy for political leadership, *petits habitants,* farmers, and small planters were firmly wedded to the political interests of the pro–Southern rights planters, a marriage that would have dire consequences in the stormy years of sectional conflict ahead.

FOUR

Secession Crisis and the Civil War

Despite the fragmentation of Acadian society during the antebellum period, as well as the increasing materialism of the nouveau riche planters, most of Louisiana's Acadians remained an insular people whose view of the world extended no farther than their parish boundaries. Affairs of national importance such as the increasing volatile slavery issue were of only marginal interest to these south Louisianians. Their self-imposed insularity was shattered by the onset of the Civil War and the establishment of military conscription by the Confederate States government. This unwelcome encroachment into their daily lives was bitterly resented by most Acadians, who, incapable of identifying with the Southern cause, passively resisted conscription. In the late 1970s, elderly Acadians still referred to the conflicts as "*la querre des Confédérés,*" or Confederates' war, in a tone inferring that the struggle was locally unpopular. The Acadian population, however, contributed three brigadier generals and a host of lesser officers to Louisiana's Confederate forces and state and parish governments.[1]

This apparent paradox was the result of the divergent interests of the various classes in Louisiana Acadian society. As war clouds gathered in 1860, these people were divided into two major ideological groups: staunchly pro-Southern Acadian planters and large farmers, who engaged in staple crop production with numerous slaves, and the farm more numerous yeoman farmers and ranchers, who had precious little interest in Southern rights, despite their traditional allegiance to the state's Democratic party. The close identification of Acadian large slaveholders with the Southern planter establishment can be attributed to the assimilation of nouveau riche Acadians, such as Louisiana governor and future Confederate general Paul O. Hébert, into the Creole planter aristocracy. These upwardly mobile Acadians consciously emulated their wealthy Creole neighbors in the 1830s and 1840s by drastically expanding their landholdings and acquiring large numbers of slaves to cultivate their new acquisitions. This evolutionary process perhaps had its greatest impact on the region's political scene.[2]

The Acadian planters, while visibly severing their ties to their cultural heritage and simultaneously seeking to distance themselves socially from the *petits habitants,* expediently courted the support of their less affluent neighbors as they sought to take their place in the state's planter-dominated politics. The insular Acadians seemingly welcomed the political leadership of the economic elite, particularly those residing on the isolated prairies, who looked to former governor and United States senator Alexandre Mouton for political guidance from the early 1840s until 1860. Unfortunately for these nonslaveholders, Mouton worked tirelessly for Southern rights and, later, for secession following his supposed retirement from politics in 1847.[3]

Because of the former governor's ideology and unblemished record of Democratic party support, the 1860 state Democratic convention elected him chairman of the state delegation to the national party assembly at Charleston. When the convention became deadlocked over the issue of mandatory federal protection of slavery in the territories, Mouton led the Louisiana delegation in bolting the meeting. Mouton's actions were subsequently endorsed by the state Democratic Central Committee, and the Pelican State delegates were instructed to attend the reconvened Democratic convention in Baltimore, Maryland. Supporters of presidential hopeful Stephen A. Douglas managed to block admission of the anti-Douglasite Louisiana and Alabama delegations, and the censured delegates, accompanied by many

Douglas opponents, held a rump convention and selected John C. Breckinridge as their standard-bearer.[4]

Upon returning to Louisiana, Mouton actively supported the Breckinridge campaign, and, through the efforts of the former governor and his cohorts, the Kentuckian carried the western Acadian parishes. Mouton's crusade for Southern rights, however, was not terminated by Breckinridge's ultimate defeat by the Republican candidate, Abraham Lincoln; on the contrary, following "Father Abe's" election and Governor Thomas O. Moore's subsequent call for a secession convention, Mouton, who had maintained a high profile in the prairie parishes throughout the presidential campaign, announced his candidacy as a secessionist delegate.[5]

Mouton's candidacy as delegate favoring immediate dissolution of Louisiana's ties to the federal government profoundly influenced the election's outcome in the prairie parishes, for, as the most prominent local politician of Acadian descent, his fellow Acadians looked to him for guidance. Running on the secessionist ticket for the senatorial seats representing the northern prairie parishes, Mouton and Lucius J. Dupré of St. Landry Parish overwhelmed their cooperationist opponents who favored the coordinated secession of the Southern slave states only if a proposed negotiated settlement of the slavery controversy failed. In the district's component parishes of Calcasieu, Lafayette, and St. Landry, the secessionists polled majorities of 96, 87, and 52 percent respectively. Only in St. Landry Parish did the Mouton-Dupré campaign receive a stern test, a challenge arising from the resurgence of the region's once dominant Whig party faction, which sponsored a slate of cooperationist candidates. Alexandre Mouton's political ally Alexandre DeClouet of St. Martin Parish conducted a victorious secessionist campaign on the lower prairie. In Vermilion and St. Martin parishes, the prosecessionist candidate received 78 and 80 percent majorities respectively.[6]

As the secessionist juggernaut rolled over the prairie parishes, Acadians Joseph A. Breaux, Edmond L. Melancon, and J. K. Gaudet led an equally successful cooperationist campaign in the river parishes. These campaigns usually originated at parish-wide political rallies. In St. James Parish, a public assembly in mid-December adopted resolutions urging the convocation of a slave state congress, which would "summon back into the Union those of the Northern States which

have withdrawn it, by violation of the Constitution." States either ignoring the call or refusing to refrain from continued transgressions
of Southern constitutional rights would be expelled from the Union.
Other river cooperationists proposed laws that were fanciful solutions
to the national political impasse over slavery, but all conceded that,
barring an improbable negotiated settlement, secession was the ultimate solution, the only viable means of protecting the South's vitally
important peculiar institution.[7]

The faint hope of a negotiated settlement offered by the cooperationists appealed strongly to the large Acadian slaveholders in the
river parishes who, like their counterparts throughout the South,
feared the potentially ruinous consequences of a voyage across the
uncharted waters of revolution and war. It is thus hardly surprising
that, with the exception of Iberville Parish, where the Acadians constituted a large minority of the free population, cooperationists dominated the delegations representing the river and Lafourche Valley
parishes.[8]

Affinity for the cooperationist and secessionist causes paled into
insignificance by January 23, 1861, when the delegates assembled in
Baton Rouge. By late January, public opinion had swung solidly in
favor if immediate secession. The erosion of public support for the
cooperationist platform was reflected in the collapse of cooperationist
opposition to a secession ordinance at the Louisiana convention. On
January 26, the assembly, by a vote of 113 to 17, dissolved "the union
between the State of Louisiana and other States."[9]

The secession of Louisiana was only one in a series of political
upheavals that culminated in early February 1861 in the establishment of a confederation of seven Deep South slave states. When
President Lincoln challenged the fledgling government's authority by
attempting to reinforce Fort Sumter in Charleston Harbor in early
April 1861, Confederate batteries bombarded the garrison into sub-
mission, thereby committing the Confederacy to an armed struggle
for independence.

The reduction of Fort Sumter by Confederate batteries was followed closely by the secession of the Upper South as well as Lincoln's
call to arms. Responding to the threat of armed Northern intervention, twelve thousand Louisiana volunteers rallied to the Confederacy's colors by June 1, but very few members of these volunteer units,

most of which were quickly dispatched to Virginia, were of Acadian descent. For example, Company C of the Sixth Louisiana Infantry Regiment, raised in St. Landry Parish by Acadians L. A. Cormier and L. E. Cormier, included only eight Acadians in its complement of ninety-four officers and men. In the river parish units, however, 27 percent of the recruits on the Donaldsonville Artillery Battery's muster roll bore Acadian surnames, though only five Acadian families resided in that Ascension Parish community.[10]

As demonstrated by the muster rolls, regional, cultural, and class differences among river and prairie Acadians continued to mold their perception of, and affinity to, the Southern way of life. Wishing only to be left alone, the insular, poor, nonslaveholding prairie Acadians viewed the war as an elitist cause, and their apathetic response to Confederate recruiting ventures is hardly surprising. As B. W. Blakewood noted in a July 1861 letter to the Confederate secretary of war, L. P. Walker: "A goodly number of our citizens can neither speak nor understand the English language. . . . Talk to them of our constitutional rights and the sires of the Revolution, they look upon you with astonishment. That portion of our citizens that are best able to endure the hardships of a campaign are not in the field."[11]

The prairie Acadians' apathy was not shared by their more affluent cousins east of the Atchafalaya River. Many river Acadians had entered the planter class and thus had a significant stake in the outcome of the war. Because of their high socioeconomic status, most Acadian planters volunteered for military service as officers, either by rising companies or regiments, as did Brigadier General Louis Hébert; through regimental and company elections; or, as in the case of future Louisiana Supreme Court chief justice Joseph A. Breaux, through appointments as aides-de-camp. Because river Acadian officers were widely distributed throughout the regiments raised in Louisiana, the number of Acadians in companies organized in the river parishes was frequently deceptively low. This is not to say that they were not well represented in these units. According to Napier Bartlett, J. O. Landry of Ascension Parish "went into the Confederate service as Lieut. Colonel of the 28th Louisiana, carrying with him five companies from his own parish, and as many blood relatives as the chief of a Scottish clan."[12]

Alfred Mouton, son of former governor Alexandre Mouton and

hero of a vigilante campaign in the late 1850s to rid the prairies of cattle and slave rustlers, also waged a successful recruiting campaign among the prairie Acadians in December 1861. But Mouton's success was atypical and must be attributed to his leadership position in the Acadian community rather than to the recruits' affinity to the Southern cause.[13]

Acadian apathy toward the war effort quickly degenerated into open hostility following the enactment of the initial Confederate Conscription Act in April 1862. Opposition to the measure was centered in the prairie parishes, where the isolated and highly individualistic Acadian farmers and ranchers viewed forced recruitment as an intolerable intrusion into their peaceful lives. Recruitment programs in southwest Louisiana were also directed by Anglo-Saxons, usually east Texans, who viewed the Acadians as social and cultural inferiors and treated them accordingly.[14]

Conscription was first brought home to the prairie Acadians by the fall of New Orleans in April 1862 and the transfer of the Confederate state government to Opelousas. Fearing Federal invasions into southwest Louisiana, the state adjutant general directed Brigadier General John G. Pratt of the state militia to establish a camp of instruction as a means of quickly processing conscripts badly needed by the Pelican State units in the Confederate service.[15]

Camp Pratt, the enrollment and training installation established by General Pratt along the northern shore of Spanish Lake[16] in May 1862, seemed a living "Purgatory" to Acadian conscripts. According to Lieutenant George C. Harding, a Union prisoner of war detained at the camp of instruction from September through October 1862, life at the installation was dismal at best for these conscripts, who wished only to remain on their prairie farms and *vacheries:* "Camp Pratt was filled with Acadiann [sic] conscripts. . . . The wants of the Acadiann [sic] are few and his habits are simple. With a bit of cornbread, a potato, and a clove of garlic, with an occasional stewed crawfish, he gets along quite comfortably, and for luxuries, smokes husk cigarettes and drinks rum—when he can get it. The Acadiann has great powers of endurance, but not much stomach for fight. Of the herd at Camp Pratt, desertions were frequent, sometimes as many as thirty or forty stampeding in a single night. But they would be caught, brought back, made to wear a barrell [sic] for a week or two, and finally broke in." Thus forcibly detained, the Acadian conscripts vented their frustrations by glaring for hours on end at Harding and his fellow Union prisoners of war, whom they apparently viewed as the ultimate source of their misfortunes.[17]

Acadian opposition to conscription, intensified by the virtual imprisonment of the conscripts at Camp Pratt, grew throughout the summer of 1862 and culminated during the early fall with the draftees' refusal to report voluntarily to the camp for processing. The Acadians' passive resistance to conscription coincided with feverish Confederate preparations to defend the Lafourche and Teche valleys from an imminent Federal invasion. To staff the regiments raised for the waterways' defense, as well as to reinforce Alfred Mouton's Eighteenth Louisiana Infantry Regiment and V. A. Fournet's Yellow Jacket Battalion, units assigned to Major General Richard Taylor's command after having seen action at the Battle of Shiloh, Taylor, the district commander, was compelled to dispatch cavalry impressment details into the prairies. By this means, approximately three thousand men were "enrolled and reported to Camp Pratt"; of this number, two thousand were assigned to Mouton's and Fournet's units. In 1862, 75 percent of the Eighteenth Louisiana's Acadian recruits were conscripts trained at Camp Pratt. As reports of impressment spread among the prairie households, many draft-age Acadians went into hiding and, in the words of General Taylor, had "to be hunted down by detachments" from his small army "and brought in tied and sometimes ironed."[18]

The effect of impressment was devastating to the already low Confederate morale in south Louisiana. An intelligence report drafted by Union Brigadier General Godefrey Weitzel states that "a refugee who came in from Attakapas this morning reports that the enemy is conscripting everybody, old and young; that they have quite a force on the Teche, but that there is great dissatisfaction among the troops." These reluctant rebels patiently awaited an opportunity to prove themselves a liability to the Confederate military, for whom they took no pains to conceal their contempt. In their baptism of fire at the Battle of Labadieville on October 27, 1862, the Camp Pratt conscripts assigned to the Eighteenth Louisiana reportedly "threw away everything they had about them, except their guns, and made back tracks, boasting as they ran, that they had not fired a gun."[19]

The poor performance of the Acadian conscripts at the Battle of

Labadieville was an ominous beginning for the Confederate defense of the Lafourche and Teche valleys. Faced by overwhelming odds and forced to rely on unseasoned troops, Dick Taylor could do little more than fight delaying actions when Major General Nathaniel P. Banks launched a full-scale invasion of south-central Louisiana in mid-January 1863, and although the Acadian conscripts performed admirably in numerous skirmishes along the lower Teche, as well as at the battles of Bisland (April 12–13, 1863) and Irish Bend (April 14, 1863), they took advantage of the Confederate retreat to return to their homes.[20] According to General Taylor, during the frantic Confederate dash to safety in north Louisiana after the Battle of Irish Bend, Brigadier General H. H. Sibley, Taylor's inept brigade commander, deserted his command, thereby permitting his men to straggle "without order over the whole line of march and adjacent country. . . . Thus commenced the scattering and straggling of our troops and falling back to Vermilion Bridge. Nearly the whole of Lt.-Colonel Fournet's battalion, passing through the country in which the men had lived, before joining the army, deserted with their arms, remaining at their homes." In Companies B and D of Fournet's Yellow Jacket Battalion, the entire Acadian contingent deserted.[21]

This reprieve from compulsory military duty was short-lived. After pursuing Taylor's rapidly dwindling army as far as Alexandria, Banks's Union invaders turned southeastward and laid siege to Port Hudson, taking with them over ten thousand head of cattle, Creole ponies, and mules from the Acadian prairie *vacheries*. In an effort to lift the siege, Dick Taylor's Texas cavalry regiments invaded the upper Lafourche and Teche valleys, and, though subsequently repulsed in the east at Donaldsonville, the rebels captured Brashear City, the strategic rail terminus commanding the entire Teche Valley.[22]

Now firmly entrenched in southwestern Louisiana, Texans, led by Brigadier General John Pratt, scoured the prairies for conscripts and deserters. Pratt and his underlings were ruthless in the execution of their duty, and a contemporary reported that the notorious enrolling officer secured recruits by "hunting them down with dogs, like slaves." These conscription forays were far less successful than their predecessors, for the majority of men subject to conscription, skulkers and deserts alike, had sought refuge either in the Atchafalaya Swamp or in the equally vast and sparsely inhabited prairie region.[23]

The prairie afforded them no natural defense, and the fugitives were compelled to organize quasi-military bands to ward off the gray-coated predators. These bands, organized immediately following the northward flight of Taylor's army in the spring of 1863, operated primarily out of western and northwestern St. Landry Parish. Called Jay-hawkers by Confederate sympathizers, these bands were such superb fighting units that they effectively banished rebel conscription units from the area west of Bayou Mallet and east of the Calcasieu River. Extant service records for the predominantly Acadian Eighteenth Louisiana Regiment and the Yellow Jacket Battalion indicate that only forty-three Acadians entered the service in 1863 (more than two thousand had been forcibly conscripted into the Confederate army one year earlier), and, of this number, thirty-four (79 percent) were conscripts.[24]

The Jayhawker bands were initially organized along ethnic lines, and the muster rolls of Ozémé Carrière's unit, provided to Confederate authorities by victims of the deserters' foraging raids, included not a single Acadian surname. The evidence thus suggests that the Acadian skulkers and deserters south refuge behind the formidable Jayhawker defensive perimeter, as did an estimated eight thousand of their counterparts from north Louisiana and east Texas. But though the prairie Acadian population benefitted from the guerrillas' presence, the Acadians, particularly the residents of present-day Acadia Parish, also bore the brunt of the latter's frequently violent foraging raids, which usually left the settlers with "nothing of value."[25]

In addition to Jayhawkers and Confederate conscription parties, the prairie Acadians were confronted by a third external threat—Union raiders. In August 1863, General Banks launched his notoriously unsuccessful Great Texas Overland Expedition, and by late September, his forty-thousand-man army had advanced to Opelousas in the face of stubborn resistance from Colonel Thomas Green's Texas calvary unit. Chafing under the "oppression" of the Texas units, the prairie Acadians greeted the Federal troops as an army of liberation. An unidentified Indiana officer, writing from a camp along the Vermilion River, reported on the Acadian reaction to the Union invasion: "The Union feeling in this portion of the state—especially among the poor class of citizens, is very strong. They are coming into our lines by the hundreds, and either volunteering or taking the oath of allegiance. Many of them say they have not been home or inside of a house for eighteen months, but have been hiding in the swamps to avoid the conscription. There is now already near three hundred of them mounted, and acting as scouts, and they are found to be very useful, as they are acquainted with every part of the country."[26]

While encamped at Vermilionville in October 1863, Union Brigadier General Charles P. Stone, Bank's chief of staff, reported that hundreds of residents in that overwhelmingly Acadian area had taken the oath of allegiance to the United States government and, having grown "heartily tired of Texan rule," wished "to arm to protect the country from further inroads on the part of the rebel forces." Major General Edward Ord speculated that, with the assistance of Acadian scouts and four prominent local Unionists—two of whom were Acadians—approximately a thousand men could be raised for the Federal army on the prairie.[27]

Most of the potential Union recruits mentioned by General Ord were former Confederate deserters. As during the first Teche campaign, the Acadian conscripts profited by the headlong rebel flight from the Federal invaders, but this time the number of deserters was far greater. On September 22, 1863, Colonel W. W. Hyatt, paymaster for Henry Gray's predominantly Acadian brigade, reported that of the unit's complement of 1,800 men, fewer than 300 were present for duty. "My company," he continued, "numbers 3 privates; that of Kelso's, one; Calvit's, 8; and Ranson's, 4." The Eighteenth Louisiana and the Yellow Jacket Battalion had sustained 2,500 desertions during the preceding twelve months. The Acadian deserters were supplemented by troops who voluntarily submitted to capture in hope of receiving a Union parole and the opportunity to return home. The Union command was only too happy to issue paroles to those willing captives for "they, with scarcely an exception, seemed glad to get out of the army, both volunteer and conscript."[28]

The euphoria pervading the Acadian population as a result of the apparent magnanimity of the new Yankee regime quickly evaporated as the invaders proved even more unpalatable that their Texas predecessors. During the long months of Confederate occupation, the rebels had seized at least ten thousand head of cattle for shipment to the armies in the eastern Confederacy. The expropriation of these cattle was, needless to say, a sore point with the local ranchers. Yet to deprive Confederate foragers of the remaining much needed supplies and to satisfy their own logistical demands resulting from an overdue supply train, the Federals appropriated and destroyed additional thousands of cattle in the heart of the Acadian ranch country and seized enough Creole ponies to mount two regiments, as well as hundreds of mules.[29]

The depletion of local herds, however, greatly exceeded the intentions of the Yankee field commanders. Many unauthorized raids were perpetrated by bored and hungry soldiers, whose commandants conveniently looked the other way as long as they received a significant portion of the "contraband." The amount of produce and livestock taken in by these renegade foragers is incalculable, but the consensus of eyewitness accounts is that the total was staggering. Private Henry P. Whipple of the Twenty-ninth Wisconsin Volunteer Infantry Regiment confided to his diary that on a single raid in late October, "eighty loads of corn and a few sweet potatoes . . . and plenty of chicken, turkey, and honey" were brought into camp. Such figures pale by comparison to the number of cattle removed from the prairies. According to several reports, foragers not only killed calves just for their tongues and brains but "destroyed animals in mere wantonness." According to Richard Irwin of the Nineteenth Army Corps, the soldiers in his company had gorged themselves on beefsteak to the extent that they "fairly loathed the sight, to say nothing of the smell, of fresh-killed beef" long before the belated arrival of the Union army's supply train.[30]

In addition to the illicit foragers, additional parties, usually entire cavalry companies, were dispatched into the field by General William B. Franklin, the local field commander. These units funneled the appropriated cattle into centrally located *vacheries* for slaughter and distribution by the commissary officer. The following account of this operation, though published in the propagandistic *Official Report Relative to the Conduct of Federal Troops in Western Louisiana*, is substantiated by hundreds of eyewitness accounts in the French and American Claims Commission records:

> During the time that a division encamped near Mr. Elise Thibodeaux, on the Vermilion [River], cattle were driven up by the hundreds and butchered before his door, and so recklessly were they shot down that the bullets used penetrated his dwelling. . . . While cutting up the carcasses, they warmed their feet at fires kindled with

his wife's hand-cards, and fed with his plough beams and her loom. The atmosphere around was infected by the stench of offal and putrified carcasses; and as soon as the division moved away, his neighbors gathered to bury the festering remains. While engaged in their work, they counted one thousand seven hundred cattle heads, lying around, in every stage of decay.[31]

Franklin's foragers were equally ruthless in seizing other livestock. A directive issued in mid-October 1863 by Acting Adjutant General J. Schuyler Crosby authorized Franklin to seize all available horses to equip cavalry in the field, and the general executed this authority with a vengeance. The exact number of horses taken is not known, but F. H. Mason of the Forty-second Ohio Infantry reported that they were seized "in great numbers" in St. Landry Parish and around Breaux Bridge.[32] Unable to speak the invaders' language or read the confiscation orders, which the foraging party commanders delighted in waving under the noses of their hapless victims, the Acadian was powerless: "he could not remonstrate—he could only suffer."[33]

The Acadian population also suffered at the hands of the black and white stragglers in the wake of Franklin's army. In Lafayette Parish, stragglers plundered the home of one Boudreaux, who was infirm and confined to bed. Narcisse Thibodeaux, a Breaux Bridge octogenarian, "was taken from his house by Federal soldiers accompanied by negroes, and beaten with sticks, until he confessed where his treasures were hidden." An undetermined number of local women was apparently raped. Such depredations became so commonplace that they were committed on a daily basis by late fall, according to one Union officer. As a consequence, Vermilionville residents were given extraordinary permission to "organize themselves into a patrol, for the protection of themselves, their families, and personal property against marauders and thieves, black or white." Nevertheless, the indiscriminate looting of civilian residences continued, forcing Assistant Adjutant Wickman Hoffman to reprimand Federal regimental commanders for failing to maintain proper discipline among their troops, "whose conduct in straggling, stealing, and maltreating women is a disgrace to the name of American soldier." Hoffman's attempt to tighten lax discipline was issued too late to be effective, for it coincided with the Union withdrawal from the northern prairie parishes in December 1863.[34]

This retrograde movement was followed closely by the advance of Confederate pickets, Colonel Louis Bush's Fourth Louisiana Cavalry Regiment. Though the prairie parishes were stripped of their enormous agricultural wealth, they remained an important source of recruits; hence, following Federal incursions into the upper Teche Valley during the Red River campaign of late March and April 1864 and the subsequent Confederate reoccupation of the area following the Battle of Pleasant Hill, the Fourth Louisiana Cavalry regularly dispatched impressment parties into the prairies, "arresting and returning to their commands all deserters that could be found."[35]

The conscripting officers also impressed all available civilians, even the walking wounded. In mid-December 1863, for example, St. Landry Parish residents were outraged when Captain W. C. Morrell pronounced Edmond Guidry, a Confederate veteran who had lost an arm in Virginia, "fit for duty" and returned him to the active duty roster.[36]

This massive recruitment campaign was surprisingly successful. Writing to his wife from Franklin on May 13, 1864, Lieutenant Colonel Louis Amédée Bringier of the Fourth Louisiana Cavalry reported: "Our Right [flank, which extended into the Attakapas prairie] is recruiting very rapidly. We now have for duty 600 men. . . . In less than one week we will have 1,000 men in the Formidable Fourth."[37]

The success of the spring 1864 recruitment campaign is attributable to several factors. The Acadian population had been enraged by the recent Union depredations, and many members of the impressment details were French-speaking residents of the river and Lafourche Valley parishes. The Francophones rejected the brutality of their Texan predecessors, and the Acadian deserters were thus more amenable to reintroduction into the Confederate service. The strategy of the officers and men of the Fourth Louisiana Cavalry, occasionally working in conjunction with local recruiting officers, is reflected in Priscilla M. Bond's May 1864 account of conscription in Vermilion Parish: "The town [Abbeville] has been kept in great commotion this week, Captain [Robert] Perry picking up deserters and conscripts. It has been quite amusing hearing of their hiding. One man could not be found till the captain seized his horse, then he came forward." Finally, on May 18, 1864, Major General Richard Taylor, the departmental commander, issued a proclamation stating that "persons who owe military service to the Confederate States and are not now in the army are hereby ordered and directed to come forward and join the Louisiana Infantry Regiments . . . on or before the 1st day of June 1864, otherwise they will be considered and treated as Jayhawkers and shot down on sight." Deserters returning to the service faced no disciplinary action under President Jefferson Davis's blanket pardon of 1863.[38]

Once restored to the Confederate service, former Acadian deserters as well as new conscripts were induced to remain in the ranks by ever-tightening discipline. Before his death in April, 1864, Brigadier General Alfred Mouton had been accused of ignoring desertions by his fellow Acadian troops, ostensibly because he feared that stern measures would scuttle his anticipated gubernatorial campaign. Such accusations were unfounded, for in early January 1864, the Acadian general ordered the execution of several deserters from the Eighteenth Louisiana Infantry Regiment. Because of the heightened surveillance as well as the increasing immobility of the Confederate units in south Louisiana after May 1864, deserting carried unacceptable risks.[39]

The overwhelming majority of Acadians in the Confederate service were thus compelled to adjust to army life. Acadians in the Fourth Louisiana Cavalry were drilled six hours daily, for Lieutenant Colonel Bringier, who assumed command of the regiment in the spring of 1864, was determined to make "Soldiers out of these *Jayhawkers, Marauders, & Skulkers.*" Facing the inevitable, the Acadian troops apparently reconciled themselves to the regimen of army life, at least in the weeks immediately following their reinduction, but during the late summer and early fall, they made every effort to return to their homes. Bringier lamented that "it is next to impossible to organize and discipline a command in the very midst of the Soldiers' homes. They *all* have excellent reasons to go home, and although I allow no non-commissioned Officer or Soldier to leave camp on horseback, except on *military* business, many ask for passes and take it on foot. Some on whom this home influence is very great, walk as far as 20 & 25 miles to spend only 12 hours at home."[40]

The brief home visits encouraged desertion, for the privates witnessed the hardships their families were enduring. The typical Acadian recruit had good reason to fear for his family's well-being. Not

only were large, active bands of Jayhawkers in the vicinity, but, because the conscripts received no pay from the Confederate army, the
typical prairie family was incapable of hiring laborers to gather the
modest fall harvest. Concern for their families preempted personal
considerations, and the number of desertions among rebel units stationed south of Alexandria skyrocketed during the late fall and winter of 1864, despite the very real threat of execution if caught. A
Union intelligence report of late January 1865 states: "Desertions oc-
cur daily. If captured the deserter is treated with rigor. Military executions take place weekly—on Fridays. Fifteen men have been shot at
one time recently for desertion."[41]

Desertions became so numerous that for the first time conscription
parties were dispatched into the Atchafalaya swamp. Bringier also attempted to arrest homeward-bound deserters from south Louisiana
units stationed north of Alexandria. Only in mid-May 1865 did the
cavalry commander's manhunt end in southwestern Louisiana, for
Bringier's regiment was ordered to Bayou Rapides, northwest of Alexandria. The prairie Acadians were free at last to return home.[42]

The prairie Acadians' unceasing efforts to join their families contrasts sharply with the Confederate patriotism of their eastern cousins. The constancy of the river Acadian officers to the Confederate
cause is indeed noteworthy. By the fall of 1863, the officer corps of
the Eighteenth Louisiana Infantry, which contained two St. James
Parish companies, seemed like a river parish planter fraternity. While
stationed with Mouton's regiment at Vermilionville in August 1863,
commissary officer Felix Pierre Poché noted in his diary visits with
eight river Acadian officers. Moreover, unlike the prairie Acadians,
many river Acadians who were captured at Vicksburg and subsequently paroled later reenlisted, usually in Confederate units stationed in southwestern Louisiana.[43]

The patriotic zeal of the Acadian officer corps was matched by that
of the slaveholding civilian population in the river and upper Lafourche parishes. The slaveholders' devotion to the Southern cause,
however, was tempered by pragmatism. Following the destruction of
Donaldsonville by Federal gunboats in early August 1862 as retalia-
tion for repeated raids on Union shipping by Captain Philippe Landry's guerrillas, a meeting of predominantly Acadian planters from
Ascension and St. James parishes decided that continued resistance

was necessary but that local Confederate guerrilla commanders must exercise greater discretion. Conforming to this decision, the Acadian planters took the oath of allegiance to the United States government so as to "retain their Negroes and purchase some provisions." They nevertheless clandestinely assisted Confederate raiders from St. Martin Parish.[44]

River Acadian planters also aided the Confederate army by operating an underground railroad that smuggled into rebel territory the handful of Acadians conscripted by, and later deserted from, the First Louisiana Cavalry (Union). Also transported across Union lines were Confederate conscripts and rebel deserters arrested behind Union lines by Lieutenant Omar Boudreaux's guerrillas. Information regarding the "railroad" is fragmentary, but it apparently operated along the eastern and southern fringes of the Atchafalaya Basin— from Oscar Ayraud's plantation near Donaldsonville, to Pierre Hébert's residence along Bayou Boeuf, to Pierre Daigle's farm along Bayou Boeuf, near Brashear City. Daigle's residence, located at the confluence of bayous Boeuf and Chemise, was a vital link in this communications system, for "all the men who go into the Confederacy" were conducted to rebel lines by Daigle and his son via the Atchafalaya Basin's network of waterways.[45]

The will to resist manifested by the river and Lafourche Valley Acadians' involvement in the underground railroad remained intense until the war's conclusion, for the network's operations apparently peaked in the spring of 1865. The intensity of the river Acadians' Confederate patriotism is also reflected in the journal of Hélène Dupuy, daughter of an Ascension Parish plantation manager. According to Dupuy, loyalty to the Confederate cause and the certainty of its ultimate success died in the river parishes only with the fall of Richmond.[46]

The cost of such fidelity to the Southern cause was high indeed. Not only did the river parish Acadian planters endure the loss of their work force through emancipation, but many Lafourche Valley plantations sustained significant battlefield damage as well. Thus at the war's conclusion, the crestfallen genteel Acadian planters of the river parishes and their plebian western cousins, the prairie ranchers, faced the same bleak future.[47]

FIVE

Declining Economic Fortunes in Postbellum Louisiana

The destruction of their farmsteads and the collapse of the social order undergirding their world were only the most tangible manifestations of the new and difficult circumstances in which Louisiana's Acadians found themselves at the war's end. The enduring nature of seemingly insoluble problems, which kept the region in turmoil for decades, held profound social, economic, and political ramifications for these people.

The drastic and sustained contraction of the local economy and the emergence of a new social order forced many changes on the Acadian community. Promulgation of harsh black codes by local governments temporarily retarded the pace of social change, as south Louisianians of all racial and ethnic backgrounds focused their attention on the far more pressing problem of economic survival.

Like most other whites and blacks in early postbellum south Louisiana, most Acadians initially regarded economic problems as preeminent. More than once in the early postwar years they faced starvation. It is thus hardly surprising that they channeled their talents and resources first into preserving and regenerating their farms and only later into general economic improvement. Yet, despite the attention, money, and energy expended by the Acadians and their neighbors to resolve the economic crisis, these problems did not go away. In *Louisiana Reconstructed,* his landmark work on postbellum Louisiana, historian Joe Gray Taylor states that "the depression which began in 1873 was almost as long in duration as the Great Depression of 1929; it lasted until 1879, and agriculture really did not recover until after 1900." Glenn R. Conrad has recently suggested, perhaps more correctly, that the Civil War created an economic recession that endured in the Acadian parishes, virtually without respite, from 1865 until World War II. Indeed, a comparison of postbellum lithographs with Depression-era photographs by the Farm Securities Administration affords ample visual evidence supporting the local oral tradition that rural south Louisianians were generally too poor to notice the Great Depression.[1]

In grappling with the postwar depression, rural south Louisianians first had to overcome the economic inertia of the war years, which had virtually paralyzed the economy of the Acadian parishes. The first step was to restore local communications. During the war, roads that in the best of times had been poorly maintained were completely neglected, becoming virtually impassable. Bridges, which also lacked proper maintenance, were frequently washed away or were destroyed by retreating armies. Permanent replacements would not be erected until well after the war and, consequently, the movement of civilians and trade goods via the local road system was no longer possible in many riverine areas. Finally, steam navigation, the quickest and most reliable form of transportation available in south Louisiana, virtually disappeared because all available vessels were appropriated by the Confederate military, and vessels introduced by the Federal navy were either warships or military transports. A few commercial steamboats returned to the bayous in the months following the war, but they were unable to reach some ports because the vessels sunk or scuttled by the Confederates constituted impassable navigational hazards. These rusting hulks and the floating debris that had collected around them would not be removed by government engineers until 1870–1871.[2]

The resulting breakdown in communications with traditional markets, the departure of adult white men (through recruitment, conscription, or desertion), and the flight of emancipated slaves permanently disrupted most local agricultural operations, which were usually reduced to subsistence gardening. Sugar production, for example, fell from a peak of 269,000 tons in 1861 to 51,500 tons in 1862, 42,500 tons in 1863, and only 5,400 tons in 1864.[3] As these figures suggest, by the war's end, most fields in the Acadian parishes had gone untended for two or three years and, in the water-bottom areas, had become so thoroughly blanketed with brush and saplings that they required clearing for cultivation. The expeditious clearing of such land was imperative because, left untended, the neglected fields would quickly revert to woodland. In addition, with the end of hostilities, thousands of rebel veterans, Confederate deserters, Jayhawkers, black camp followers, and former slaves returned to their south Louisiana homes, severely taxing the area's meager food resources. Many former Confederate soldiers, already home, were disabled and incapable of supporting themselves. By the summer of 1865, the population of the Acadian parishes hovered dangerously close to starvation. Individual food stocks were low, and grocery stores were generally unable to obtain provisions until late fall. Commenting on the situation along the Mississippi River to his daughter on September 3, 1865, Captain James A. Payne noted: "I very much fear the Whole [population] will starve. . . . Want is staring so many . . . in the face."[4]

Such desperate circumstances demanded swift remedies, but clearing the fields and resuming normal agricultural operations proved a thorny problem. Confederate foraging and the Union invasions of 1863 had resulted in the wholesale destruction of agricultural processing equipment, implements, and draft animals. Large numbers of cotton gins, sugar mills, and warehouses were destroyed during the war, and hundreds were unserviceable after years of inactivity. Sugar mills and warehouses had been prime targets for Union marauders, and they sustained a disproportionate amount of damage. Louisiana sugarcane growers had operated 1,291 mills on the eve of the Civil War but only 175 at the end of the conflict. Fewer than 300 of these factories were in operation by 1870.[5]

Compounding the loss of processing equipment was the generalized destruction of farm implements and draft animals. In the sugar bowl parishes, the number of horses and mules listed in the decennial agricultural censuses declined by 48 and 43 percent respectively. The loss of mules was particularly crucial, for, by the Civil War era, they had replaced oxen as the most commonly used draft animal. The demand for mules in south Louisiana was so high that by 1867, the price had risen to nearly $250 per head.[6]

Few farmers could pay the exorbitant prices, even though the survival of their farms often hinged on such purchases. Most farmers and planters lacked the necessary cash or sufficient credit to obtain enough draft animals to satisfy their farms' needs. The liberation of most slaves in south Louisiana during the Union occupation and the emancipation of the unfortunate few remaining in bondage at the end of the war deprived former slaveholders not only of their crucial labor supply but of much of the collateral necessary for loans to replace lost or stolen animals and equipment as well as loans to pay the wages of freedmen and whites willing to work as day laborers.[7] According to the 1870 census, Acadian personal property holdings, which had served as collateral for many antebellum loans, declined by 73.86 percent overall and by 85.97 percent in the river parishes (table 1). The equally drastic depreciation of farmlands throughout the Louisiana sugar and cotton belts further reduced the amount of collateral available for badly needed loans (table 2). Excessive personal debts accumulated by most south Louisiana planters during the prosperous 1850s, when many ambitious farmers invested in steam mill equipment and large numbers of slaves, compounded the former slaveholders' credit problems.[8]

Farmers able to obtain some credit (usually at 10 to 15 percent interest) channeled their efforts into production of staple crops requiring the least amount of labor and producing the greatest profit margins, but major problems restricted resumption of sugar operations in the sugar bowl parishes. A considerable amount of capital had to be raised by individual farmers to clear, redike, and cultivate the land and plant the crop. Skilled laborers were in short supply, creating an artificially high wage scale. In addition, there was a shortage of seed cane. Sugar crops, which in Louisiana are grown on a three-year rotation schedule, generally reach their peak sucrose production only in the second year after planting.[9] "So difficult was it to resume sugar planting, and so unprofitable were operations which were undertaken, that many planters and, especially, smaller farmers in the sugar region" turned to other crops. Most farmers, regardless of their prewar background, opted for cotton production because it was far less labor-intensive and the artificially high prices produced by wartime shortages made it a more attractive investment for banks and private investors.[10]

These novice cotton farmers made their first attempt at large-scale staple crop production in 1866. Their efforts were generally unsuccessful because of difficulties in adjusting to the new wage labor system, as well as armyworm invasions, epidemic diseases, unseasonal weather, and a series of major floods. Under normal circumstances, most seasoned farmers undoubtedly could have overcome the perennial problems of labor, insects, weather, and disease, but the combination of these difficulties, coupled with the devastating effects of repeated flooding and two nationwide recessions, ultimately overwhelmed most agriculturists.[11]

Flooding, which greatly exacerbated south Louisiana's bleak economic situation, provided the coup de grace to many of these economic casualties. Weakened by wartime neglect and, in some instances, by fighting along the waterways, Louisiana's levee system was no longer capable of performing its protective function. In 1865, breaks in the levee system caused flooding in the low-lying regions of south Louisiana, destroying crops and further weakening the levees. Flooding the following year was far more severe, as the Chinn and Robertson crevasses above Baton Rouge produced a flood comparable to the 1927 "high water." At their height, floodwaters extended fifty miles in width and one hundred miles in length, stretching from the west bank of Bayou Teche to the Mississippi River. These floodwaters disrupted the flow of the Red River, causing that major tributary to overflow its banks.[12]

Though damage was extensive in the Red River Valley, the flooding was far more destructive in the sugar bowl parishes. The cane and cotton crops planted on south Louisiana's best farmlands were covered for months by ten to twelve feet of water and ruined. One planter residing along the Mississippi River informed a friend that "the land, formerly covered by abundant crops of sugarcane, now presents to the view a vast and melancholy expanse of ruins and swamps, in which the waters of the Mississippi seem permanently to reside." Armyworm invasions that followed in the flood's wake destroyed not only those fields that escaped the high water but also the second cotton crop planted in early summer by flood victims.[13]

The cost of flood and insect damage to the south Louisiana economy has been calculated at $30 million, but the cost in human terms is incalculable. In September 1865, federal authorities estimated that one to two thousand civilians were receiving government rations, but by May 31, 1866, the number of Louisianians needing government assistance—primarily members of the white and black laboring classes—had grown geometrically, with estimates ranging from twenty to fifty thousand.[14] But the starving masses were only the most visible symptom of the misery wrought by the flood. Though better able to feed themselves during the crisis, hundreds of farmers were financially ruined by the disaster, and, lacking the resources to start again, they faced certain foreclosure, eviction, and adaptation to a new way of life. Other farmers, primarily those along the periphery of the Atchafalaya Basin, found that the perennial flooding had rendered their lands unsuitable for agriculture and were forced to seek a new means of livelihood. Some turned to fishing and lumbering in the swamps and along the coast.[15]

Farmers who survived the trials of 1866 looked forward to a more prosperous 1867. Because of wartime shortages, cotton prices had remained artificially high, and farmers were confident that an average crop would reverse their declining fortunes. But once again, fate intervened. As in 1865 and 1866, springtime brought severe flooding and in its wake armyworm infestation. Cotton production again declined dramatically. Though south Louisiana cotton crops were devastated, other cotton-producing areas offset the local shortfall and helped satisfy the national demand for the fiber. As a result, the price of cotton fell precipitously, and when the Acadian farmers sent their processed bales to market in New Orleans they reaped a paltry return on their investment. Unable to satisfy their debts, they were also often unable to secure credit to continue their farming operations. The onset of a national recession not only reduced the availability of credit but further devaluated their farmlands, which were used as collateral with state banks, the traditional source of agricultural credit. State banks were reluctant to extend additional credit to such high-risk borrowers, and the Louisiana banks most capable of extending credit to financially strapped farmers, the new national banks created at New Orleans after 1865, were legally forbidden to lend money when real estate was used as security. Thus, at worst, these demoralized farmers faced bankruptcy and eviction; at best, they anticipated an ever-declining standard of living and the probable sale of some or all of their lands.[16]

Finding prospective buyers for farmland, however, grew increasingly difficult with each passing year. Armyworm infestations in 1868, 1870, and 1871 inflicted heavy damage on the cotton crops in the prairie region, adding scores of farmers to the region's already lengthy list of postwar economic casualties. Facing inevitable loss of their lands, these individuals, like most of the newly poor around them, suspended farming operations and awaited foreclosure either for delinquent loan payments or for back taxes. By the end of 1868, approximately twenty thousand acres of arable land were idle in Lafayette Parish alone.[17]

The region's festering economic crisis and its sociological consequences had disastrous results for the Acadian community. The social leveling that universal economic adversity fostered left no one unaffected. As Dr. Clarence Ward, editor of the *Plaquemine Iberville South,* lamented in the aftermath of the conflict: "The fortunes of war have brought well nigh all of us to the same estate, and that condition is one of startling, and in many instances, distressing poverty. The rich of yesterday are poor to day, and the ever poor are poor indeed."[18]

The 1870 census of Louisiana bears grim testimony to Ward's observation. On the eve of secession, the Acadians had collectively constituted, after the Anglo-Americans, the most affluent group in rural south Louisiana. By 1870, the economic underpinnings of this distinction had been erased. As in Louisiana society as a whole, the effects of the depression were felt most severely at the polar extremes of the Acadian community's socioeconomic spectrum. Census reports, conveyance records, newspaper accounts, and other sources bear abundant testimony to the economic hardships of the gentry class, concentrated in the water-bottom areas of the bayou country.[19]

Worst hit were residents of the Acadian Coast, the parishes most dependent on farm credit and slave labor. Securely tied to staple crop production, these parishes were also most sensitive to the vagaries of the nation's commodities markets. The hope of economic rejuvenation afforded by high commodities prices in the wake of the Civil War proved illusory, and many formerly successful Acadian farming ventures failed. Such farms were inevitably offered for sale, either by the owners or by their creditors, but few buyers could be found and depressed prices were driven even lower by the constantly increasingly supply of available farmland. Between 1860 and 1870, Acadian real estate holdings declined in value, on average, by 52.15 percent, but in the Acadian Coast parishes, depreciation in property values was a catastrophic 77.24 percent (table 2).[20]

The loss of equity built over generations was devastating to the formerly prosperous Acadian planters and large farmers of the Acadian Coast, consisting of West Baton Rouge, Iberville, Ascension, and St. James parishes. By the criteria used earlier to identify planters, the 1870 census shows the economic impact of the postwar depression. The Acadian planter class virtually disappeared in the Acadian Coast. In the most extreme example, West Baton Rouge Parish, which boasted twenty-five Acadian planters in 1860—22 percent of the parish's Acadian freeholders—was home to only one Acadian planter in 1870 (table 3).

The virtual extinction of the Acadian planter class, however, did not signal the disappearance of successful Acadian farmers. Many former Acadian planters were reduced to the status of large farmers, while numerous others maintained their prominent prewar economic position despite the challenges of the postwar era. According to the 1870 census, owners of farms valued at $1,500 to $9,999 constituted at least 25 percent of all Acadian households in six parishes. These medium-to-large farmers constituted at least 40 percent of the Acadian households in three parishes (table 4). As one would expect, concentrations of these farmers were greatest in the plantation parishes and lowest in the prairie region, where ranching had supplanted agriculture as the leading economic activity.[21]

The economic impact of the postbellum depression took a far greater toll at the lower levels of the socioeconomic spectrum. Unlike the trials of the gentry, the tribulations of the Acadian "ever poor" are largely ignored by the documentary record; yet the 1870 census indicates their precarious economic situation. Tenantry was practically nonexistent in the prewar Acadian communities, even in the most impoverished areas. Yet many Acadians of modest means found it increasingly difficult to survive economically, especially in the last two decades of the antebellum period, when many yeomen became day laborers.

This change was caused in part by Louisiana's forced heirship laws and the uninterrupted inflation in land prices in the late antebellum years, which made both maintenance and acquisition of farmsteads large enough to support a family nearly impossible. Others, gradually drawn into the materialistic culture that surrounded them and increasingly dependent on manufactured goods, were eventually forced to change from being seasonal to permanent day laborers to support themselves and their families. As Joe Gray Taylor has noted: "They had never been subsistence farmers in the pure sense of the word. Before 1860 they had depended on cotton, sugar, rice, or in a few instances, tobacco, citrus fruit, or cattle as a source of ready money. Apparently this dependence was intensified after the war. To obtain the goods necessary to sustain life, they were as dependent on the merchant as was the lowliest sharecropper."[22] This trend was especially pronounced in the bayou country east of the Atchafalaya River. By 1860, day laborers formed a significant portion of the Acadian work force in the Lafourche Basin: 19.5 percent in Ascension Parish, 27 percent in Assumption, 28 percent in Lafourche, and 49 percent in Terrebonne. In the Mississippi River parishes and in the parishes west of the Atchafalaya, day laborers remained a negligible portion of the local work force, with the exception of St. Mary and Vermilion parishes, where they constituted 11.6 and 22.5 percent respectively of all gainfully employed Acadians.[23]

By 1870, day laborers constituted a majority of the Acadian agricultural work force (consisting of farmers and day laborers) in ten of the fifteen original Acadian parishes. After touring Lafayette Parish in January 1870, prominent Louisiana journalist Daniel Dennett noted that "at Vermilionville . . . I learned that nearly half of the labor of the parish is now performed by white men, and that about one-eighth was performed by white men before the war."[24] Acadian day laborers were drawn from two basic groups—the rapidly growing landless class and the increasingly beleaguered and rapidly dwindling small farmer class (tables 5 and 6). The landless were well represented in the 1870 census of the Acadian parishes. In twelve of the fifteen parishes, more than 40 percent of all Acadian households were landless, as were more than 60 percent of the households in six parishes. Concentrations of the landless were highest in the plantation parishes, where real estate prices had put landownership beyond the reach of all but the most affluent, and in St. Landry and Terrebonne parishes, to which Acadians displaced by the riverine plantation systems had migrated in large numbers in the late antebellum period. Only in Calcasieu Parish, where cheap public land was plentiful, did the landless constitute a relatively small percentage of Acadian householders.

The landless formed the largest component of the Acadian laboring class. Many small farmers served (and would continue to do so until well into the twentieth century) as day laborers on a seasonal basis. As one historian has reported, in 1870, many white cotton farmers along Bayou Teche neglected their own harvest "in order to earn two or three dollars a day making sugar." The landless were forced to make a profoundly different arrangement with their employers. Though classified as day laborers (or farm laborers) in the 1870 census, most landless Acadians were actually share renters. This arrangement, entered into by the most prosperous landless farmers, both black and white, offered significantly greater rewards than traitional sharecropping because the tenant provided his own work stock, animal feed, fertilizer, and tools as well as the labor of himself and his family. Though required to buy at the plantation store like other sharecroppers, share renters exercised greater control over their farm operations as well as the selection of crops to be grown on the rented farmland. The rents were negotiable, but the levies generally involved one-fourth of the staple crop production and one-third of the corn produced.[25]

The Panic of 1873 altered the status of most share renters. Because of falling commodity prices, many share renters lost their draft animals and equipment to foreclosure. They were joined in their descent to sharecropper status by yeomen, who also lost everything during the depression. On April 4, 1874, the *Thibodaux Sentinel* complained that "we have never seen Thibodaux possess so fine a delegation of vagabonds as have been visiting the streets of late." Most of these vagabonds were recently dispossessed small farmers. This trend of downward mobility paralleled that in the South as a whole. By the end of the nineteenth century, white sharecroppers would outnumber their black counterparts in the former Confederate states.[26]

Acadian sharecroppers found themselves in a particularly bad economic position. Sharecropper contracts, like share-rent agreements, were negotiable, but, unlike the more endurable levies imposed on share renters, sharecroppers were generally obligated to provide their landlords as rental payments a portion—often one-half—of their crops. Their reduced income, coupled with their complete dependence on the plantation stores that exacted exorbitant prices and high interest rates condemned the Acadian sharecroppers—like sharecroppers throughout the South—to virtual peonage from which they had little hope of ever extricating themselves.[27]

Far less numerous than share renters and sharecroppers were the small farmers whose landholdings were appraised by census takers at up to $1,500 in value. In only three parishes—Calcasieu, Cameron, and Vermilion, all of which were primarily ranching areas—did they constitute more than 20 percent of all Acadian households. In agricultural parishes, small farmers made up a tiny fraction of the Acadian community—less than 10 percent of all Acadian households in eight of the fifteen parishes.

The downward mobility experienced by most Acadian small farmers during the postbellum era was traumatic. Regardless of their status, most Acadian day laborers were forced for the first time into the indignity of working for another man and the social stigma that such employment conveyed. Shortly before the Civil War, Frederick Law Olmsted observed that, in the Deep South, "to work industriously and steadily, especially under the direction from another man, is, in the Southern tongue, to 'work like a nigger.'"[28] For Acadian day laborers their employment as manual laborers, working alongside freedmen under the direction of white men only marginally better off than themselves, was not only a loss of economic independence but also a significant social demotion (table 7).[29]

The loss of economic independence necessitated changes in lifestyle. The loss of prestige added to the bitterness of witnessing the destruction of their world. Members of the new Acadian proletariat had been accustomed to dictating their own leisurely work pace. Forrest McDonald and Grady McWhiney have noted that "of all the comments made by contemporary observers the most universal was that Southerners loved their leisure—or, as hostile observers said, they were lazy." The typical Southern yeoman, like the typical Acadian yeoman, aspired only to have a comfortable existence, not wealth. McDonald and McWhiney have demonstrated that in 1850 Gulf Coast yeomen not only supported themselves and their families but also produced a small cotton surplus for sale by working the equivalent of eleven forty-hour weeks. Corn, the mainstay of the nineteenth-century Acadian diet, required considerably less maintenance than staple crops. Hogs, the main source of protein for the Acadian middle and lower classes, also yielded a bountiful return with little investment or upkeep. This source of protein was supplemented by hunting and fishing, favorite pastimes of the yeomen.[30]

The personal independence on which this life-style was based ended with employment as wage earners. In addition to working their own fields, day laborers now had to plant, cultivate, and harvest their employers' crops. In an effort to extricate themselves from their undesirable economic situation, many day laborers began to grow more cotton, requiring considerably more work, and less corn, thus producing less food for their families and their livestock. The result was a steadily declining standard of living. By the 1890s, lower-class Acadians were reduced to bartering eggs and hens for "city goods" at local stores.[31]

Though bitterness undoubtedly dampened their work ethic, already considered lax by contemporary Protestant standards, Acadian day laborers readily found employment with local farmers who evidently considered them more reliable and industrious than the freedmen, who reputedly worked only grudgingly. Most postbellum Louisiana employers believed, as historian J. Carlyle Sitterson has noted, that "many Negroes considered themselves emancipated not only from slavery but also from the status of manual laborers." White farmers also "complained endlessly" about what they perceived to be the "freedmen's reluctance to work hard."[32] Though the economic impact of these pervasive attitudes and the negative reaction they elicited is the subject of a heated scholarly debate, the most recent scholarship on the subject indicates that the local black labor supply declined by approximately 50 percent in the early postwar years. White employers consequently tried unsuccessfully to introduce European and Chinese laborers into their agricultural operations. Indeed, Louisiana's agricultural interests pressured the state legislature into establishing a state Bureau of Immigration in 1866 to undertake the necessary recruitment effort.

Private and public efforts brought to the Pelican State thousands of prospective laborers, but the transplanted workers generally remained on their employers' farms for only one harvest season. Quickly disenchanted with the climate, the hard work, the low wages, and their landlords' frequent harsh attempts to regiment them, the immigrants usually sought a better life in New Orleans. Disillusioned employers hired ever-increasing numbers of Acadian day laborers even after hundreds of freedmen began to return to work, often for their former masters. Increasing competition for the shrinking pool of available jobs, coupled with growing Acadian frustration over the social leveling wrought by circumstances beyond their control generated considerable racial friction (Chapter 7).[33]

The frustrations of the lower classes were shared by small farmers sliding slowly toward the edge of the economic precipice. Nudging these small farmers toward bankruptcy and admission into the ranks of the impoverished, frequently landless masses was the continuation of the seemingly endless economic slumps and natural disasters that had begun with the war's conclusion.[34]

Perhaps the greatest challenge faced by the surviving Acadian farmers was the Panic of 1873, which virtually paralyzed the nation's economy. National economic expansion halted abruptly in late summer 1873, when the nation's banks discovered that the American financial market was saturated with bank bonds. Simultaneously, the leading financial institutions learned that the American railroad system, which had doubled in size between 1865 and 1873, was overbuilt. The banks' inability to secure additional capital to cover bad debts to railroads brought numerous major banks to the verge of insolvency. On September 18, 1873, a major creditor of Northern Pacific Railroad, Jay Cooke & Co., failed. On the following day, nineteen additional banks closed and the securities market collapsed, necessitating the temporary closure of the New York Stock Exchange. The shock waves from the New York monetary crisis were quickly felt in European money markets, which were already reeling from the repercussions of a panic on the Vienna market. The result was a deep and enduring worldwide depression, the effects of which were felt on a global scale until 1896. In the United States, "with the first scare, both stock and commodity prices fell, bonds went into default, over-extended bankers failed, and credit began to contract."[35]

These national trends negated the very modest economic gains made by Louisiana farmers since 1865. On September 24, 1873, four

days after news of the New York securities crisis reached New Orleans, Crescent City banks suspended currency payments. Early the
following month, the city's financial institutions stopped issuing loans
and ordered their debtors to rush their crops to market so New Orleans factors could repay their bank loans. The payment of these
debts permitted the New Orleans banks to engage in some limited
financial intercourse, but only for those individuals desperate or fool-
hardy enough to accept the usurious interest rates, which during the
fall and winter of 1873 and most of 1874 fluctuated between 12 and
30 percent.[36]

The financial crisis in New Orleans and the resulting shortage of
farm credit were magnified by the flight of carpetbag investors who
had decided to cut their losses and retreat northward with their remaining liquid assets. The lack of statistical data regarding unemployment and foreclosures makes it difficult to assess the human cost of
the depression. One historian has estimated that five thousand New
Orleans families were threatened with starvation as a result of chronic
unemployment in 1874–75. Similarly, numerous Iberville Parish residents went hungry, malnutrition being particularly evident among the
laboring classes.[37]

Landowners were better able to feed themselves, but their already
depressed land values declined precipitously and, because of the exorbitant interest rates in effect throughout 1874, they found it nearly
impossible to obtain credit for their farm operations. Reduced credit
availability and depressed commodity prices forced into bankruptcy
many marginal farmers who had managed to survive the difficult
early postbellum years. Describing the depressed economic situation
in the river parishes, a Baton Rouge cotton factor lamented in October 1874, "I am Getting along poorly Making Collections Cotton
Crops is poor and the people have Got so far behind that I fear there
will be many failures." Many others were forced out of business by
the floods of 1874 and 1876, both of which equaled the destruction
of the 1867 high water.[38]

Frequent flooding and seemingly endless economic reverses quickly
transformed Acadian society by economically polarizing the population. Before the Civil War, the Acadians constituted a highly stratified and diversified socioeconomic group. The community contained
planters, prosperous small slaveholding farmers, ranchers, urban

professionals, rural artisans, independent yeomen, and landless day laborers. In the postbellum period, however, Acadian agriculturalists divided into two basic groups: a small upper and upper-middle class that was largely co-opted by the region's dominant Anglo-American culture, and the impoverished, poorly educated, but culturally steadfast masses. Only the latter retained its Acadian identity so that the group's ascriptive characteristics and standing in the region's social and cultural hierarchies changed fundamentally. The division influenced not only how the Acadians viewed themselves but also how they were perceived by others. Because of the co-optation of wealthy Acadian farmers and less affluent but highly educated professionals—the Acadian community's natural leadership elements—Acadians came to be almost universally regarded by outsiders as a poor and ignorant people, a distortion that has persisted to the present.

Alcibiades DeBlanc, leader of the postbellum White League movement. Courtesy of the Center for Louisiana Studies, University of Southwestern Louisiana.

Alexandre Mouton, U.S. Senator, first Democratic party governor of Louisiana, vigilante leader, and southern "fire-eater." From Alcee Fortier's *History of Louisiana* (New York: Manzy Joyant and Company, 1904).

The Lafayette Parish Courthouse, built at Vermilionville in 1859, was an important symbol of vigilante rule in the prairie parishes. Courtesy of the Center for Louisiana Studies, University of Southwestern Louisiana.

Black troops guarding the New Orleans, Opelousas, and Great Western Railroad in South Louisiana's bayou country. From *Harper's Weekly*.

The Battle of Bayou Bourbeux (known to Union writers as the Battle of Grand Coteau), 3 November 1863. No Cajun conscripts took part in this major battle in the heart of Cajun country. From *Leslie's Illustrated Weekly*.

An 1863 caricature of a Cajun conscript by a Union war correspondent. Note that the conscript is shackled to a tree to prevent him from deserting. From *Leslie's Illustrated Weekly*.

W. L. Sheppard's postbellum sketch of black electioneering in the Deep South. Such meetings were carefully monitored by Democrats in the Acadian parishes. Courtesy of the Center for Louisiana Studies, University of Southwestern Louisiana.

Opposite: Jayhawkers, seen here robbing a well-to-do traveler, were a thorn in the Confederacy's side in Louisiana's prairie region. From *Harper's Weekly*, 24 December 1864.

Federal foraging parties returning to camp, 1863. From *Harper's Weekly*, 14 May 1864.

The St. Landry Parish courthouse, seen here in 1863, functioned briefly as the state capitol in 1862 and as a Union prison and Signal Corps station in 1863. From *Leslie's Illustrated Weekly*.

Though most of their opulent antebellum homes are now gone, Acadian planters left ample evidence of their wealth in South Louisiana cemeteries in the form of monumental funerary architecture. In river parish cemeteries, Acadian planters' tombs were actually replicas of small Greek Revival houses, like the tomb pictured here in Donaldsonville's Catholic cemetery. Courtesy Carl Brasseaux.

Above: These young women, seen here making coarse corn meal, were drawn by a *Harper's Weekly* illustrator to depict the poverty then pervasive in the early postbellum South's white society. From *Harper's Weekly,* 24 December 1864.

At left: This elderly man's late 1870s costume reflects the increasing Cajun dependence on manufactured clothing and the corresponding conformity with national clothing styles. Sketched by Allen C. Redwood. From *Scribner's* magazine, 1879.

"Washing-Day among the Acadians on the Bayou Lafourche, Louisiana," Waud's most notorious Louisiana illustration. A. W. Waud, artist/correspondent for *Harper's Weekly,* was perhaps most responsible for creating the negative national stereotype of the Cajuns, because of his dark sketches which emphasized his personal revulsion for the region's strange landscape and its even more exotic inhabitants. Note the exposed legs of the washer-women, the corn cob pipe clenched in the matron's mouth, and the evident laziness of the Cajun man. The *battoir* in the hands of the woman in the foreground was used to beat the dirt out of clothing. From *Harper's Weekly,* 20 October 1866.

SIX

Cultural Integration, Transformation, and Regeneration

The declining economic fortunes of Acadians following the Civil War accelerated the processes of sociological and cultural change under way within the community since the early antebellum period. The course of this metamorphosis was shaped in part by local demographic and cultural factors and in part by universal laws of social dynamics. The interaction of dominant and subordinate cultures has been the subject of intense scrutiny in recent decades, and much of the research regarding social dynamics, particularly studies focusing on interethnic relationships, has been heavily influenced by the writings of Richard Alonzo Schermerhorn. According to Schermerhorn, "the best two indicators of the current state of ethnic relations are the degree of stratification (inequality) and the degree of cultural distinctiveness (lack of assimilation) of the groups concerned." The amount of inequality and distinctiveness among groups in any society, Schermerhorn maintains, is determined by the "mass or degree of enclosure of each ethnic group, the type of interaction between the groups, the goals of each group, and the extent to which they are in agreement about goals." Mass is the critical component of the Schermerhorn model, for it directly influences the significance of the other variables.[1]

These sociological theories have served as the bases for the best recent studies on the interaction between dominant and subordinate cultures. The most relevant of these works have focused on the inter-relationship between Canada's dominant Anglo community and its major Francophone minorities—the Quebecois and the Acadians. The relationship of these Canadian ethnic groups during the late nineteenth and early twentieth centuries as described in these works bears striking resemblance to the corresponding situation in postbellum Louisiana. As in Louisiana, Anglos have traditionally constituted a majority of the general white population but a minority in most areas occupied since colonial times by persons of French descent. But also like Louisiana, Anglo economic dominance has been pervasive, even in French-majority areas.[2]

Perhaps the most balanced and insightful analysis of Canada's deep and abiding cultural divisions and their impact on the country's rival ethnic groups is that of Canadian sociologists Raymond N. Morris and C. Michael Lamphier. Following the Schermerhorn model, they have determined that mass is the most critical element in maintenance of cultural integrity and ethnic identity. Mass, as defined by Morris and Lamphier, consists of a group's basic demographic features: "its size, its compactness, and its institutional completeness."[3]

Though Morris and Lamphier maintain that "strength in one or more of these [areas] enables a group to maintain itself when surrounded by a larger and more dominant group," it is abundantly evident from their writings that a group's overall size is the major determining factor for maintenance of culture and identity. Indeed, it would appear from their findings that a group must constitute at least 20 percent of any local community if it is to have any chance of survival. As Morris and Lamphier note, "Where francophones outnumbered anglophones, loss of the French language was very unusual, even though many if not most male francophones also knew English. Where francophones were a substantial minority, say 20–40 percent, one could expect that significant numbers of their children would adopt English as their first language. Where the percentage of francophones fell below fifteen, almost all would learn English and over half might assimilate."[4]

Morris and Lamphier's findings are supported by numerous ethnographic, sociological, and demographic studies of late nineteenth- and early twentieth-century Canada. Approximately 90 percent of all Francophones assimilated in provinces where French-speakers constituted less than 2 percent of the total population. In areas where French-speakers constituted 3 to 8 percent, 49 to 70 percent were absorbed by the dominant culture. But wherever Francophones constituted more than 25 percent of the local population, assimilation rates declined dramatically. In New Brunswick, where Acadians composed approximately 35 percent of the population, only 14 percent were absorbed into Anglophone society.[5]

Assimilation of these Francophones into Anglophone society was largely voluntary and economically motivated. Canadian English-speakers have traditionally wielded a disproportionate amount of economic power. Morris and Lamphier indicate that between 1871 and 1971, Francophones, who composed more than one-fourth of the national population, consistently constituted less than 10 percent of Canada's economic elite. Thus "the francophones who reached the top in Canada would be those who conformed most closely to the expectations of anglophones, the culturally dominant majority. Francophone culture would remain a handicap, and francophones could . . . improve their chances of reaching the top [only] by abandoning their culture." Stanley Lieberson agrees, noting that "with an overwhelming concentration of economic power in the hands of English speakers, it is clear that the avenue to the top is in this tongue."[6]

Assimilation, however, was not confined to upwardly mobile Francophones seeking economic success. Despite significant and enduring class and cultural differences reminiscent of Louisiana's Acadian-Creole conflicts, Acadian migrants into Quebec and Quebecois transplants in New Brunswick were quickly absorbed into the dominant French-speaking culture in their new homelands. The assimilation process that transformed these immigrants also changed the dominant host cultures that absorbed them, though often very superficially.[7] The Canadian experience serves as a paradigm for multicultural Louisiana. As in Canada, Anglos constituted a statewide majority of Louisiana's postbellum white population but a regional minority in the rural French parishes. Yet they controlled most of the real estate and liquid capital, even in the areas of French demographic domination. The result was a highly stratified multicultural society in which culture and language provided the basis for social distinctions. Indeed, throughout the nineteenth century, class lines and cultural boundaries coincided in rural south Louisiana. Upwardly mobile Acadians of the late eighteenth and early nineteenth centuries entered the "aristocratic" Creole domain. Moving still further up the socioeconomic ladder in the antebellum period, the most successful Acadians found themselves on an economic plateau dominated by extremely wealthy Anglo-American immigrants from the Carolinas and Virginia. Anglo landholdings in the Acadian parishes in 1870 possessed a cumulative value 339 percent greater than the collective appraised value of Acadian properties. Acadians owned more real estate in only two parishes—Lafayette and St. Martin. Similarly, Anglo personal property was appraised at 2.26 times the aggregate value of Acadian personal property in the fifteen-parish area. Only in Lafayette, St. Martin, and St. James parishes did Acadian personal property holdings exceed those of the local Anglos (tables 8 and 9).[8]

These lines of cultural and social demarcation became more and more significant as the nineteenth century progressed. During the first two decades of the century, when the region's English- and French-speaking communities were locked in a bitter struggle for economic and political control of Louisiana, cultural boundaries served as the principal markers dividing the area's antagonistic native and immigrant communities. These markers remained the principal cultural dividing lines in south Louisiana well into the twentieth century, but the ethnic antagonisms became muted, at least within individual classes, once the Anglo-Americans had achieved overwhelming numerical superiority within the state.[9]

The Anglo-American influx into the present state of Louisiana began in the late 1770s, when religious refugees from Fort Pitt made their way to the Attakapas and Opelousas districts. They were later joined by loyalist émigrés, East Coast merchants, and land-hungry frontiersmen. Until the Louisiana Purchase, however, Anglo-American immigration into rural south Louisiana constituted a steady trickle. Despite its notable but localized impact on present-day St. Mary, Vermilion, and St. Landry parishes, the migration did not significantly alter the composition of the population in the original Acadian settlement areas. Nor would it fundamentally alter the demographic composition of the future state.[10]

It has been estimated that in 1803 French-speakers enjoyed a seven-to-one numerical advantage over English-speakers among Louisiana's free population. By the time of Louisiana's admission to the Union in 1812, the ratio had fallen to three to one, despite the influx of nearly ten thousand Saint-Domingue refugees in 1809. Anglo-American immigration, primarily from the Southeast, continued unabated throughout the antebellum era. By 1860, English-speakers constituted 70 percent of the Pelican State's free population. This remarkably disproportionate population growth was achieved despite uninterrupted French immigration throughout the antebellum period.[11] Shielded by the Atchafalaya Basin and by the high antebellum land values for prime riverine properties, most of south Louisiana's fifteen Acadian parishes did not receive the full impact of the Anglo invasion. As late as 1870, Acadians outnumbered Anglos in nine of the fifteen principal Acadian parishes (table 10). Only in Calcasieu and Cameron parishes, areas adjacent to Texas and possessing large quantities of cheap public land, did Anglo percentages approach those of the Anglo-dominated portions of north Louisiana.[12]

Nor were the Anglo settlers in the bayou country representative of Anglo-American immigrants as a whole. The Anglo-settlers who had begun migrating into rural areas of Louisiana in the 1780s were generally poor and of Celtic extraction. Through hard work and persistence, they usually achieved modest success as farmers and ranchers. The antebellum Anglo settlers of the bayou lands were generally of English descent and better educated and far more affluent than the English-speaking immigrants to north Louisiana. These individuals, many of whom were planters, professionals, and merchants, wielded greater economic influence than their number would suggest. Because of the Anglos' influence and prestige, the Acadian upper and upper-middle classes gauged their success by their acceptability to the region's new elite.[13]

It is hardly coincidental that the decline of the French language occurred when the Anglo elite emerged—generally in the late 1830s and 1840s. The best available account of this linguistic metamorphosis focuses on Baton Rouge's small Catholic congregation, approximately half of which consisted of the region's Acadian and Creole gentry. The study, undertaken by Gabriel Audisio of the Université de Provence, examines dissension within the council of churchwardens for St. Joseph Catholic Church stemming from pastor J. N. Brogard's November 1843 decision to deliver his homilies exclusively in English. (Before that date, the St. Joseph pastors had given their sermons in French and English on alternate Sundays reflecting the roughly equal distribution of French and English contingents of the congregation.) The dispute, which quickly evolved into a contest over secular control of the clergy, brought to light the changing linguistic patterns of the Acadian and Creole elements of the congregation. The *Baton Rouge Gazette,* a staunch supporter of Brogard and his linguistic policies, justified the pastor's decision by noting that "when he preaches in that language [English] he has a congregation, when he preaches in French he speaks to empty pews." [14]

The controversy appears to have ended with the March 22, 1844, council election in which all of the proponents of French usage were displaced. At the first council meeting following the election, the new churchwardens ordered that homilies be given in English and directed that the minutes, which previously had been published exclusively in French, be broadcast only in English. English remained the dominant language of the congregation despite the preponderance on the council by Acadians and Creoles through much of the late 1840s and 1850s. In 1851, for example, Acadians and Creoles held four of the council's five seats, and Acadian A. Theriot presided over the body. As Audisio has concluded, "It is thus obvious that, after 1847, French-speaking members of the council accepted the English-language's ascendancy in the council." [15]

Parallel developments occurred in local journalism. The *Baton Rouge Gazette,* which had been a bilingual weekly since its establishment in 1819, announced on May 13, 1843, that it would henceforth restrict the French language to advertising, and then only on demand. The newspaper's abrupt change in policy was a direct response to recently adopted legislation. On April 28, 1843, Acadian Alexandre Mouton, Louisiana's first Democratic party governor, signed into law "An Act Relating to the Advertisement of Judicial Sales and Monitions," which removed from state journalists the obligation to publish judicial advertisements. Because many of the announcements for sheriff's sales were issued in French by local sheriffs, elimination of this requirement freed journalists from publishing a bilingual paper to satisfy state publishing regulations. And many journalists moved quickly to divest themselves of what had become an expensive albatross—the French portion of their weeklies. As the editor of the *Baton*

Rouge Gazette lamented on November 24, 1843: "Since in the hands of the present proprietor, the French side of the Gazette has been a dead expense; and yet the management of the French has been at no time entirely confided to another. . . . But this is a portion of his labor for which he has received no adequate compensation; on the contrary money gained on the English side has been lost on the French."[16]

As the *Gazette*'s editor bitterly observed, the French readership in most rural south Louisiana parishes was small and unstable. Nineteenth-century French immigrants who congregated in the area's towns bought the local papers for the European news in their French sections, but their children, who tended to assimilate as quickly as possible, did not. Though the trickle of "Foreign-French" immigrants throughout the nineteenth century provided a steady source of readers, they were never numerous enough to support a bilingual newspaper in any of the rural south Louisiana parishes. This painful lesson was learned by numerous French immigrant entrepreneurs who established French- or European-oriented bilingual newspapers in the country parishes after 1843. With a few notable exceptions, these newspapers usually survived only one or two years.[17]

Country editors were thus forced either to publish exclusively in English or to build a diverse French readership, including the native Creoles and Acadians, by translating more local news into French. Most lower-class Acadians and Creoles, however, were illiterate. The educated elite could read the French portion of the local papers but generally were not interested in the European news that appeared there. Perhaps more important, the elite had internalized the social stigma associated with all things French by the early 1840s. For example, on greeting a French immigrant of lower socioeconomic status in 1859, Acadian Sarrazan Broussard of Vermilion Parish reportedly stated, "I am only an Acadian and I am not educated [like you]."[18] As happened in the church's language controversy, abandonment of the French language elicited no outcry or opposition from the literate Acadian elite. Frenchman Victor Tixier, for example, noted, while traveling through the Acadian Coast in the late 1830s, that "the French Creoles [meaning the local Acadian and Creole gentries] are losing their national character from day to day; they even pretend to submit to the invasion of Americans, whose language and manners they adopt by preference."[19]

The quiet acceptance of the English language in ecclesiastical and secular affairs was symptomatic of upwardly mobile Acadians' obsessive drive toward mainstream culture throughout the bayou country. For these people, acculturation was simply a matter of adapting to new socioeconomic realities. By the 1840s Anglo-Americans had attained a position of social and economic leadership within the state and, through their overwhelming numerical advantage, exercised considerable political power. Leaders of the Pelican State's French-speaking communities thus found it expedient first to deemphasize the ethnic friction that had characterized early Louisiana political contests and, later, as the numerical disparity became indisputable, to wed themselves, sometimes literally as well as figuratively, to the new majority.[20]

This tendency was almost universal among the antebellum Acadian elite, many of whom became bilingual (English- and French-speaking) of their own volition. A significant minority took English-speaking wives, often of Irish descent. Unlike the New Orleans Creoles, who continued to educate their children at French schools, Acadian planters routinely sent their children, particularly their sons, to English-speaking schools and universities.[21] Father J. N. Brogard noted that by the early 1840s in his parish there were "no Creoles [persons of French descent] from 10 to 25 years of age for whom the American language is not the common language."[22] This phenomenon was by no means confined to Brogard's church parish. Jean Mouton, a prominent Acadian politician, land speculator, and town developer, sent his son, future U.S. senator and Louisiana governor Alexandre, to Georgetown University. Alexandre's English-language skills served him well when he subsequently read law in Judge Edouard Simon's law office, for, after adoption of the 1812 state constitution, Louisiana's rules of judicial procedure had specified that all cases before the state courts be tried in English. Mouton, however, did not use English exclusively in business affairs. His first wife, Zelia Rousseau, was a Creole; his second, Emma Kitchell Gardner, an Anglo. Though he corresponded with his first wife in French, his letters to his second wife are in English. The personal correspondence between Alexandre Mouton's children was also written consistently in English. Particularly notable among these children was the eldest son, West Point graduate and future Confederate brigadier general Jean-Jacques Alexandre Alfred, who, as a toddler, bore the Anglo nickname "Buck."

Though raised by a mother whose first language was French, bilingual Alfred Mouton used English for much of his personal correspondence and for all of his professional writing, first as a railroad engineer and later as a Confederate general. Thus by the time of the Civil War, the Mouton family was functioning within the Anglo-American mainstream.[23]

The Mouton saga has numerous striking parallels in the family histories of the Héberts, Landrys, and many other genteel Acadian families from the river parishes. For example, Amant Hébert, "a sort of chief and leader" along the Second Acadian Coast, served as a delegate to the 1812 Louisiana constitutional convention. His son Valéry Hébert, was treasurer of the Iberville Parish police jury, an Iberville Parish police juror, a state representative, and, finally, a state senator. The son of Valéry Hébert and Marie Clarisse Bush, a woman of Irish descent, Louis Hébert was a West Point graduate, an antebellum chief state engineer, a Confederate general, and a postwar educator. Louis Hébert's professional writing, his wartime reports, his personal letters, and his unpublished memoirs are all written in flawless English. It is thus hardly surprising that, although he married a woman of mixed Creole and Acadian ancestry, Louis Hébert's sons, named Burton and Ellis, evidently used English as their first language.[24]

Like scores of other struggling young Acadian professionals throughout south Louisiana, an impoverished Louis Hébert found that his linguistic skills and education were the only tools with which he could make his way in the world. But without the financial assistance necessary to resuscitate labor-intensive farming operations or to establish a business, these tools were of little value, particularly for professionals such as engineers, who were highly dependent on political patronage for employment. Having been highly visible supporters of the Confederacy, Acadian professionals could count on precious little assistance from the state's Republican regime without the intercession of powerful allies. Louis Hébert's experience made this dilemma abundantly clear. After evidently being unemployed in 1866, Hébert took a job as editor of the *Plaquemine Iberville South* in 1867. When the paper was sold the following year, he worked in a variety of teaching jobs—as a tutor and as a teacher in short-lived private and public schools—for nearly three decades. He died a pauper.[25]

Hoping to avoid Louis Hébert's cruel fate, many members of the Acadian professional and gentry classes, who publicly opposed the state's Reconstruction government, privately courted the support of Louisiana's new financial and political power brokers, who, often as not, were scalawags and carpetbaggers. Writing from Plaquemine on March 5, 1867, carpetbagger George E. Harris informed his friend William B. Benson that "there are many here of the higher class of french who are the equal of the 'Cow tow' Americans in refinement & their [they're] thus superior in politeness. I am pleased with the people & the country & I was a Stranger & they took me in, not in the Pleasant Hill acceptation of the term, but in the meaning that was implied by the expression in Holy writ."[26]

The gentry's move into the Anglo-American mainstream is perhaps seen most clearly in its tendency not only to embrace but to promote publicly the goals and aspirations of Anglo businessmen. In the wake of the Civil War, Anglo-American business leaders urged their fellow Southerners to demonstrate initiative and work their way out of their economic predicament. In the prairie region, prominent Acadian farmers such as Colonel William Mouton echoed these sentiments, spearheading a drive to rejuvenate the local agrarian economy by organizing an industrial fair association.[27]

The Acadian gentry's drive toward assimilation was given impetus and urgency in the 1850s by the increasingly virulent and public Francophobia of the new dominant culture. As is abundantly evident from the personal correspondence of Governor W. C. C. Claiborne and other influential American officials, Francophobia had been rife within Louisiana's Anglo-American community since the Louisiana Purchase.[28] Public manifestations of Francophobia, however, remained restrained until the 1850s, usually taking the form of cultural and linguistic chauvinism as in the following quotation from a newspaper: "[We possess] a sincere desire that their progress in the predominant language of the land, will enable us soon to communicate with them through the medium of that impressive tongue in which the constitution and laws of our country are written."[29]

All pretenses at tempering such condescension with tact, however, ended with the nativist movement of the 1850s. Large-scale European immigration resulting from the Irish potato famine and the European revolutions of 1848 prompted a violent nationwide backlash against all things "foreign." Opponents of immigration coalesced in the mid-1850s to form the American party (better known as the Know-Nothing party), the purpose of which was to arrest and reverse "the corruption of American institutions by the foreign-born."[30]

Though short-lived as a national institution, the party enjoyed some of its most notable political successes in Louisiana. Despite the party's anti-Catholic and anti-"foreign" national platform, which by implication also meant anti-Louisiana French, numerous prominent Acadians, primarily former Whig sugar planters, became leading members of the American party's south Louisiana chapters, as did many notable Creoles. Partly as a result of Acadian and Creole support, the Know-Nothings scored impressive electoral victories in St. Landry Parish, where they controlled the police jury, in 1854. The American party fared poorly in the 1855 general election, however, largely as a result of the Democratic party's successful exploitation of the religious issue. Most Louisiana Catholics, evidently including most middle- and lower-class Acadians, voted the Democratic ticket. Yet the Know-Nothings demonstrated exceptional strength where Acadian Whigs had formerly been most numerous, registering majorities in West Baton Rouge, St. James, and St. Martin parishes. The Know-Nothings also carried Donaldsonville and Thibodaux in the heart of the Acadian sugar belt.[31]

The cultural apostasy of the Acadian nativists, manifested in their support of the American party, belied their changing cultural and linguistic orientation and presaged the wholesale postbellum migration of the Acadian gentry into the Anglo-American mainstream. This flight across cultural lines would be undertaken in response to the vitriolic public denigration of their mother culture. The Acadian yeoman and laboring classes, however, lacked the cultural, linguistic, and educational wherewithal—and evidently the inclination—to join the cross-cultural migration. As the sole heirs to their ethnic identity, they became an object of national and regional derision.

The dominant culture's changing attitude toward the Acadians, evolving from condescension in the 1840s to disgust in the 1850s and 1860s, reflected increasingly hostile national attitudes toward America's linguistic and cultural minorities. Despite the dissolution of the American party following its miserable showing in the 1856 national election, intolerance toward individuals and groups whose culture and language differed from national norms increased. The sectional crisis, the commencement of the Civil War, and the patriotism that they engendered created heightened pressures for conformity in both North and South. Persons outside the boundaries of either dominant subregional culture were considered fair game. Southerners frequently ridiculed the sanctimony, materialism, and meddling tendencies of their sectional adversaries. Northerners generally viewed Southerners collectively as a debased, backward, and morally bankrupt people who had been left behind culturally, economically, and technologically by their more industrious, ambitious, and aggressive neighbors to the north. As one student of sectional attitudes has noted, "no quarter of Southern culture managed to escape the negative [Northern] evaluator."[32]

Regional animosities were compounded by growing middle- and upper-class resentment of less affluent and less well-educated social elements, whose low socioeconomic status was attributed to laziness, ignorance, and, worst of all, lack of ambition. In the eyes of mainstream whites, lower-class Acadians embodied the worst of all possible attributes. Because they were Southerners, they were "debased and tainted" by their archaic and unjust social system as well as their climate; because of their different cultural and linguistic characteristics, they were perceived as inherently inferior; because they commonly aspired to only a comfortable existence, they were lazy and unambitious; because of their Catholicism, they were priest dominated, intolerant of other faiths, and pawns in the pope's perceived quest for world domination; because of their strong extended family ties and tendency toward residential propinquity, they were thought to be dangerously inbred; because of their lack of formal education, they were ignorant (often stupid); because they failed to embrace materialism, exemplified by acquisition of the latest consumer goods, they were backward. Worst of all, because they refused to assimilate, they were un-American.[33]

Albert Rhoads, a writer for *Galaxy* magazine, expressed this viewpoint most clearly and succinctly:

> The American is only satisfied when all foreign elements are thrown into the national turning shop and come out turned to his own exact proportions. The Creoles [i.e., Cajuns] for generations have steadily refused to be planed, and this irritates the American. He of Anglo-Saxon stock regards American civilization as the highest in the

world, and insists that this Creole native shall square himself to it, but he persistently refuses—he prefers his own. Elsewhere the turning shop works successfully. The Indians are shaved down almost to annihilation; Mexicans of California and Texas assume the national shape; Alaskans even are being cut down to the required model; and as for the Irish, they are hardly landed on the Battery before declarations are filed and they are turned out after the approved pattern. The Creole alone resists, and to the urgent demands of the Anglo-Saxon neighbor his "Non, monsieur," comes back as unerringly as the refrain of Poe's raven.[34]

It is hardly surprising that the Acadian parishes shared with the Appalachian region a "peculiar onus," shaped to a large extent by the widely circulated writings of such unsympathetic outsiders.[35]

The basic elements of the resulting negative stereotype are clearly evident in the reports of Northern correspondents sent to cover the devastation in postwar Louisiana. Perhaps the most notorious of these reports was penned by the internationally famous lithographer A. R. Waud, who, like many other influential observers, was enchanted by south Louisiana's natural beauty but repelled by its French-speaking denizens.

> These primitive people are the descendants of Canadian French settlers in Louisiana; and by dint of intermarriage they have succeeded in getting pretty well down in the social scale.
>
> Without energy, education, or ambition, they are good representatives of the white trash, behind the age in every thing. The majority of all the white inhabitants of these parishes are tolerably ignorant, but these are grossly so—so little are they thought of—that the niggers, when they want to express contempt for one of their own race, call him an Acadian nigger. Their views of the future life are principally confined to the prospect of meeting Monsieur VULSIN, a prominent man among them, who departed this life a good while ago. Some of them are devout Catholics, to which Church they are all attached.
>
> To live without effort is their apparent aim in life, and they are satisfied with very little, and are, as a class, quite poor. Their language is a mixture of French and English, quite puzzling to the uninitiated. During the Civil War, although forced into the Confederate ranks, they were considered Unionists, and were kind to those who needed their help.
>
> With a little mixture of fresh blood and some learning they might

become much improved, and have higher aims than the possession of land enough to grow their corn and a sufficiency of "goujon" (gudgeon). They have suffered a great deal by the overflowing waters, even to making their escape from their houses in boats, or knocking the upper works off and floating to safety on the floor for a raft.[36]

Lest any reader miss the point, Waud included with his short article a woodcut showing two Acadian washerwomen, their legs exposed to mid-thigh, a clear message of cultural and moral depravity to Victorian America. The image also featured prominently a woman smoking a corncob pipe and an idle (and thus manifestly lazy) man holding a small net used for recreational fishing, watching the women work nearby.

Waud's comments were echoed, though with less vitriol, by numerous other Northern visitors to postbellum Louisiana. The following account is perhaps the most representative:

The Acadians—abbreviated to "Cajens" by our laconic race—form a small portion of the Creole population. They first settled in Nova Scotia, and thence proceeded to Louisiana, where they have clung to their little possessions with tenacity ever since. They turn up the soil and cultivate the cane like the first settlers, and are but meagerly successful. They detest innovation, and the steam plough and the new-fangled sugar-house are not in favor. To adopt them involved outlay, risk, much thinking and fretting. It is simpler to give them a wide berth, and digest well by day and sleep well at nights. This is Acadian philosophy.

The American employs the word Acadian in an uncomplimentary sense. A Utopian dreamer and idler is implied—one who sits on the skirts of progress. The reproaching American delves and digs in the shadow of life while his cheerful neighbor pleasantly basks in the sunshine. To one, the world is a workshop; to the other, a great fair. The Acadians are the least intelligent of the Creole population, and occupy small patches of land along bayous and the coast, which are just sufficient in extent to satisfy the wants of their simple lives. Their dwellings usually contain two chambers, are of one-story, and barely peep above the bayou ridge and the level coast. A curtain frequently hangs across the doorway to keep out the mosquitoes. This is an object of luxury, for, however much these insects annoy strangers, they trouble the indigenes very little. . . .

Generally the little house of the Acadians is surrounded by a small orange grove, which is the principal support of the family. Before the oranges are ripe, cunning fruit-vendors from the city buy them on the tree for future delivery. The part behind the house is usually devoted to the cultivation of cane, which some more affluent neighbor grinds for the owner on shares. To make one hogshead of sugar is usually the height of Acadian ambition; to make two is to bathe in Pactolian waters.[37]

Critical views of the Acadians, such as those of Rhoads and Waud, were not restricted to contemporary Northern journalists. Southern Anglos shared most of the ethnocentric biases of their Northern antagonists. Southerners' anti-Acadian complaints centered on the same perceived character flaws attacked by Waud: laziness, lack of ambition, ignorance, backwardness, and an unrelenting refusal to assimilate.[38] These attitudes had crystallized by the early 1850s, when Frederick Law Olmsted observed them while traveling through the Acadian Coast.

> At one corner of Mr. R's plantation, there was a hamlet of Acadians (descendants of the refugees of Acadia), about a dozen small houses or huts, built of wood or clay, in the old French peasant style. The residents owned small farms, on which they raised a little corn and rice; but Mr. R. described them as lazy vagabonds, doing but little work, and spending much time in shooting, fishing and play. He wanted very much to buy all their land, and get them to move away. He had already bought out some of them, and had made arrangements to get hold of the land of some of the rest. He was willing to pay them two or three times as much as their property was actually worth, to get them to move off. As fast as he got possession, he destroyed their houses and gardens, removed their fences and trees, and brought all their land into his cane plantation.
>
> Some of them were mechanics. One was a very good mason, and he employed him in building his sugar works and refinery; but he would be glad to get rid of them all, and should then depend entirely on slave mechanics—of these he had several already, and he could buy more when he needed them.[39]

The Acadian targets of Anglo vilification appear to have held their tormentors in equally low esteem. The few contemporary writers who commented on the attitudes of working-class Acadians toward Anglo-

Americans all agree that the relationship was acrimonious. It would appear from all accounts that the *gens d'en bas* considered the *Américains* haughty, meddlesome, and unscrupulous, often dishonest. R. L. Daniels noted in the late 1870s that "of Americans, as a class, they have not the highest opinion. Southerners as well as Northerners are 'Yankees,' unless regarded with exceptional favor. If one of their own people is shrewd or tricky in business transactions, he is unceremoniously designated a 'Yankee.'" George Washington Cable agreed, noting that Acadians "don't trust or follow *Américains*."[40]

Because of these mutual antagonisms, intercultural contact was minimal and helped preserve the Acadians' linguistic integrity. They also made it difficult for former Acadian yeomen now trapped in tenantry to escape their fate, for economic success was increasingly linked to credit from Anglo-American businessmen. Minimal contact in turn gave rise to stereotypical images of both rival cultures, particularly the tendency for each group to view the other as monolithic, devoid of internal class, cultural, and religious distinctions. This attitude is evident in the epithets used by both groups—*Américain*, implying swindler, and *Cajun*, signifying white trash.[41]

As the negative inference of the term suggests, *Cajun* was used by Anglos to refer to all persons of French descent and low economic standing, regardless of their ethnic affiliation. By the end of the nineteenth century, this class alone retained its linguistic heritage. Hence poor Creoles of the prairie and bayou regions came to be permanently identified as Cajun, joining the Acadian ever poor and *nouveau pauvre*. Eventually swelling their ranks were significant numbers of chronically poor and downwardly mobile Anglos and Foreign French (nineteenth-century French) immigrants. Like the Acadians, the Creoles and Foreign French—the other major elements of the local white population—generally existed on an economic plane separate and distinct from that of the Anglo elite. Though the Creole and Foreign French elite appears to have endured the economic trials of war and Reconstruction somewhat more successfully than their Acadian counterparts, few individuals attained the lofty economic heights of the planter caste. As in the Acadian community, a small upper middle class, consisting of large-scale farmers and prominent merchants, complemented the Creole and Foreign French planters. But, as also in Acadian society, yeomen of increasingly marginal economic status and landless individuals composed an overwhelming majority of the Creole and French immigrant populations (tables 11 and 12).[42]

The term *Cajun* thus became a socioeconomic classification for the multicultural amalgam of several culturally and linguistically distinct groups. In several parishes, these groups constituted an absolute majority of the white population—approximately 57 percent of all white households in the fifteen-parish Acadian area (table 13). Over the course of the next half-century these groups would coalesce to form the synthetic, Acadian-based culture that presently pervades south Louisiana.

Creation of the new sociocultural amalgam was a result of the component members' common bonds of poverty. Following the Civil War, rural neighborhoods became increasingly multicultural as French-speaking families of culturally heterogenous sharecroppers came together to work adjoining tracts of large farms (tables 13, 14, and 15).[43]

Increased daily contact led to a fundamental change in intergroup relations. By 1870, multicultural households were not uncommon in numerous Acadian parishes, particularly in the water-bottom areas, as non-Acadian orphans, immigrants, and, increasingly, in-laws came to reside in Acadian households. Traveling through the Acadian region around 1880, George Washington Cable observed that "Acadians take care of helpless & orphans, very commonly. Often see them with members of family of no relation." Seventy Acadian households in Lafourche Parish, for instance, contained at least one Creole occupant, while fifty-two boasted an Anglo resident. These close and persistent social contacts were complemented by a dramatic rise in marriages between members of disparate "Cajun" subcultural groups.[44] Exogamy was pervasive among Acadians of all social and economic backgrounds. The Mouton family, perhaps the most illustrious antebellum Acadian family, is representative of the gentry class. The Catholic church recorded marriages for twelve Mouton men between 1866 and 1868. Six of them married Acadians, four married Anglos, and two allied themselves with Creoles. Mouton women exhibited an even greater tendency to marry outside the group. Of the ten Mouton brides who married between 1866 and 1868, eight entered into exogamous unions—three with Foreign French grooms, three with Anglos, and one each with Canadian and Creole men.[45]

The Guidry family's marital patterns are far more representative of the lower socioeconomic strata in the traditional Acadian settlement areas. Between 1866 and 1868, fifteen of the twenty-three (65 percent) Guidry grooms married within the Acadian community. Five others (approximately 22 percent) married Anglos, and the other three (13 percent) married Creole and Foreign French brides. Guidry brides were far more likely to marry outside their group. Only eight of eighteen Guidry women (44 percent) took Acadian spouses between 1866 and 1868, while six (33 percent) married Creoles. Three of the four remaining Guidry brides married Foreign French men. Only one Guidry bride married an Anglo.

Acadians living in peripheral areas exhibited the most pronounced tendency toward exogamy. The Pitre family, clustered in northwestern Imperial St. Landry Parish, a prairie Creole bastion since colonial times, married almost completely outside the Acadian community. Of the ten Pitre grooms between 1866 and 1868, nine took Anglo, Creole, or Foreign French brides. In addition, nine Pitre women married during the same period, all forging alliances with Creole and Anglo families.

Exogamous marriages involving Acadian women are especially important, for intermarriage was the cultural vehicle most responsible for the gradual assimilation of the other elements of the Cajun amalgam. Mothers have traditionally been the principal intergenerational transmitters of culture, and local oral tradition indicates that Acadian women in intercultural marriages invariably raised their children as Acadians, even when their spouse was of Anglo-American background. The Caruthers family, for example, was so thoroughly assimilated that its name was gallicized to Credeur by the late nineteenth century. The Miller, Abshire, Choate, Theall, Venable, Clark, Johnson, and Kidder families were similarly drawn into the Acadian fold. Joining them were numerous Foreign French (François, Faul, Dubois, Jacquemoud, and Herpin) and Creole (Barras, Domingue, and Louviere) families.

The reverse process operated in intercultural households dominated by Acadian men, resulting in the assimilation of the children into the non-Acadian mother's cultural milieu. Unlike the antebellum period, when endogamous marriages by Acadian men were largely responsible for preserving the group's cultural integrity, only marginally fewer Acadian men married outside the group than Acadian women. A minority of Acadian men and women married within the Acadian community on both sides of the Atchafalaya River. In postbellum southwestern Louisiana, approximately 45 percent of all Acadian men entered into endogamous marriages. In the Lafourche Basin, only 42 percent of all Acadian grooms took Acadian brides, and 37 percent of Acadian brides married Acadian men. These endogamous unions were often with cousins, particularly in the bayou regions, where social stratification was most pronounced. Approximately 15 percent of the Acadian grooms in southwestern Louisiana during Reconstruction carried the same surname as their brides.

The sudden and dramatic increase in exogamous marriages fundamentally altered Acadian society. In the many south Louisiana parishes where Acadians constituted a minority, even limited intermarriage undermined the group's precarious cultural existence. The very small numbers of Acadians who had moved to parishes on the periphery of the original Acadian settlement areas were particularly vulnerable to rapid assimilation into the dominant Anglo- and Creole-based cultures on their new domiciles. For example, the Acadian settlers in Avoyelles and Pointe Coupée parishes—numbering 220 and 237 respectively—constituted the largest contingents of Acadians transplanted in the peripheral, rural parishes, but even these groups made up only 1.6 and 1.8 percent respectively of the total parochial populations. Even less secure were the Acadians in Plaquemines, St. John, Jefferson, St. Charles, St. Bernard, and Livingston parishes, who numbered respectively only 80, 44, 33, 20, 11, and 10 persons. The growing body of urban Acadians faced perhaps the greatest threat of assimilation (table 17).[46]

Following the Civil War, scores of unemployed and underemployed Acadian professionals, merchants, and craftsmen made their way to the towns and cities of south Louisiana. Most congregated in their local parish seats. The 1870 census indicates the professions and numbers of gainfully employed Acadians residing in Vermilionville: merchant, 6; attorney, 2; carpenter, 1, clerk, 1, cook, 1, doctor, 1, physician, 1, saddler, 1, state tax collector, 1; and wheelwright, 1. But the most ambitious established themselves, at least temporarily, at either Baton Rouge or New Orleans (table 18). The 1870 census records 44 such individuals in Baton Rouge, then a city of 6,498, and 306 in New Orleans, a metropolis of over 191,000. The Acadians who

remained in the city were inevitably drawn into the American mainstream. Perhaps the best barometer of their cultural transformation
is the change in naming practices. Seventy-three percent of all Acadian children living in the New Orleans suburbs in Jefferson Parish
carried distinctly Anglo given names, such as Arthur, Edgar, Albert,
William, or Walter. None of the Acadian children there bore such
distinctly French names such as Jacques, Alcée, Alcide, Ozémé, François, Hippolyte, and Théophile then much in vogue in the rural
French-speaking community. The remaining 7 percent carried biblical names such as David, the spelling of which is identical in French
and English.[47]

Acadians living in New Orleans followed the same trend; 52 percent of all Acadian children living in the city bore Anglo names.
Unlike the suburbanites, many New Orleans Acadians—37 percent—
bore distinctly French names, apparently as a result of the lingering,
albeit rapidly declining, influence of the Crescent City's white Creole
minority.[48] Acadian residents of the parish seats confronted less overwhelming odds, but they faced equally certain assimilation into the
Anglo-American mainstream for, with the end of hostilities, English
had become the primary language of business even in the most remote Louisiana hamlets.[49]

The economic incentive that drew the Acadian urbanites into the
American mainstream was less compelling for rural agriculturists.
Constituting the lower orders of the region's white socioeconomic hierarchy, struggling Acadian yeomen and sharecroppers generally
lacked the skills, the capital, and often the initiative necessary for up-
ward mobility into the economic orders dominated by Anglos. Approximately 60 percent of the marriageable Acadian men and
women, however, experienced horizontal mobility by crossing previously rigid cultural boundaries through exogamous marriages.[50]

Exogamous marriages were critical to maintenance of mass in the
Cajun cultural equation. They were particularly crucial in such parishes as Terrebonne, where Anglos enjoyed an overwhelming numerical advantage. There, the Acadians tended to assimilate into the
dominant culture. By 1870, 56 percent of Acadian children in working-class households carried Anglo given names. Where Creoles predominated, as in Plaquemines, Pointe Coupée, St. John, and St.
Charles parishes, the small Acadian minority was quickly absorbed

into the lower socioeconomic strata of white Creole society, thereby preserving their French character. Unlike the urbanites, 54 to 75 percent of these rural Acadians continued to endow their children with French given names, and it appears from scant evidence that equally large percentages continued to speak French. In traditional settlement areas such as St. James, St. Landry, and St. Martin parishes, where Acadians were heavily outnumbered by Creoles but Acadians and Creoles together outnumbered Anglos, Acadians faced less pressure to assimilate into the larger French-based culture. Though intermarriage between members of these Francophone groups would persist in these areas, the Acadian and Creole minorities for some time remained largely undissolved elements in the emerging Cajun amalgam. Cultural persistence is evidenced in the continuing mutually antagonistic group attitudes, each group's linguistic viability, and the enduring dominance of traditional given-name practices (table 19).[51]

But even in areas such as St. Landry and St. Martin parishes, where vestiges of the original Acadian and Creole communities have survived to the present, the cultural integrity of the Francophone subgroups continued to erode through exogamous marriages.

The cultural exchanges resulting from intermarriage gradually transformed the base culture, even in areas of Acadian demographic and cultural domination. Exogamous marriages, for example, were largely responsible for the introduction of Creole and European folklore, music, and cuisine into Acadian culture. Cross-cultural transfers through intermarriage were also responsible for the gradual linguistic homogenization of all working-class Francophone groups in rural south Louisiana, including the Acadians. By the early twentieth century, Cajun French had become the lingua franca among the lower classes in the prairie and bayou countries.[52]

Cajun French is a linguistic hybrid including vocabulary drawn from Acadian French, Creole French, nineteenth-century Standard French, and English. Although the dialect's basic structure is consistent throughout the rural Francophone parishes, various idioms are subregionally specific. There are also significant subregional variations in pronunciation. In regions such as the Pierre Part area of Assumption Parish and the lower prairie sections of Vermilion Parish, where the Acadian population remained the dominant cultural force and intercultural marriages were limited, the archaic (seventeenth-century) French pronunciation patterns of predispersal Acadia were preserved. French idioms and pronunciation in these parts of Louisiana remain remarkably similar to those of Acadians in the Canadian Maritimes. In Avoyelles Parish and in present-day Evangeline Parish, the equally distinctive pronunciation patterns introduced by eighteenth-century French and Canadian pioneers were, and would remain, predominant. A more modern variety of French is spoken along bayous Lafourche and Teche, along the Vermilion River, and in the middle prairie region westward from present-day Sunset, Scott, and Broussard. Postbellum sharecroppers and intercultural marriages were most numerous in these areas, and communications with New Orleans, the nation's second leading port of entry for French immigrants, were far easier there than in the northern and southern prairies. The number of Foreign French agriculturists was consequently largest in these areas. It is thus hardly surprising that the bayou country and central prairies came to use nineteenth-century French constructions and pronunciation patterns.[53]

As linguistic pattern suggest, the process of cultural integration, transformation, and regeneration was most widespread in the Lafourche Basin and in the prairie regions below present-day St. Landry Parish. Yet even in areas where the Acadian presence was limited and intermarriage was far less commonplace, the change in ethnic identity for the lower economic strata of Francophone society was slowly but surely taking place. A great deal of confusion regarding this group existed among outsiders, who in postbellum times sometimes labeled them Creoles, sometimes Cajuns.[54] But by 1900, *Américains*, particularly newspaper and magazine writers and authors of popular nonfiction, had succeeded in permanently affixing the Cajun identity to poor Francophones in Avoyelles and northwestern Imperial St. Landry Parish, even though members of these groups did not identify themselves as such. Samuel Lockett, for example, makes no distinction between the various components of the new Cajun community in his geography of postbellum Louisiana, published in 1873: "We will now turn to that [part of Louisiana] which to me . . . is the most pleasing part of the state. I mean the region of the prairies. This region lies almost entirely west of the Bayou Teche and South of Bayou Cocodrie, making up the old Opelousas and Attakapas countries. . . . Most of the population of the Prairies is of Acadian origin, and, with but few notable exceptions, they are a rather thriftless people."[55] Residents of French descent in Evangeline and Avoyelles parishes today still privately concede their Creole background. Yet when northwestern Imperial St. Landry seceded from its mother parish in 1910, it was dubbed Evangeline Parish by the state legislature in honor of the region's correspondingly mythical Acadian heritage.[56]

SEVEN

Politics and Violence
in the Reconstruction Era

The pressures created by rapid socioeconomic change, exacerbated by precipitous downward mobility, resulted in increased violence both within the Acadian community and between the Acadians and their neighbors. Violence had been an integral part of Louisiana Acadian life since the 1755 dispersal. Neighbors frequently quarreled over land boundaries, crop damage caused by stray livestock, and bad debts. Confrontations often degenerated into fistfights. Like their counterparts throughout the antebellum South, Acadians of all social classes considered violence an acceptable means of settling personal disputes. No moral impediment existed for fistfights or duels. Indeed, as George Washington Cable observed, Acadians "can't understand how a fistfight can be an assault." Nor did the combatants acquire a social stigma.[1]

Local society did, however, establish acceptable limits for violence, even in "affairs of honor." Homicide, for example, was acceptable only for self-defense. Thus though combatants frequently threatened one another with firearms, such engagements were seldom lethal. Instead, conflicts were usually resolved peaceably, either informally through the intercession of a disinterested third party, often an elder in the community, or, more commonly, through the local court system.[2]

The Acadians' willingness to settle disputes by legal means caught the attention of several antebellum observers familiar with the more violent English-speakers in other southeastern states. Whenever local police and judicial authorities proved incapable of dealing with the criminal element, these Southerners habitually took it upon themselves to quell real or perceived threats to life and property. Richard Maxwell Brown, author of the most comprehensive study of extralegal violence in American history, states:

> Violence has been the determinant of both the form and the substance of American life. The threat to the structure of society mounted by the criminal and the disorderly has been met energetically by the official and unofficial violence of the forces of law and order. Often perceiving a grave menace to social stability in the unsettled conditions of frontier life and racial, ethnic, urban and industrial unrest, solid citizens rallied to the cause of community order. . . . Not confining themselves to passive approval of police action, these upright citizens revealed their deep commitment to community order by their own violent participation in lynch mobs and vigilante movements and other extralegal bodies. Violence, thus employed, has been socially conservative. Whether used legally or extralegally, it has been used to support the cohesive three-tiered structure of the American community with its upper, middle, and lower classes and its underlying social values of law and order and the sanctity of property.[3]

These characteristics remained constant in American vigilantism between the establishment of the Back Country Regulators, America's first vigilante movement founded in South Carolina in 1767, and the end of the nineteenth century. The South Carolina vigilantes served as a model for parallel movements subsequently organized in other eastern seaboard colonies. From these hotbeds, the vigilante impulse "followed the sweep of Anglo settlement toward the Pacific," making its way to Louisiana by the 1830s.[4]

Despite geographic and chronological differences between individual groups, vigilante organizations and activities remained fundamentally unaltered throughout the late eighteenth and nineteenth centuries. Vigilante movements were usually organized and led by members of the local socioeconomic elite. Under their guidance, alleged ne'er-do-wells were rounded up, flogged, and ordered to leave the country. Persons failing to depart were executed once their deadline had passed. These floggings and executions were intended to serve as warnings to local outlaws that they would be given no opportunity to erode "the established values of civilization."[5]

In the late eighteenth century, such vigilante retribution was a common feature of frontier areas. But vigilante floggings and lynchings of ne'er-do-wells became more and more frequent in developed and developing areas as the nineteenth century progressed. Indeed, the peak of vigilante activity in the first half of the nineteenth century occurred in the late antebellum period—the late 1830s, the early 1840s, and between 1857 and 1859.[6]

Louisiana's Acadians were not immune from these national trends, and their attitudes toward law and order changed dramatically in the late antebellum period. Indeed, the level of violence increased geometrically as the period drew to a close, primarily because of corruption and intimidation of the local judicial system in the late 1850s, the disruptive influences of the Union invasions and Jayhawker activities during the Civil War, and the political, social, and economic upheavals of Reconstruction. Violence during these periods took three separate and distinct forms: violence within the community; violence to suppress criminality; and violence to achieve social control.

The catalyst for this metamorphosis was the apparent collapse of local law and order in 1858 and 1859. By the late 1850s, southwestern Louisiana criminals boasted publicly of their ability to intimidate public prosecutors and manipulate juries through perjury, and, according to some contemporary accounts, suspected burglars, rustlers, and murderers were acquitted with notorious frequency. Indeed, believing themselves virtually immune from prosecution, thieves and cattle rustlers brazenly plied their nefarious trades by daylight in 1858 and 1859. Property rights were sacred to the Acadians, as they were to landholders of all ethnic backgrounds throughout the South. Crimes against property thus drew an immediate and forceful reaction from the Acadian community.[7]

Like their fellow Southerners, Acadian landholders believed that good fences make good neighbors. Property owners looked upon any violation of boundary lines, for whatever reason, as a threat to their independence and security. The Acadians consequently were particularly aggressive in asserting and maintaining their territoriality. Indeed, maintenance of property rights had constituted the focal point of legal disputes involving Acadians since the seventeenth century.[8]

Finally, nineteenth-century Acadians of all social classes despised all forms of dishonesty, usually severing relations with those who proved to be less than scrupulously honest. Even petty thieves were not tolerated. For example, though their nineteenth-century card games were reportedly played for small stakes, Acadians did not abide cheating. George Washington Cable indicates that cheaters at cards were "ostracized [by Acadians] as . . . criminal[s] against society." Far harsher punishment was reserved for thieves, particularly in the late 1850s, after Acadian property holders of all classes were victimized by penniless European immigrants and landless Acadians and Creoles, who engaged in petty thefts, cattle rustling, and distribution of stolen property. The most affluent victims quickly mobilized to protect their belongings, and unlike their late eighteenth- and early nineteenth-century counterparts, who dealt with such problems individually, late antebellum Acadian property holders joined paramilitary vigilante groups to deal with the outlaws.[9]

Prairie Acadians turned to vigilance committees perhaps because of their recent use by Lafourche Basin Acadians in response to an anticipated servile insurrection in 1856. The Lafourche Basin Acadians, in turn, had drawn upon Anglo precedents in creating their vigilante organizations. It appears that the Lafourche vigilantes drew their inspiration from the nationally publicized activities of the 1851 and 1856 San Francisco committees of vigilance, which were the best organized and most powerful in American history.[10]

The Louisiana vigilance committees that followed in the wake of the Lafourche Basin vigilantes, however, not only drew their inspiration but also modeled their organizations and their activities after the San Francisco committees of vigilance. Unlike its predecessors, the San Francisco vigilante movement did not focus exclusively on the local outlaw element. Fed by incipient nativism, the movement also provided a violent outlet for class, ethnic, and racial animosities. "Catholics, Jews, immigrants, blacks, laboring men and labor leaders, radicals, free thinkers, and defenders of civil liberties" all became their targets. South Louisiana's vigilance committees rivaled those of

San Francisco in both size and political influence. According to statistics compiled by Richard Maxwell Brown, the 1859 vigilante movement of southwestern Louisiana, which boasted a membership of approximately four thousand men at its zenith, was the second largest vigilante movement in nineteenth-century America and the third largest movement in United States history.[11]

The oldest of the Attakapas committees of vigilance, the Côte Gelée chapter at present-day Broussard, organized on February 4, 1859, in response to a wave of thefts from local homes and businesses. The twelve organizers included Acadians Charles Duclize Comeau, Alexandre Bernard, Eloi Guidry, Don Louis Broussard, Raphael Lachaussée, Joseph Guidry, Valsin Broussard, and D. Guidry. Drawing on long-established vigilante precedents, these men first established an extralegal court, presided over by the group's "captain." This court entertained charges brought by any member of the vigilante group against any member of the local community. Defendants were usually tried in absentia, with all attending members of the vigilante organization serving as jurors. Once a verdict of guilty had been rendered, the vigilantes armed themselves and set out as a group, generally consisting of ten to twenty persons, to dispense their own brand of justice. These vigilantes usually arrived at a person's home in the middle of the night and roused their victim from bed. Brought before his accusers, often at gunpoint, the "convicted" malefactor was given an ultimatum. Depending on the severity of his supposed crimes, he was given one to thirty days to leave the area under penalty of death by hanging. Unarmed individuals resisting either capture or the order of banishment were flogged; armed resisters were shot. With one notable exception, this modus operandi served as a model for the dozens of vigilante chapters that sprang up in southwestern Louisiana between February and August 1859. In late spring 1859, the St. Martinville committee of vigilance evidently incarcerated many of its victims in an extralegal makeshift jail as a means of forcibly extracting information from them. Once the most notorious "criminals" had been evicted, the committees established night patrols to maintain law and order. On May 7, 1859, for example, the executive committee of Lafayette Parish's Society of Mutual Protection divided the Vermilionville area into districts and appointed "chiefs" to supervise armed patrols in their respective areas. District patrol chiefs were authorized to summon to their assistance as many Vermilionville vigilantes as they deemed necessary to make an arrest.[12]

The Attakapas night riders launched their activities on the evening of February 4, 1859. They used traditional forms of retribution—physical and psychological intimidation coupled with threats of physical harm, later the lash, finally, the hangman's noose, but frequently focused on nontraditional targets—particularly European immigrants—legitimized by the San Francisco vigilante movement. Twelve of the first twenty-two local victims (54.54 percent) of vigilante justice were either European immigrants or children of immigrants. Two others were the sons of immigrants. Their inaugural victim, August Gudbeer, the son of German (probably Alsatian) immigrants, is perhaps representative of the individuals who would fall victim to the vigilante lash. Though all of the victims were either reputed criminals who had managed to evade justice or persons who had harbored fugitives from vigilante justice, these supposed ne'er-do-wells were persons deemed socially or politically unacceptable by the local gentry. Gudbeer allegedly was a petty thief, but this outcast was also the son of immigrant parents and the consort of a mulatress born of the union of a black man and a white woman—the antebellum South's ultimate social taboo. However serious Gudbeer's alleged crimes may have been, it is clear from Alexandre Barde's official history of the Attakapas vigilantes that his social transgressions, particularly his sexual liaison with the mulatress and his familial background, weighed heavily in his "conviction" by his extralegal judge and jury.[13]

The Côte Gelée committee initially arrested and expelled individuals such as Gudbeer who were suspected of criminal activities. Because these suspects could not resist the overwhelming force brought to bear against them, the Côte Gelée committee enjoyed impressive initial success, forcing numerous individuals into exile in Texas, New Orleans, and distant Louisiana parishes. These successes prompted other rural communities to organize their own vigilante committees. By late August 1859, at least eighteen such organizations had been established in Lafayette, St. Martin, Vermilion, and Calcasieu parishes. (Alexandre Barde states that nine or ten committees existed in St. Landry and Calcasieu parishes, but he identifies only four.) Membership in individual chapters ranged from approximately two hundred to several dozen (table 20).[14]

Acadians constituted disproportionately large numbers of both the leadership and general membership elements of these organizations. For example, all but one of the executive officers of the two-hundred-member Vermilionville committee, officially called the Society of Mutual Protection, were Acadians: Alexandre Mouton, president; André Valerien Martin, vice-president; A.D. Boudreaux, secretary; Ignace Mouton, marshal; Edmond Guilbeaux, deputy marshal; Jules Dugat, deputy marshal; Auguste Murr, deputy marshal; and Valéry Breaux, deputy marshal. Acadians constituted 61.67 percent of all known Attakapas vigilantes.[15] Regardless of their standing in individual organizations, these Acadian vigilantes were members of the local upper and upper-middle classes (table 21).[16]

Targets of the Acadian vigilantes and their *confrères* were drawn from the lower strata of local white society—occasionally small landholders but more frequently landless individuals (table 22). It is clear from Barde's chronicle of vigilante activities that once persons most responsible for crimes against property had been removed from the local scene, vigilantes focused their attention on social control, choosing as victims poor whites and free blacks who threatened the social status quo by harboring fugitive slaves, by conducting indiscreet sexual liaisons, or by challenging contemporary concepts of white superiority. In the most flagrant example of social control, vigilantes from Anse-la-Butte, apparently assisted by reinforcements from neighboring committees, drove from their homes twenty-one members of the Coco family, a mixed-race clan formed by the polygamous union of a free black man and two white sisters. Though accused of prostitution, petty theft, and distribution of stolen goods, their only real crimes may have been their open rejection of local social norms and racial attitudes as well as their ownership of desirable lands. Offering no resistance to the vigilantes, the Coco family soon migrated to Avoyelles Parish.[17]

Not all victims succumbed peacefully to vigilante ultimatums. Indeed, by late spring 1859, the vigilantes began to encounter significant resistance, as former victims and potential victims joined to oppose the night riders' terror tactics. Organized resistance centered in two areas: the Cypress Island region of St. Martin Parish and along St. Landry Parish's extensive southwestern boundary, bordering northern Vermilion and Lafayette parishes. The birth of antivigilante groups forced individual vigilante chapters to join forces to subdue their now much more formidable opponents. The first major confrontation occurred on May 31, 1859, when approximately two hundred vigilantes from St. Martinville, Côte Gelée, and Fausse Pointe encountered about fifty armed men and their wives and children at Pierre Romero's fortified home at Cypress Island. Bloodshed was averted because most of the defenders fled upon the vigilantes' arrival, and Romero and Tiburse Hulin, a suspected criminal sought by the vigilantes, surrendered in the face of overwhelming odds.[18]

The use of extralegal justice against individuals suspected of criminal behavior, the gradual escalation of violence in vigilante attacks against these people, and the forced exodus of victims from the state's south-central parishes prompted Louisiana's governor, Robert C. Wickliffe, to issue a proclamation on May 28, 1859, ordering the vigilante groups to disband. In a meeting on June 18, 1859, in response to the proclamation, the assembled vigilante delegates, led by Alexandre Mouton, voted to defy the governor. Realizing that prolonged resistance would compel Wickliffe to use the state militia to force compliance with his directive, however, the vigilante leaders authorized a single massive assault against the "undesirable" elements remaining in the area. A "council of war" consisting of Pierre Z. Doucet, Desire Landry, Placide Guilbeaux, Don Louis F. J. Broussard,[19] Jean-Jacques Alexandre Alfred Mouton, Pierre R. Breaux, Alexandre Latiolais, Gerassin Bernard, John R. Rigues, and Charles Z. Martin was established at Vermilionville on July 16 to plan and coordinate the proposed offensive. The principle targets of the attack would be the many individuals who had sought refuge just across the St. Landry Parish line following banishment from Lafayette, Vermilion, or St. Martin parishes.[20]

The antivigilantes, meanwhile, were mobilizing for a strike against their tormentors. Realizing that the substantial political influence wielded by the vigilante leadership effectively shielded the night riders from either criminal prosecution or government intervention, antivigilantes sought to end the reign of terror by force of arms. Organized by Acadian Olivier Guidry *dit* (called) Canada, his two sons, and a nephew—all of whom had been banished from Lafayette Parish for alleged aggravated assault, banditry, and harboring fugitive slaves—the antivigilantes sought popular support for their cause by promoting it as struggle by the poor against the oppression of the area's increasingly aggressive and intolerant "rich classes." Prisoners subsequently taken at the September 3, 1859, vigilante raid at Emilien Lagrange's Bayou Queue de Tortue residence, for example, consistently believed that "the Committee of Vermilionville . . . [was] hostile to the poor . . . [and] was going to sweep all [poor persons] from Lafayette Parish." The apparent righteousness of their cause attracted numerous landless prairie dwellers and yeomen to the antivigilante banner. Among the first to join the Guidrys was Jean-Baptiste Chiasson, alias John H. Jones, an Acadian landowner and small slaveholder who reportedly coordinated the plan of attack with the antivigilantes remaining in the Cypress Island area. But as events would later prove, many of these were vigilante spies. Indeed, most of the antivigilantes were non-Acadians, including large numbers of recent French immigrants and poor white Creoles. Most either reputedly had criminal records or had previously been vigilante victims. Perhaps the most notable member of the latter group was Emilien Lagrange, whose home was transformed into a fortified antivigilante bastion by a former French noncommissioned officer.[21]

Throughout the late summer, the antivigilantes prepared for their assault by acquiring arms and gunpowder from various suppliers in Louisiana and Texas. These arms agents reported and vigilante spies apparently confirmed their claims that the antivigilantes were preparing to do battle with their enemies. This attack, the vigilantes believed, would be launched following a barbecue at Emilien Lagrange's house on September 3, 1859, at which one Dr. Wagner, a prominent antivigilante, was expected to issue a call to arms. "If the [vigilantes] did not present [themselves]," the vigilante intelligence reports stated, the antivigilantes "would go and plant [their] flag . . . on the steeple of Vermilionville and turn the town red with blood and fire." To this disturbing news was added inflammatory, though apparently unfounded, reports of antivigilante efforts to incite a servile insurrection on September 3.[22]

The Vermilionville vigilantes responded by launching a massive preemptive strike against the antivigilantes. While mobilization orders were dispatched to all vigilante organizations in southwestern Louisiana, the Vermilionville committee moved quickly to divide and neutralize the opposition. Communications between the antivigilante groups along Bayou Queue de Tortue and near Cypress Island were disrupted by night patrols, and reputed antivigilante agents supposedly attempting to agitate the local slave population were banished from Lafayette Parish. The town of Vermilionville was virtually transformed into an armaments factory, as townspeople prepared to use the community's ceremonial cannon. Vigilantes converged on the town in anticipation of the coming battle, filling the local hotels.[23]

Additional vigilantes converged on Vermilionville on the morning of September 3. By 5:00 A.M., seven committees of vigilance—from Côte Gelée, Vermilionville (two), La Pointe, Pont Breaux, Grande Pointe, and Anse-la-Butte—were riding in formation toward the Emilien Lagrange residence. They were joined en route by numerous vigilantes from Vermilion, St. Landry, and Calcasieu parishes.[24]

Upon arrival at the Lagrange residence, West Point graduate Alfred Mouton, named by the Vermilionville committees to lead the assault, positioned most of the six hundred assembled vigilantes for a frontal attack. The Foreman and Vermilion committees from Vermilion Parish and the Prairie Robert and Faquetaique committees from St. Landry Parish were deployed along the prospective avenues of retreat for the antivigilante defenders, who, Barde maintained, numbered two to three hundred men.[25]

Once his men were in position, Mouton first resorted to psychological warfare. The ceremonial cannon was unlimbered in full view of the defenders, and the chief cannoneer went to great lengths to frighten the defenders by making a show of loading the fieldpiece and preparing the fuse and wick. The cannoneer's antics had the desired effect, and numerous antivigilantes fled into the woods lining the adjacent coulee as the wick was slowly lowered toward the fuse. These fugitives were quickly intercepted and arrested by the St. Landry and Vermilion units.[26]

When some of the defenders took flight, the cannoneer "lowered the wick and awaited new orders." Hoping to capitalize on the resulting confusion within the antivigilante camp, four vigilantes—former governor Alexandre Mouton, the chiefs of the Côte Gelée and St. Martinville committees, and an unidentified fourth party—approached the Lagrange home and conferred with Jean-Baptiste Chiasson and Emilien Lagrange, the antivigilante leaders. The antivigilantes initially rejected demands that they surrender Olivier

Guidry *dit* Canada, his sons, and his nephew and that they all lay down their arms. Governor Mouton's expressed concerns regarding the safety of the women and children taking shelter within the La-grange house, however, persuaded the defenders to capitulate. Two hundred vigilantes were then stationed along the palisade surround-ing the Lagrange residence, while an additional twenty-four night riders arrested and disarmed an equal number of antivigilantes.[27]

Once disarmed, the antivigilante prisoners, who now numbered ap-proximately eighty persons,[28] having been joined by the antivigilante fugitives captured in the woods, were completely at the mercy of the vigilantes, who took full advantage of the situation. Prisoners were bound and brought before a vigilante tribunal, composed of two rep-resentatives of each committee participating in the raid. Called indi-vidually before their extralegal judges, who held court in a nearby grove of trees, the "defendants" were summarily convicted after per-functory defense statements. The vigilantes then began to dispense their own brand of justice. Alexandre Barde, the vigilantes' official historian, insists that "the committees had not assumed the right to drown in the blood of the vanquished, especially since the victory had not been disputed." According to Barde, the captives were sentenced to "punishment with the whip and exile in five days." Accounts of the ensuing mass "chastisement" published in antivigilante newspapers, however, suggest that the beatings quickly degenerated into a homi-cidal orgy. The antivigilante *Franklin Planters' Banner* indicates that three antivigilante leaders were beaten to death. Barde himself con-cedes that six antivigilante leaders were each given 120 lashes. Their cohorts were given either 20 or 40 lashes, depending on the extent of their participation in the abortive antivigilante campaign. The *Banner* further notes that "several cadavers were [subsequently] found in the prairies." The provigilante *Opelousas Courier* also hints that the death toll was heavy, stating that the captives were transported to Lafa-yette Parish, near present-day Scott, Louisiana, where they were "tried by Judge Lynch"—that is, lynched. In addition, Geneus Guidry, a suicide victim according to Barde, was evidently murdered by his captors.[29]

The September 3, 1859, incident led to a second confrontation be-tween the Attakapas committees of vigilance and Governor Wickliffe. Wickliffe, accompanied by Adjutant-General Maurice Grivot, commander of the state militia, went to south-central Louisiana to restore order to that troubled region. These state officials apparently met with vigilante victims in St. Landry Parish, then conferred with the Attakapas area's vigilante leaders at Vermilionville. Though the conversation between the governor and the vigilantes was not recorded, it is clear that Wickliffe threatened to use the Louisiana militia if the outrages continued. Unwilling to give the governor further cause for state intervention, which, it was commonly believed, would permit the fugitives to return to their homes, Alexandre Mouton publicly called for the Attakapas committees of vigilance to desist from further acts of violence. Mouton's conciliatory gesture, however, appears to have been strictly for public consumption. He apparently was responsible for blocking Wickliffe's intention of destroying the Attakapas vigilante organizations and, in doing so, provided the local vigilantes the means for continuing their normal activities, albeit more discreetly. As the *Baton Rouge Advocate* noted, "It is difficult to say just how this promise [to refrain from further violence] will be carried out. We place little faith in it until the committees are dissolved, something which the [vigilante] leaders are not obliged to do. " The *Advocate's* insightful observation proved prophetic. All available evidence indicates that the activities of the Attakapas committees continued unabated. Exiles attempting to return home were arrested and punished, and at least one was killed while resisting arrest by vigilantes.[30]

The St. Landry committees, evidently composed largely of prairie Acadians, also disregarded Mouton's order to disband, choosing instead to expel forcibly the Attakapas exiles now living in their midst. The continuing antivigilante purge was centered in the southern and southwestern portions of the parish. This task was quickly accomplished, for by October 1859, many victims of the September 3 raid had reportedly been forced to seek refuge in Pointe Coupée Parish. Emulating others throughout the South, the local vigilantes then turned their attention to other "undesirables," whom they persecuted with a vengeance. The *Opelousas Courier* reported in late April 1860: "The vigilants [*sic*] are in motion! From Faquetaique, Plaquemine Brulée, Bois Mallet, Gros Chevreuil, even to Washington, the cry is they are marching calmly, quietly, but determinedly to the accomplishment of their purpose." St. Landry Parish's prosperous free persons of color bore the brunt of the continuing vigilante activities, and hundreds of free blacks were driven out of the parish by night riders. Some of these fugitives preferred relocation in Mexico and Haiti to eventual resettlement in their native parish.[31]

Only the beginning of the Civil War and the enlistment of many former vigilantes into the Confederate army brought a brief hiatus in the extralegal violence in the prairie parishes. By the end of 1863, night riders were once again active on the southwestern Louisiana prairies. Large numbers of poor prairie Creoles conscripted into the Confederate army in 1862 deserted when their units retreated north through their home parishes during the Union invasion of the bayou country during the spring of 1863. After deserting, many of them organized on the northern prairie "10 to 18 miles west" of Opelousas to resist reinduction into the rebel army. During the summer of 1863, Ozémé Carrière welded the deserters into a tightly knit quasi-military force. Once organized, Carrière's "battalion"—Jayhawkers as they were dubbed by Confederate sympathizers in Louisiana's prairie country—became a haven for the ever-growing number of south Louisianians deserting General Richard Taylor's dwindling army. The deserters were joined by fugitive slaves and, after July 1864, by free men of color escaping Confederate attempts to impress them into work crews in north Louisiana. The admission of blacks into the formerly all-white group appears to have been Carrière's decision, for before the war, he had cohabited with two free women of color.[32]

As Carrière's forces grew, he confronted overwhelming logistical problems. To arm and feed his men, Carrière ordered raids on isolated prairie residences from Plaquemine Brulée to the southwestern outskirts of Opelousas. These predominantly Acadian areas were probably singled out because of the recent Acadian participation in vigilante raids that had targeted free persons of color and their white sympathizers, like Carrière.[33]

The loss of horses, cattle, and saddles had a demoralizing effect on area farmers and ranchers, prompting local civilian and military authorities to stage a punitive strike against the marauders. As the following report from the *Opelousas Courier* indicates, the results were less than satisfactory: "On Sunday last, a company of mounted troops joined, it appears, by some citizens, started in pursuit of the jayhawkers, and when arrived in their quarter, dismounted and leisurely laid down, waiting for something or other, when, all at once, here come the jayhawkers pouncing upon them and throwing dismay among the crowd. Firing commenced, running too commenced, and from what we can learn we had one man killed and several wounded, one of whom has since died. We know not the loss of the other side." [34]

Their victory over the combined Confederate and Home Guard forces made Carrière's Jayhawkers the undisputed masters of southwestern Louisiana's upper prairie region. Having grown to approximately one thousand men by February 1864, Carrière's battalion established a defensive perimeter stretching from Prairie Mamou to upper Vermilion Parish, a barrier deemed so impermeable by contemporaries that eight thousand Confederate deserters reportedly sought refuge in the prairie country behind it. [35]

The Jayhawkers' defensive posture, however, quickly changed following the withdrawal of Confederate forces from St. Landry Parish in late winter 1864. Resorting to common banditry in mid-February, Carrière's men "swept over the country known as Plaquemine Ridge [near present-day Church Point], robbing the inhabitants in many instances of everything of value they possessed, but taking particularly all the fine horses and good arms they could find." Even more disconcerting than the widespread thefts was the fact that, for the first time, the Jayhawkers had dared to go "about publicly in daylight robbing citizens." It was perhaps more noteworthy that the raiders left their victims unharmed. Though the thieves frequently threatened to shoot their victims, as well as "every damned Confederate" they could find, they injured no one at the farmsteads of T. P. Guidry, Felix Dejean, Madison Young, Terence Jeansonne, and François Savoy. [36]

Though the raids were a source of concern, particularly for the area's propertied classes, the absence of bloodletting left intact the Jayhawkers' image as champions of resistance against the Confederacy. Indeed, according to Confederate authorities at Opelousas, by February 1864, the St. Landry Jayhawkers were seen as heroes by "discontented whites and free negroes [as well as] slaves already demoralized by the Yankees." According to Captain H. C. Morell, Confederate enrolling officer at Opelousas, "Carrière is daily becoming more and more popular with the masses, and that [popularity] every day serves to increase his gang. These men [Carrière and his lieutenants] are making the ignorant and deluded suppose that they are their champions, that the object they follow . . . is to bring the war to a close, and tell them if they could only make everybody join them the war would soon be brought to a close."[37]

Carrière's activities also attracted the attention of the Union military command. During the second Union invasion of the Teche Valley in late October 1863, General Charles P. Stone directed Major-General William B. Franklin, field commander of the expedition, to offer Carrière a commission in the Union army. Carrière apparently refused, for during the short-lived Union occupation of St. Landry Parish in late March 1864, Franklin was ordered to obtain from Judge B. A. Martel, a Union sympathizer, "the names of reliable men who [could] control and make valuable to you as scouts that large body of men known as jayhawkers—more than 1,000." An early postwar news report indicates that mulatto Martin Guillory, one of Carrière's lieutenants, accepted a Union commission as captain of a Jayhawker band known to Federal authorities as Les Eclaireurs Indépendants du Bayou Mallet. Franklin, like his Confederate counterparts, was unable to dislodge Carrière from his leadership position within the Jayhawker bands.[38]

Because of Carrière's enduring threat to the civilian population of St. Landry Parish, local civil and military leaders issued numerous petitions for military aid to Major General Richard Taylor, the department commander. Taylor responded in May with a proclamation directing Confederate soldiers to shoot Jayhawkers on sight and dispatched Colonel Louis Bush's Fourth Louisiana Cavalry into the area to deal with the Jayhawker menace.[39]

The Fourth Louisiana's campaign against the Jayhawkers was directed by Bush's executive officer, lieutenant Colonel Louis Amédée Bringier, who from May 1864 to May 1865 conducted a personal vendetta against Carrière. During his initial tour of duty in St. Landry Parish (October 1863 to January 1864), Bringier's men had executed more than a hundred Jayhawkers. Upon reassignment to "lower Louisiana" in April 1864, Bringier gleefully informed his wife that he would soon "exterminate the Jayhawkers." Bringier's subsequent raids on Carrière's Bois Mallet headquarters, however, failed to neutralize the Jayhawker threat. Indeed, the futile Confederate attacks appear to have merely served to escalate the violence. In early September 1864, sixty-three-year-old Bosman Hayes of Plaquemine Brulée was murdered by Don Louis Godeau while attempting to resist

eight Jayhawker horse thieves. Three weeks later, Napoleon Franchebois, also from the Plaquemine Brulée area, was killed by James Veillon during a nocturnal Jayhawker raid. Finally, in early November,
Carrière's men maliciously burned the residences of Charles Derosier,
Sylvin Saunier, and Joseph B. Young, "leaving their respective families to take care of themselves as best they could, and prevented them
even of saving the most necessary clothing."[40]

The Jayhawker rampage cost Carrière and his followers most of
their grass-roots support. Their position was further undermined
by the end of Confederate conscription in southwestern Louisiana,
which deprived them of their raison d'être. As a consequence, the
once formidable Jayhawker battalion rapidly disintegrated. Only fifty
men reportedly remained under Carrière's command when the Jayhawker leader was ambushed and killed by Confederate soldiers in
May 1865.[41]

Carrière's death did not signal the end of lawlessness and extralegal
violence in south Louisiana. Rather, a new phase began. The end of
the war, however, did provide Jayhawker victims with an opportunity
to avenge the wartime depredations of the former conscript evaders.
Evidently believing that their brief Union service and the presence of
a Union military garrison at nearby Washington provided adequate
immunity against both legal and extralegal retribution from St. Landry's now largely hostile population, surviving Jayhawker leaders began to return to their homes in late summer 1865. But local vigilantes
almost immediately initiated efforts to eradicate the former marauders, targeting as their first victim Martin Guillory, the most prominent
surviving Jayhawker. An undetermined number of night riders cor-
nered Guillory at his home near Opelousas and, in the course of a
brief but heated gun battle, mortally wounded him. Taken by his wife
to the Union garrison's headquarters at Washington for medical attention, Guillory filed a formal complaint against his attackers before he
died, resulting in the arrest of five St. Landry residents. But the subsequent release of Guillory's alleged assailants, who evidently were
never brought to trial, cleared the way for continued eradication of
former Jayhawkers. Sporadic news reports from the *Opelousas Courier*
suggest that the remaining marauders were either killed or driven
from St. Landry Parish by early February 1866.[42]

The extermination of the former Jayhawker leadership marked a watershed in south Louisiana violence. Before St. Landry's anti-Jay-hawker campaign concluded, violence had been confined almost exclusively to the lower strata of the local free population—poor Acadians and white Creoles, landless immigrants, and free people of color. Some of this violence stemmed directly from interpersonal disputes, conflicting land or property rights, overt or perceived insults, and other petty causes. Petty controversies frequently degenerated into family feuds of long duration, with devastating consequences for subregional Cajun communities. The following report from the *Thibodaux Sentinel* of May 29, 1875, affords rare insight into this evolutionary process:

> On the night of July 23, 1870, at a ball at the residence of Theodule Savoie in Bruslee St. Martin, Parish of Assumption, some six or eight miles above and back of Paincour[t]ville, a misunderstanding occurred between Charles Landry, brother of the accused, and a daughter of Euzelieu Theriot, concerning an engagement for a quadrille, in which Landry made some remarks which were construed by the young lady into an insult, and she so informed her brother Camille, who was present. Some words passed between Theriot and Landry on the subject, in which Landry said that he was not able to fight Theriot. The matter thus stopped for the night.
>
> It appears that when Landry reached home he informed his brother Catoir what had occurred, who told him that if he [Charles], was not strong enough to fight the Theriots, that he himself was not afraid of them.
>
> The next morning, Sunday, the Landry Brothers, between 7 and 8 o'clock, went to the house of Euzelieu, about one mile distant, and called the Theriots into the road in front of the house.
>
> Catoir Landry then stated that he had come over to settle the difficulty of the night previous. Euzelieu Theriot said that it was [not] what he wanted, that it was unpleasant for neighbors to be disputing, etc.
>
> After consultation the difficulty appeared to be amicably arranged but a dispute again arose—by whom commenced is in doubt—in which Catoir stigmatised the Theriots as a set of d——d sons of b——c——s.
>
> Euzelieu Theriot remarked that that was rough language and ought not to be used.
>
> Catoir drew a pistol and aimed it at the old man's head, who was

sufficiently near to lower the weapon with his hand to cause the bullet to pass between his leg[s]. Nichols Theriot, his son, then put himself between Catoir and Euzelieu, and begged the former not to shoot his father. Catoir then shot Nichols in the breast, causing his death in about 20 or 30 minutes.

After threatening to shoot Hypolite Theriot if he came near him, he [Catoir] retired to Paincour[t]ville, boasting along the road that he had "killed a bull," and surrendered himself to Justice Lauve.

Catoir says that the pistol accidently went off the first time, and that he only fired the second shot in self-defense.

After being confined for some time in jail he escaped.

On the 24th of July, 1870, the Grand Jury found a [true] bill against Catoir Landry for murder. This presentation was signed by John A. Cheevers, District Attorney, but was never filed in the office of the Clerk of Court. Subsequently a new indictment was found.

After his escape nothing was heard of him, so as to effect a recapture, until two weeks ago when he was found to be incarcerated in the prison of St. Mary's Parish, where, as we stated last week, he was found and brought to Assumption for trial.

It is said that he came to his home about Christmas last, when one of the Theriots found it out, took a gun and went to his house, saw him through a window by the light of a lamp, and raised his gun to shoot him, but at that moment a little girl sat down between him and the window, thus saving his life.

Such conflicts persisted throughout Reconstruction, but the violence they engendered escalated geometrically, indicating the almost universal acceptance and institutionalization of violence within local white society. Writing shortly after the end of Reconstruction in Louisiana, George Washington Cable noted that the once peaceful Acadian *bals de maison* were now "apt to end in rows outside." The novelist was also struck by a "growing disposi[tio]n to carry weapons" in Acadian society, observing also that "deadly weapons [were] in use much & only since the war."[43] It is thus hardly surprising that Acadian disputants resorted to guns and knives at least as often as their fists. Indeed, a random sample of thirty-two postbellum homicides in the Acadian parishes suggest that Acadians were directly responsible for eleven of the killings. This number easily eclipses the homicides committed by all other groups in the region during this period (table 23).

As in the late antebellum period, private quarrels were overshadowed by extralegal attempts to maintain law and order. Indeed, by the late 1850s, most local violence resulted from confrontations between vigilantes and their opponents. This trend had continued throughout the Civil War, when antivigilante forces temporarily gained the ascendancy, and the postbellum era, when antebellum vigilantes reasserted their control over the area. As in the prewar years, the vigilantes operated almost exclusively in the prairie parishes, dispensing "justice" to reputed burglars, rustlers, and "undesirables." In a major departure from prewar practices, however, the local vigilantes appear to have summarily executed their victims without first delivering the customary admonition to leave the area. The December 4, 1869, issue of the *Opelousas Courier,* for instance, reports that "on last Sunday night a band of armed men called at the house of Mr. Paul Fontenot, at Plaquemine Brulée, took him from his house, and shot him down in cold blood." Such raids increased in frequency in the 1870s, when vigilantes justified homicides on political grounds. By the mid-1870s, the former antivigilante forces apparently constituted most of the white element of the local Republican party. According to reliable sources, many of these poor white Republicans from the Cypress Island area of St. Martin Parish were hanged by vigilantes ostensibly for "stealing chickens or cattle, or something of that kind," but almost without variation, these alleged petty thieves and rustlers were "white Republicans." During the same period, only one black man was hanged by local vigilantes for the same reasons.[44]

Though poor whites and former free persons of color remained frequent targets of vigilante raids, southwestern Louisiana's postbellum vigilantes increasingly began to attack the recently freed local bondsmen. This redirection of their activity was the result of forces present before the Civil War and the socioeconomic and political changes wrought by the war. As the 1859–60 vigilante campaigns of terror and violence against free people of color in St. Landry Parish and in the Attakapas region indicated, the vigilante-antivigilante struggle had evolved from a crusade for law and order into a class struggle with strong racial overtones. But unless directly involved in some illicit activity, slaves were usually spared the vigilante lash and rope because of their significant value as chattel. The importance of race in the evolution of extralegal violence was magnified by the secession crisis, the onset of the Civil War, the 1863 Union invasions of south Louisiana and the resulting emancipation of large numbers of slaves, the biracial nature of local Jayhawker bands, and the emancipation of all remaining slaves at war's end.[45] The freedmen were a special source of concern to postbellum whites, and vigilantes eventually channeled most of their energies into suppressing them. Relations between whites, particularly upper-class whites, and slaves had been chronically poor in south Louisiana. The harsh slave regime established by ambitious planters, including Acadians, spawned abortive slave insurrections in Lafayette and Iberville parishes in the early 1840s and in Assumption Parish in 1856. The brutal repression of these generally illusory threats belied the intensity of white fears regarding the black underclass, fears that would persist after the Civil War.[46]

The most basic concern of the vigilantes and of the local white population in general was the intimidating size of south Louisiana's African-American population, which easily overshadowed its white counterpart (table 24). In the river parishes, freedmen and former free persons of color collectively constituted 66.2 percent of the total population, outnumbering Acadians by a ratio of 10.6 to 1. The differential was narrower in the Lafourche Basin, where blacks constituted 47.67 percent of the population. But even here they outnumbered Acadians by a ratio of 2.76 to 1. Blacks were considerably less numerous in the prairie regions, constituting 39.75 percent of the population. The latter figure is deceptive, however, for blacks made up only 16, 19, and 21 percent of the population in the three parishes where ranching was the main agricultural pursuit. Only in Vermilion Parish did Acadians outnumber blacks.[47]

The sheer size of the black population had tremendous cultural ramifications for the region's whites. African-Americans heavily influenced the development of Cajun music, folklore, cuisine, folk medicine, and folk religion.[48] In the postbellum period, however, these cross-cultural contributions were overshadowed by the political ramifications of emancipation for the former servile population. Yet the political impact of emancipation was, paradoxically, not readily apparent because African-Americans were barred from political involvement until their enfranchisement in 1867. Hence in the months immediately following the war, white concerns regarding blacks centered on the difficulty of adapting to wage labor and rampant criminality widely attributed to freedom.[49]

Because most whites regarded the former bondsmen as the principal remaining threat to law and order, the campaign to eradicate the Jayhawkers constituted merely one facet of the popular backlash against lawlessness that swept through south Louisiana during and immediately after the Civil War. The roots of this backlash can be traced to the sporadic Union invasions of south Louisiana, when residents of the prairie and bayou countries had been terrorized by the depredations of the Union armies' black camp followers, which touched all segments of local society. A more persistent and insidious threat, however, confronted property owners in the months immediately following the war's conclusion. Hunger was pervasive among freedmen, and many blacks reportedly killed livestock to avert starvation. Occurring in the midst of the economic crisis of 1865–67 and the specter of famine it raised, the loss of livestock was a major source of concern to Acadian landholders. Far more disconcerting, however, was the seemingly endless series of muggings and burglaries suffered by whites, usually at night.[50] The white population believed that most of these crimes were committed by the temporarily idle and hungry freedmen. Though contemporary crime reports indicate that freedmen were guilty of many of the crimes with which they were charged, they were not responsible for all the mischief attributed to them. Assaults and burglaries appear to have been particularly numerous in the areas where Federal troops had been stationed, ostensibly to maintain law and order. Not only did the garrisons prove incapable of checking the rash of criminal activities, much to the chagrin of the local white population, but, as the editor of the *Renaissance Louisianaise* lamented in late summer 1865, some of the soldiers participated in the pilferage.

> The deplorable situation created by the Negro garrisons for the residents of Lafourche Parish has grown intolerable. During the most difficult moments of the [Federal] occupation, in the days of combat which the region endured, often finding itself in a crossfire, there was nothing comparable to the brigandage and murders inflicted there by armed bandits. . . .
>
> During the night of the ninth of the present month, M. De-

zauche's house was the scene of an orderly raid. At each door of the residence, an armed bandit held the family at bay, threatening [them] with death, while the other thieves rummaged through drawers and closets, taking everything, trinkets, clothes, *vaiselle de prix,* &c. M. Dezauche, a old man sixty-four years of age, having attempted to stop the looting, was thrown to the floor [and] struck several times with clubs and bayonettes. . . . These wretches withdrew after having gathered their spoils, with an estimated value of $2,500. Their tracks led to Camp Vicocq, several miles away, where the 75th Regiment was encamped.[51]

Thefts and burglaries persisted after the temporary withdrawal of the overwhelmingly black Federal garrisons from St. Landry and Lafourche parishes, however, reinforcing the prevailing white belief that former slaves were responsible for the unrelenting criminal assault on property and property owners. Sensational reports of arrests and convictions of freedmen in south Louisiana newspapers lent credence to these popular beliefs, as did more mundane official judicial reports carried by the local press. Eighteen freedmen, for example, were convicted of burglary or larceny in the January 1868 session of St. Landry Parish's district court, while only three whites were found guilty of the same crimes.[52]

The absence of an effective local deterrent against crime and its pervasiveness elicited fears of anarchy.[53] The white population took it on itself to curb crime and simultaneously reassert the social control ended by emancipation of the servile population by adopting stringent black codes to regulate the movement and activities of freedmen. Opelousas, in St. Landry Parish, was among the first Louisiana communities to adopt a postbellum black code.[54] Promulgated during the summer of 1865, this body of regulations, which was little more than a reenactment "of the municipal regulations in force for slaves in 1860, sharply circumscribed the freedoms of newly liberated freedmen." As Leon Litwack has noted:

> To enter the town, a black person needed his employer's permission, stipulating the object of the visit and the time necessary to accomplish it; any freedman found on the streets after ten o'clock at night without a written pass or permit from his employer would be subject to arrest and imprisonment. No freedman could rent or keep a house within the town limits "under any circumstance," or

reside within the town unless employed by a white person who assumed responsibility for his conduct. To hold any public meetings
or to assemble in large numbers for any reason, blacks needed the
mayor's permission, as they also did to "preach, exhort or otherwise
declaim" to black congregations. Nor could they possess weapons or
sell, barter, or exchange any kind of merchandise without special
permits. A freedman found violating these ordinances could be
punished by imprisonment, fines, and forced labor on the city
streets.

The Opelousas black code served as a model for other municipal and
parochial black codes throughout rural south Louisiana.[55]

White efforts at social control continued even after the region's economic situation slowly improved and the incidence of burglaries and
livestock rustling gradually subsided. But the focus of these activities
shifted as the enfranchisement of blacks in 1867 and 1868 gave rise
to a more serious problem in the estimation of whites—the first political challenge to their domination of the region. The impact of
black enfranchisement—magnified by the reluctance of many whites
to register as voters in early postbellum Louisiana—was both immediate and dramatic. With the exception of the western prairie parishes, black voters came to constitute a majority of the electorate
throughout south Louisiana. In St. Landry Parish, for example, the
registrar's office reported 1,986 white and 3,068 black registered voters, although the freedmen and former free persons of color together
constituted only 42 percent of the population. The political implica-
tions of the emerging black political power base were immediately
obvious to incumbent politicians and their white supporters in the
Democratic party, who did everything in their power to encourage
eligible white voters to register. Their initial efforts, supported by
Democratic newspapers, evidently bore little fruit, as the following
editorial from the *Opelousas Courier* suggests: "We would again advise
our readers and friends to get registered. They need not fear that by
so doing they will be implicated or compromised in any manner. Neither should they yield to that feeling of repugnance which seems to
pervade each breast, for if they follow its promptings they will lose
the unrestrained political power . . . . Let them get registered, or they
will most undoubtedly repent of their obstinacy or neglect."[56]

The discouraging results of the initial white voter registration campaign drove to desperation local politicos who had experienced the difficult birth pangs of the newly regenerated local Democratic party. Even south Louisiana Democrats prominent in the late antebellum period—including numerous Acadians—often encountered surprising difficulty while testing the political waters in the 1865 and 1866 local elections. The changing political situation boded ill for long-term health of the party that had traditionally championed white supremacy in local elections. Only by resuscitating the issue of race would south Louisiana's Democratic party experience a resurgence.[57]

The race issue centered on the threat to white supremacy posed by black political power. "Maintenance of white supremacy, and the old order generally," as a leading student of postbellum violence has noted, "was a cause in which white men of all classes felt an interest." The sparse extant writings as well as the actions of "white men of all classes" in south Louisiana consistently reflected their belief that black political domination was an intolerable threat to the social underpinnings of the world they dominated.[58] These sentiments are stated perhaps most clearly and succinctly by Captain James A. Payne, a Northern-born Baton Rouge merchant with extensive business contacts in the Acadian Coast area. Writing on September 1, 1867, he states: "Perhaps all of you May think it strange that I should break up housekeeping So Soon . . . but this Country is changing So rapidly that it is Impossible to point out the future[.] My prejudicies [sic] against Negro equality can Never be Got over[.]   it is coming about here that equality is so far forced on you that you May protest as much as you please but your Childrens Associates Will be the Negroes[.] The Schools are equal[.] The Negro have the Ascendency and can out Vote the Whites on every thing."[59]

Despite the gravity of the problem, rural white south Louisianians were slow to react to the perceived "Negro Ascendency." Whether because of their preoccupation with the states economic crisis, intimidation by the military authorities who had governed Louisiana since the beginning of Radical Reconstruction, or "perhaps because it took time for [white] Louisianians to believe the unbelievable," there was "no organized attempt at intimidation of Louisiana blacks in 1867."[60]

Whites also may have naively anticipated far more pliability on the part of the black electorate than they encountered. White Democrats first attempted to manipulate the black vote by nonviolent means, but it soon became apparent that black adherence to the Republican party, the Radical faction of which had been responsible for their en-franchisement, was unshakable, and politically conservative whites then resorted to less peaceful means of neutralizing the new elector-ate. Like the white supremacists who organized the Ku Klux Klan at Pulaski, Tennessee, in 1866, these white south Louisianians were motivated by the "shock of 'Negro supremacy' and the threat [which it posed] to the 'southern way of life.'" And like their Tennessee counterparts, they turned to the most effective weapon at their dis-posal—the region's recently reactivated vigilante organizations—to intimidate and manipulate the independent black electorate.

Political violence was by no means an innovation in south Louisiana politics. Violence had been an integral part of local elections before Reconstruction, and it would remain so long after the Federal occu-pation of the state had ended. Writing about the prairie Cajuns in the late 1870s for *Scribner's* magazine, R. L. Daniels stated: "Elections are attended with great excitement. Primed with their favorite tafia, or cheap whisky which they call 'rote-gut'—rot gut—the voters are noisy and turbulent. Free fights are the order of the day, but, to their credit be it said, no weapons are used except such as are furnished by na-ture. To give his foe a black eye, or to make him cry *'Assez!'* is sufficient glory for the Acadian."[61] For the first time, however, political violence would be directed against blacks. Though the Ku Klux Klan would not exist in Reconstruction Louisiana, unnamed vigilante groups, the Knights of the White Camelia, and the White Leagues would serve the same function.[62]

Unnamed vigilante groups appear to have been most active in the early postwar period, primarily in the Lafayette-St. Martin-Vermilion Parish area and in the former region of St. Landry Parish now en-compassed by the borders of Acadia Parish. In testimony before the Joint Committee on Reconstruction, Thomas Conway, director of the Freedmen's Bureau in Louisiana, declared that vigilantes had de-stroyed all black schools along the lower Teche and along Bayou La-fourche shortly after withdrawal of Federal troops from those areas in late 1865 and early 1866. Destruction of black schools, a primary concern of Louisiana vigilantes throughout the postbellum period, was a direct consequence of the falling economic status of lower-class whites, which translated into increases in the already high illiteracy rates for south Louisiana's white population (table 25). Historical geographer Lawrence Estaville has determined that "Louisiana was . . . the only state in the nation in which white literacy declined between 1880 and 1890." Rising black literacy, vigilantes evidently feared, would result in the economic liberation of the laboring masses, if not the eventual economic domination of the African-American population.[63]

The larger and better-organized vigilante movements were politically oriented, at least during major election years. Most of the vigilantes in the Acadian parishes appear to have joined the Knights of the White Camelia in late 1867 and 1868. That group was established at Franklin, Louisiana, on May 22, 1867, by Alcibiades DeBlanc, a veteran of St. Martinville's antebellum vigilante committee and a former Confederate officer, who, at the end of the Civil War had used his military authority to reestablish antebellum controls over freedmen, and Daniel Dennett, editor of the *Franklin Planters' Banner* and perhaps the most prominent journalist in rural south Louisiana.

As with the 1859 vigilante movement, men of high social stature dominated the organization throughout its existence. Indeed, in the prairie parishes, many local leaders of the Knights of the White Camelia appear to have been former leaders of the 1859 vigilante movement, and the previous movement also appears to have served as an organizational model for the new clandestine organization.[64] Like the Ku Klux Klan, the Knights of the White Camelia was a secret society with elaborate ceremonies, signs, rituals, and passwords and, more important, an avowedly racist purpose. According to the "Charge to Initiates," the organization's "main and fundamental objective" was the "maintenance of the supremacy of the white race in this Republic."[65] Because of its racist appeal, the secret society was an immediate and unqualified success. Chapters were organized throughout the state, as whites rallied in response to the black political assault on the social status quo. Most of the rural membership, however, resided in the Acadian parishes. It has been estimated that half the adult white male population in this area belonged to the movement, but in St. Martin, St. Landry, Calcasieu, Vermilion, and Lafayette parishes, where Acadians constituted a substantial portion of the white population, "almost the entire white population was involved with the Knights of the White Camelia." The St. Landry chapter alone boasted a membership of three thousand men by the fall of 1868. Most of the initiates joined after the April 1868 ratification of a controversial new state constitution which established "universal desegregated education, a prohibition of racial discrimination in public places, and severe disfranchisement of 'disloyal' voters."[66]

The Knights almost immediately initiated a campaign of violence against blacks and Republicans. All available evidence suggests that this violence was part of a master plan designed by Democratic leaders in Lafayette, St. Landry, and St. Mary parishes to ensure a Democratic victory in the November 3, 1868, election. Most of the violence appears to have begun following a series of Democratic barbecues and rallies held in St. Landry Parish in August and early September 1868. Though both blacks and whites were publicly invited to these meetings, the addresses—delivered in English by Alcibiades DeBlanc, Colonel William Mouton, and Judge Charles Homer Mouton—attacked the liberal racial policies of the Republican party. Alcibiades DeBlanc delivered a particularly inflammatory address. After recounting his long years of service in the Confederate army, DeBlanc reportedly told his large audience that he "would be ready to fight again in a year or six months, or now if you say so, boys! Why do you not kill these carpetbaggers? There are only five or six in each parish! We are a hundred to one. What are you afraid of?" DeBlanc's call to arms generated an almost immediate response that ultimately led to the expulsion of most carpetbaggers from the Acadian prairie parishes. In September "bands of armed men . . . regularly patrolled country roads on horseback and town streets on foot, and made the rounds of Negro cabins" in St. Martin, Lafayette, and Vermilion parishes. Though members of some patrols wore disguises and policed their "districts" only at night, most of the Knights "traveled without concealment and in broad daylight."[67]

The purpose of the patrols and other activities of the Knights of the White Camelia was to intimidate Republicans of all racial backgrounds. When stronger measures were deemed necessary to attain this goal, the Knights of the White Camelia did not hesitate to use them. Collaborating with the Knights of the White Camelia were members of the Seymour Knights, a less secret group organized in the summer and fall of 1868 by the Louisiana Democratic party on behalf of the Democratic presidential campaign. Together these groups maintained a reign of terror over much of Louisiana. Republican leaders were threatened with death if they remained politically active, Republican meetings were disrupted, and the Republican press was muzzled. Vigilantes destroyed the *Attakapas Register's* presses and forced the editors to seek refuge in New Orleans.[68] The *St. Landry Progress* of Opelousas, another Republican organ, was also silenced. On September 28, 1868, three Seymour Knights entered the Negro school of Emerson Bentley, the eighteen-year-old, Ohio-born, English-language editor of the *Progress,* and demanded that he publicly retract his editorial attacking Democrats for attempting to protect from hostile Republicans blacks who had recently entered the Democratic camp after crossing party lines. When Bentley refused, he was beaten with a cane. According to Republican sources, the Northerner was horsewhipped in front of his students. Bentley then signed a retraction, and his assailants departed.[69]

The incident caused several groups of armed blacks to converge on Opelousas. Evidently panic-stricken, the Opelousas municipal government dispatched a white posse to intercept them. Encountering approximately twenty-five blacks at the Paillet farm on the outskirts of southern Opelousas on the afternoon of September 28, the posse ordered the "invaders" to lay down their arms. The blacks refused, and firing began. In the ensuing gun battle, three whites were wounded and four blacks were killed. An additional twelve were taken prisoner and incarcerated in the Opelousas jail. Determined to crush all black resistance, approximately two thousand Knights of the White Camelia assembled at Opelousas on the morning of September 29. Sometime during the day, a white mob broke into the office of the *St. Landry Progress* and destroyed the press and printing materials. A group of Seymour Knights then entered the town jail and seized eighteen Negro prisoners, including the twelve captured the preceding day. Together with one Durand, the French editor of the *Progress,* the captives were marched to a nearby woods and executed.[70]

What followed is enshrouded in conflicting evidence. Democratic sources claimed that twenty-five people, including two whites, died during the Opelousas incident. They also maintained that, following the executions, white patrols peaceably disarmed the parish's black population. Republican sources, however, maintained that whites systematically killed all armed Negroes they encountered. According to these Republican sources, two to three hundred people were killed during the vigilante rampage. A recent historical study has put the black death toll at forty to fifty. Armed whites also attacked and drove out of St. Landry Parish prominent white Republican leaders. Historian Ted Tunnell has estimated that as many as two hundred St. Landry Republicans may have sought refuge in New Orleans following the clash.[71]

Sources also disagree about the next move by the Knights of the White Camelia and the Seymour Knights. Oscar A. Rice, former agent for the Freedmen's Bureau in Lafayette and Vermilion parishes, stated in public testimony; "After that [the Opelousas incident of September 1868] the democrats of Lafayette and Vermilion parishes commenced a system of terrorism, violence, murder, and driving of all persons of the republican party who took any active part in opposition to the democrats, under pretence that they feared a rising of the colored people: they [white Democrats] formed armed patrols all over the said parishes. In the parish of Vermilion, these patrols committed numerous outrages on the freedmen, shooting, and driving them from their homes. Reports were brought to me constantly from that parish of the outrages committed there on all persons said to be republicans."[72] Leading Republicans also reportedly were killed in St. Mary Parish in October 1868. Other sources suggest the use of less violence by vigilantes, but all agree about its main purpose: to demoralize the black population, which rendered far more effective the existing vigilante control over all internal lines of communication within the prairie parishes. Between the so-called Opelousas riot and the November election, freedom of movement was denied all blacks lacking passes signed by the local leader of the Knights of the White Camelia. Blacks remaining in the area were required to acquire "protection papers" and to register them with a designated vigilante authority. To obtain protection papers, blacks were required to register as Democratic voters. Beverly Wilson, an Opelousas freedman, subsequently testified that he did "not know a colored man that did not do it, as they thought that if they did not they would be looked on with suspicion, that is as Radicals, which [was] equivalent to being an escaped murderer in this parish." In this way, the Knights of the White Camelia and their cohorts controlled voting in the November 1868 presidential election. Republican presidential candidate Ulysses S. Grant garnered the paltry total of thirty-seven votes in the prairie parishes of Calcasieu, Lafayette, St. Landry, St. Martin, and Vermilion. To put this figure in perspective, one need only compare the results of the state and local elections in St. Landry Parish in April and September 1868. In April, Republicans outpolled their Democrats by 2,624 to 2,309, but in November all 4,787 of its votes went for Horatio Seymour, the Democratic presidential candidate (table 26).[73]

Though south Louisiana's vigilante activity was largely confined to the prairie region, violence was by no means restricted to that corner of the state. Only parishes bordering the state's principal waterways or having permanent Federal garrisons appear to have been spared the terror campaign, which reached its zenith shortly before the fall 1868 national election. Because of vigilante terrorism, seven north Louisiana parishes recorded less than ten votes for Grant. In addition, Republican state officials reported that 784 people were killed and another 450 were either wounded or "mistreated" during the reign of terror. Although these figures were undoubtedly inflated for political purposes, there is no question that anti-Republican violence was widespread in Louisiana and that the toll in lives and human suffering was high. The resulting popular outcry was so shrill that Congress launched an investigation into the matter.[74]

Yet the vigilantes' efforts were for nought. Though Seymour comfortably defeated Grant in Louisiana by a margin of 80,225 to 33,263, Grant carried the nation. Disappointed by the outcome most Knights of the White Camelia left the organization, and by mid-1869 the terrorist group had ceased to exist. Undoubtedly more disappointing to the erstwhile vigilantes, however, was the state government's response to the 1868 campaign of fear and intimidation. Under the leadership of Governor Henry Clay Warmoth, the state's Republican administration established a new electoral system designed to keep the party in power even in the face of further vigilante intimidation of the black Republican electorate. Under the new system, governor-appointed registrars controlled registration of voters; a constabulary appointed by the governor policed voting precincts throughout the state on election days with the authority to arrest anyone accused of interfering with the election; and gubernatorial appointees to the new returning board could invalidate electoral returns from any precinct deemed to have been influenced by political fraud or violence.[75]

The new system worked as intended. Compared to the election of 1868, the 1872 election was relatively free of violence, although attempts were made to manipulate voting results. The state's increasingly confused political situation contributed significantly to electoral fraud and voter manipulation. On August 27 or 28, the Louisiana Democratic party, the Reform party, and the Liberal faction of the state Republican party joined to put forth a common slate of candidates—called the Fusionist ticket—in an effort to defeat the regular Republican candidates in the 1872 general election. John McEnery, tapped earlier as the Democratic candidate for governor, headed the Fusionist ticket, with Colonel D. B. Penn, a Liberal Republican, as his running mate. The Fusionists mounted an aggressive campaign, but Warmoth's new electoral machinery prohibited them from resorting to the terrorism the Democrats had employed so effectively in 1868. The Enforcement Acts of 1870 and 1871, which made interference with civil rights or suffrage rights federal offenses punishable by fine or imprisonment, served as additional impediments against the use of intimidation.[76]

Despite the paucity of violence on behalf of the Fusionist ticket, "fraud and trickery were used extensively by both parties" before and during the election. Before the election, most of this fraudulent activity was focused on the offices of the local registrars of voters. The registrars of voters throughout Louisiana were Warmoth appointees loyal to the former governor, who was then feuding with the regular Republicans. Aware that the registrars were the key to the election, Fusionists attempted to mobilize these Warmoth appointees on their behalf. Pro-Fusionist registrars responded by reducing the number of polling places in Radical Republican wards and making ballot boxes more readily accessible in Democratic and pro-Warmoth areas. The registrars also attempted to reduce to an absolute minimum the number of new Negro voters, who were expected to register as Republicans. On election day, ballot boxes were stuffed by both parties, eligible voters were denied ballots in some precincts, and "the Fusionists engaged in deliberate and unconcealed fraud in a number of sure Republican parishes, especially Iberville, St. James, St. Martin and Terrebonne"—all of which had significant pro-Fusionist Acadian populations. Consequently, according to Joe Gray Taylor, "the [Louisiana] election of 1872 was so shot through with fraud that no one ever had any idea who actually won."[77]

The final but unofficial returns gave the election to McEnery. Republicans immediately contested the results, and the party's incumbent officeholders—divided in their allegiance to the Fusionist and Republican tickets—created rival returning boards to certify the recent balloting. Unable either to certify or throw out precinct returns because the pro-Fusionist board denied them access to the ballots, the Republican returning board successfully challenged the legitimacy of the incoming Fusionist administration in federal district court. President Grant responded immediately by extending recognition to the Louisiana republican candidates, thereby stealing the election for the national Republican party.[78]

The Fusionists refused to acknowledge defeat or the legitimacy of the state's new Republican government, dominated by Governor William Pitt Kellogg, and McEnery established a shadow government, complete with a legislature, at New Orleans. Inflamed by growing frustration over Grant's demonstration of partisan politics, Fusionists in state militia units commanded by the McEnery government unsuccessfully attempted to seize control of New Orleans and oust the state's Republican administration. Their defeat at the so-called Battle of the Cabildo on March 5, 1873, in which the insurgents attacked the statehouse, forced the Fusionist government to dissolve.[79] Popular resistance to the Kellogg government nevertheless continued in the rural areas, particularly in those Acadian parishes that had experienced the most intense anti-Republican violence in 1868. The resurgence of anti-Republican activity was largely the result of the establishment of the White League.

Joe Gray Taylor attributes the formation of the Louisiana White League movement to establishment of the *Alexandria Caucasian,* which began publication on March 28, 1874. The editors of the *Caucasian* urged Louisiana's white men to forget their petty political differences and unite to defend the Southern social order against the architects of social change—freedmen and their unscrupulous white leaders. In its April 4, 1874, editorial the *Caucasian's* editor exhorted white Louisianians to join the cause, stating that "there will be no security, no peace, and no prosperity for Louisiana until the government of the state is restored to the hands of the honest, intelligent, and tax-paying masses; until the superiority of the Caucasian over the African in all affairs pertaining to government, is acknowledged and established."[80]

The *Caucasian's* call to battle elicited a quick response. On April 27, 1874, the first White League chapter was organized at Opelousas. The group's charter, which served as a model for the numerous chapters subsequently established around the state, clearly sets out the White League's objective: race warfare to secure the end of Louisiana's black political domination. From Opelousas, the organization spread rapidly throughout the state, but chapters were organized wherever local racial tensions were chronically poor. Numerous White League "clubs" were established in north Louisiana, where the open racial warfare had already claimed untold numbers of black victims. An equally large number of chapters were established in the Acadian parishes, where racial tensions had been intense since the late antebellum period. An organizational meeting for the first club outside St. Landry Parish was held at Breaux Bridge on June 14, 1874. The principal rural settlements in all of the prairie and Bayou Teche parishes soon followed suit. By the end of the summer, there were fifteen White League chapters in Lafayette Parish alone. As in previous vigilante movements, White League chapters were led by local social, economic, and political leaders, and Acadians constituted a disproportionately large percentage of their memberships (tables 27 and 28).[81]

Joe Gray Taylor concludes: "The most effective work of the White League organizations was in forcing Radical [Republican] parish officeholders to resign. Here violence was usually not necessary." Though White League activities were widely distributed throughout Louisiana, perhaps the most notable early efforts to dislodge Republican officeholders, including a handful of Acadian scalawags, were in the Attakapas region.[82]

These efforts grew out of White League participation in the prairie region's tax resistance campaign of 1873. Responding to President Grant's recognition of the Kellogg administration, McEnery partisans throughout Louisiana initiated a program of passive resistance to the state's Republican administration. In meetings held at Abbeville on March 17 and 22, 1873, area Democrats established a Tax Resisting Association "for the purpose of resisting the payment of all illegal taxes, and diverting the revenues of the State to the support of the legal government headed by John McEnery." Local attorneys offered free services to any resisters seeking injunctions against Kellogg tax collectors. Lafayette Parish followed suit in April.[83]

By late June the campaign of passive resistance had proven ineffective, and newspapers reported that many local politicians had joined the Kellogg camp. Democrats then opted for more persuasive methods of dealing with area politicians. Sometime during the morning of May 5, the rival forces clashed. District court adjourned, and the town was evacuated. Negotiations between leaders of the rival camps failed when the tax resisters demanded that all local officials be commissioned by McEnery and that the Metropolitans withdraw from St. Martinville.

Hostilities resumed, and DeBlanc's forces, which had grown to four to six hundred men by May 6, took the offensive, moving to positions only two blocks from the St. Martin Parish courthouse and laying siege to it. Only when United States Army troops were dispatched to St. Martinville did DeBlanc direct his troops to disperse to avoid direct confrontation with the Federal authorities. On May 9, columns of resisters were reported moving toward Vermilionville, Breaux Bridge, and Fausse Pointe.[84]

On May 11, DeBlanc and his lieutenants were arrested by Federal marshals, charged with violating the Enforcement Acts by "intimidating Negroes," and sent to New Orleans for trial. After receiving a hero's welcome in the Crescent City, DeBlanc and his fellow defendants were tried, acquitted, and released. But two hundred Federal troops were subsequently stationed in the St. Martinville area to prevent any further resistance and to ensure the collection of taxes by the Kellogg government.[85]

Though the presence of Federal troops broke the tax resistance movement, it apparently did little or nothing to suppress local organized resistance to the Kellogg regime. On July 25, 1874, Charles Homer Mouton, a White League officer in the Lafayette organization, delivered a fiery anti-Kellogg address to the Iberia Parish chapter. In August 1874, five to seven hundred White Leaguers—including large numbers of volunteers from Lafayette and St. Landry parishes—armed with "revolvers," "double-barreled shot-guns and rifles" and under the command of Alcibiades DeBlanc forced from office all of the Radical Republicans in St. Martin Parish. Seven hundred White Leaguers, also apparently under DeBlanc's command, extracted resignations and forced from office several Iberia Parish Radicals, banishing two of them from the parish. Only the river parishes and Lafourche Basin areas appear to have been spared extensive White League violence.[86]

Confrontations between the White League and the Kellogg regime continued throughout August and early September 1874, culminating with the defeat of the Metropolitans at New Orleans in the Battle of Liberty Place on September 14, 1874. These armed conflicts served three purposes. First, they placed unrelenting pressure on incumbent Radical Republican officeholders to resign, thereby greatly limiting the state government's effectiveness. According to Taylor, "The resignation of local officials weakened the Kellogg government. Many appointees refused to accept positions. A perusal of Kellogg's correspondence shows, however, that the thirst for office was not altogether quenched by danger. There were applicants for most vacancies as soon as they developed. But local officials who remained in office, as well as new appointees, functioned with the knowledge that they could be ousted at almost any time. Thus they did as little as possible. As a result, Kellogg ceased to govern most of Louisiana."[87] By the end of 1874, New Orleans was filled with former Republican officeholders from the rural parishes who sought refuge from the White League onslaught.

Second, the size and aggressiveness of the White League force intimidated the small Seventh Cavalry detachment assigned to preserve the peace in the upper Teche and prairie regions. Though fully aware of the White Leaguers' activities, the Federal troops conspicuously avoided all contact with the vigilantes—even when the rival patrols faced one another on the area's many back roads. Thus assured of a free hand, the White Leaguers moved quickly to neutralize the local Republican vote. Planters in the Vermilionville-Breaux Bridge-St. Martinville area threatened to fire every employee—white or black—who voted Republican in the forthcoming election. Then, in a series of nocturnal raids throughout the area and as far south as Iberia Parish, the terrorists disarmed the local Negro population and admonished their victims to stay at home on election day.[88] According to one eyewitness, the White League delivered threats to blacks in

French in hopes of concealing their activities from Federal officials and army officers who were almost universally monolingual English-speakers. In testimony before congressional investigators, Lieutenant Charles C. De Rudio, responding to the question, "What effect has this turbulent spirit of the whites had on the blacks?" stated: "They are totally scared. They do not see any protection for them in any way. Although the military has been up there, yet I have heard many of the White Leaguers speaking French. I have the advantage that I speak French . . . and in that way I have had an opportunity to hear a great deal more than any one could who did not understand French. I have heard them say to the negroes, 'Oh! you need not mind about the military. They will be away in a few days. They only came here to get you to vote; and a few days after you have voted they will go away, and then we will fix you. They will not be here to defend you. They will have to go away, and then we will fix you."[89] To prove the ineffectiveness of the military in protecting the freedmen, vigilantes drove into the swamps near Breaux Bridge on the eve on the election an undetermined number of black Republicans. On election day, bands of White Leaguers each consisting of eight to twenty armed riders patrolled the country roads in a largely successful attempt to intercept any Republican voters bound for the polls.[90]

Third, they had the effect of embarrassing President Grant, who had already been disgraced by numerous political scandals, and concomitantly eroding Northern support for continued military occupation of Louisiana. White Leaguers thus gained more freedom to employ intimidation as a means of influencing the outcome of the 1876 presidential election in Louisiana.[91]

As in 1872, the apparent Democratic victory was disputed. The Democrats claimed victory on the basis of the returns, but the state's Republican returning board invalidated 13,211 Democratic ballots to give the Republicans the election. The Republican candidates, led by gubernatorial hopeful Stephen B. Packard, then established a government at New Orleans. As in 1873, gubernatorial candidate Francis T. Nicholls and the other Democratic candidates established a rival government in the Crescent City. Because the White League controlled most rural parishes, recognition by Washington was essential if the Packard regime were to survive.[92]

But Grant not only refused to mobilize Federal troops to install

Packard in power, he also moved most of the troops to New Orleans, thereby effectively conceding the rural areas to the White League. In early January 1877, Nicholls recognized New Orleans area White League units as the state militia. These forces were employed to seize the state arsenal, the New Orleans police stations, and the state supreme court building. Nicholls then appointed all new justices to the state bench, and, on January 9, had himself sworn in as governor.[93]

Democratic control of Louisiana was recognized by the national government through the terms of the negotiated settlement to the inconclusive national presidential election. Under the terms of this agreement, forged on February 26, 1877, the Republicans retained the presidency in return for the withdrawal of the remaining forces of occupation from the former Confederate states and for recognition of the Nicholls government. The agreement was followed by Nicholls's successful efforts to lure away from the Packard government sufficient Republican legislators to form a quorum in the Democratic-dominated general assembly. A quorum was achieved on April 21 and, unable to conduct business legally, the Packard government collapsed by April 26, when Nicholls took possession of the statehouse. The installation of the Nicholls government and the simultaneous withdrawal of Federal forces from Louisiana marked the end of Reconstruction in Louisiana and the official demise of the White League.[94]

Vigilante justice, however, would remain a fact of everyday life along Bayou Teche and in the prairie parishes for another generation. By the end of Reconstruction, violence had become so institutionalized that it influenced all facets of social interaction in Acadian society. Acadian men routinely carried guns and knives following the Civil War, and towns in the Acadian parishes did not prohibit civilians from brandishing weapons until the second decade of the twentieth century. Individuals would continue to carry knives and handguns conspicuously in such prairie settlements as Pointe Noire and Marais Bouleur well into this century. There was, not surprisingly, a corresponding rise in the level of interpersonal violence. Confrontations settled by fistfights before the war were usually settled with weapons in the postbellum era, often resulting in the killing or maiming of combatants.

Of equal importance was the changing Acadian attitude toward violence, particularly homicide. As William Lynwood Montell has demonstrated in his notable study of Southern violence, people exposed to the ravages of the Civil War, the depredations of guerrilla bands and camp followers, and politically based confrontations came to accept violence—and particularly homicide—as a means of solving problems.[95] The levels of violence remained undiminished following the end of Reconstruction. Between 1878 and 1890, the town of Vermilionville (which was renamed Lafayette in 1884) was invaded on three occasions by armed vigilantes. Acadians—particularly those from the Bayou Teche and prairie regions—consequently experienced parallel changes in attitudes regarding violence in general and homicide in particular. This is perhaps the most enduring legacy of nineteenth-century violence in Louisiana's Acadian society.

Conclusion

The Acadian community that emerged from the turbulent Reconstruction era bore little resemblance to the dynamic and highly stratified prewar society, much of which had been upwardly mobile both economically and socially and was becoming integrated into the American mainstream. The postwar Acadian community became essentially a two-tiered society in which status and wealth were polarized between a small educated and influential gentry caste and a large and growing underclass of landless sharecroppers. This society resembled that of modern Third World countries lining the Caribbean rim. The socioeconomic polarization caught the attention of Louisiana resident W. H. Sparks, who maintained that "the population is either very rich or very poor."[1] Separating the upper class from the underclass was a small and steadily dwindling group of economically beleaguered urban professionals and yeoman farmers.

Acadians on the lower rungs of the socioeconomic ladder found it increasingly difficult to improve their lot as the region's festering economic crisis solidified the changes wrought by the economically disastrous Reconstruction era. Nor could the poor Acadians look to their more prosperous neighbors for assistance. Acadian sharecroppers and their Acadian landlords were separated by a broad and ever-widening gulf of economic and cultural differences. Upper-class Acadians increasingly wished to avoid the onerous social stigma borne by their poor relations, identified increasingly as Cajuns (an Anglo cor-

ruption of Acadians) in the postbellum period. Even the newly emancipated freedmen, who formerly constituted the doormat of local society, quickly emulated their former masters in viewing their Cajun
neighbors with derision.

Scorned by rival groups, abandoned by their own natural leadership element, and under mounting pressure to conform to the Anglo-
American norm, poor Acadians were ill-equipped to meet the challenges of life in the postbellum South. Economically ruined by the
war, some Acadians were forced to abandon their traditional agricultural pursuits and to seek their livelihoods first as cypress lumber-
jacks, later as fishermen and trappers in the Atchafalaya Basin and in
the coastal marshes. Many more were reduced to tenantry by the end
of the nineteenth century. It is perhaps not coincidental that the incidence of alcoholism and the general consumption of whiskey among
Cajuns escalated tremendously during the postbellum period.[2] Those
drawn into poverty soon discovered that they could not escape. They
and their descendants would remain mired in tenantry until the in-
dustrialization of Texas's Golden Triangle in the first two decades of
the twentieth century provided well-paying jobs and the promise of a
better life to thousands of Cajun sharecroppers. Throughout the late
nineteenth and early twentieth centuries, the tenants' reduced circumstances forced them to interact daily with black fellow tenants—
despite mounting pressure for segregation—and the resulting cultural interchanges produced both modern Cajun music and Cajun
cuisine (as well as zydeco music in the black Creole community). Such
interchanges, which were particularly numerous in the Eunice, Louisiana, area, helped to blur, at least in the eyes of outside observers,
the long-standing but rapidly decaying cultural cleavages between the
Acadians and their prairie Creole neighbors to the north. By the turn
of the twentieth century, these poor prairie Creoles who, like the Acadians, had been abandoned by their own ethnic leadership element,
gravitated culturally, economically, and politically toward the Acadians south of present-day Eunice, with whom they shared an increasingly common life-style. This metamorphosis was largely completed
by 1910, when the original prairie Creole settlement was officially designated Evangeline Parish.

Poor Creoles east of the Atchafalaya River, and particularly in the
Lafourche Basin, also adopted the Cajun identity as they became ac-

culturated through intermarriage. Indeed, the assimilation of the eastern Creoles into the Lafourche Acadian community has been so complete that such families as the Quatrevingts (originally Achtzigger), Chauvins, Himels, Verrets, Cantrelles, and Haydels are generally unaware that their German and French ancestors arrived in Louisiana fully one-half century before the Acadians.

Many members of the up-and-coming antebellum gentry were also profoundly affected by the Civil War and its aftermath. The war claimed most of the prominent young Acadian politicians. Not until the turn of the century would the gentry reassert a modicum of its antebellum influence on the state and regional levels. Although a Cajun would not again occupy the governor's office until 1972, Acadian political influence at the dawn of the twentieth century was substantial. Acadians Joseph A. Breaux, Robert Broussard, and Edwin Broussard would serve respectively as chief justice of the Louisiana Supreme Court, United States senator, and United States congressman and, later, senator. Numerous other Acadians functioned as police jurors, sheriffs, district attorneys, district judges, state representatives, and local functionaries.

This resurgence in political power stemmed in no small part from Acadian participation in efforts to eradicate the local Republican party. The political violence of the postbellum era, which secured the Democratic party's return to undisputed power, was merely part of a sustained effort, based in the prairie parishes, to maintain social control in a rapidly changing world. The region's postwar economic instability stemming from the ravages of Union invasions, Confederate foraging, wartime vandalism by freedmen, postwar natural disasters, epidemics, and recurring economic slumps fueled the insecurity of the vigilantes who enforced the regional social code. Most severely affected by the reverses were the antebellum Acadian planters and yeoman farmers, as well as planters' sons who grew to manhood just before or during the conflict. Unable to find a niche in agriculture, many of these young Acadians migrated to south Louisiana's farming villages such as Vermilionville, Plaquemine, and Thibodaux, where they formed a new professional class. Falling back on their classical educations, these urban Cajuns generally developed comfortable existences as sugar and cotton factors, attorneys, dry goods merchants, clerks, bill collectors and teachers.

This movement into the mercantile sector of the south Louisiana economy accelerated long-established social and cultural trends within the Acadian upper class. For postbellum Acadians, as in New Orleans, the language of business was English, and the Acadian social climbers who had formerly aspired to the heights of Creole society moved rapidly into the Anglo-American mainstream. Because of the social stigma now associated with less affluent Acadians, the Acadian gentry made every effort to disassociate themselves from their heritage and, concomitantly, their poor relations, by wrapping themselves in the ennobling mantle of the Evangeline legend and ultimately identifying themselves simply as "American."

The children of these acculturated Acadians were in the vanguard of the early twentieth-century movement to Americanize the Acadians. Focusing on public education as the best means of bringing the state's illiterate French-speakers into the national mainstream, the movement was propelled by the compulsory education act of 1916 and by the compulsory English educational provisions of the 1921 state constitution. Though the authors of these laws were Anglos, most of the teachers who implemented the English instructional program were drawn from the Acadian gentry caste. These teachers showed no more sympathy than their Anglo colleagues for Louisiana French, and French-speakers in their care were chastised and publicly humiliated for using their mother tongue on the school grounds. For much of the twentieth century, the Acadian/Cajun community would remain a society at war with itself as a result of socioeconomic and cultural changes wrought during the volatile nineteenth century.

Appendix

Table 1.

A Comparison of Acadian Personal Property Holdings,
1850 and 1870

PARISH	1860	1870	PERCENT OF REDUCTION
Acadian Coast/River Parishes			
Ascension	$6,581.00	$240.74	96
Iberville	1,625.00	348.38	79
St. James	9,006.67	728.53	92
West Baton Rouge	1,068.30	245.13	77
Lafourche Basin			
Assumption	$1,268.09	$735.58	42
Lafourche	2,196.85	386.03	82
Terrebonne	2,044.41	588.92	71
Prairie Parishes			
Calcasieu	$3,164.44	$911.53	71
Lafayette	6,444.16	615.46	90
St. Landry	4,741.44	437.86	91
St. Martin	4,564.06	221.88	95
St. Mary	1,511.75	743.17	51
Vermilion	535.14	242.19	55

Source: 1870 census, Population Schedules, Ascension, Assumption, Calcasieu, Cameron, Iberia, Iberville, Lafayette, Lafourche, St. James, St. Landry, St. Martin, St. Mary, Terrebonne, Vermilion, and West Baton Rouge parishes. All tables are from this source except where otherwise indicated.

Table 2.
Median Acadian Real Estate Holdings, 1860 and 1870

PARISH	1860	1870	PERCENT OF REDUCTION
Acadian Coast/River Parishes			
Ascension	$10,330.98	$1,024.78	90
Iberville	15,500.22	4,694.04	70
St. James	6,281.95	2,340.99	63
West Baton Rouge	8,327.16	1,129.25	86
Lafourche Basin			
Assumption	$2,579.61	$1,310.00	49
Lafourche	1,714.24	1,649.23	4
Terrebonne	1,857.37	2,063.64	−11
Prairie Parishes			
Calcasieu	$524.19	$265.26	49
Lafayette	1,849.13	1,506.05	19
St. Landry	1,347.63	783.85	42
St. Martin	12,241.26	2,406.07	80
St. Mary	4,935.93	881.25	82
Vermilion	535.14	242.19	55

Table 3.
Acadian Planters of the First and Second Acadian Coasts, 1860 and 1870

PARISH	1860		1870	
	NUMBER	PERCENT*	NUMBER	PERCENT
Iberville	43	31	10	5
Ascension	17	8	4	2
West Baton Rouge	25	22	1	0
St. James	18	13	3	2

*Percentages are based on total Acadian households in each parish.

Table 4.
Acadian Large and Medium-Sized Farms, 1870

PARISH	TOTAL HOUSEHOLDS	FARMS VALUED AT $1,500 TO $9,999	PERCENT
Acadian Coast/River Parishes			
Ascension	192	8	4
Iberville	213	44	21
St. James	183	41	22
West Baton Rouge	165	43	26
Lafourche Basin			
Assumption	595	120	20
Lafourche	473	119	25
Terrebonne	301	66	22
Prairie Parishes			
Calcasieu	84	8	10
Cameron	55	4	7
Iberia	153	52	34
Lafayette	691	377	55
St. Landry	407	62	15
St. Martin	313	126	40
St. Mary	100	87	87
Vermilion	289	9	3

Table 5.
Landless Acadian Households, 1870

PARISH	TOTAL HOUSEHOLDS	LANDLESS HOUSEHOLDS	PERCENT
Acadian Coast/River Parishes			
Ascension	192	93	48
Iberville	213	145	68
St. James	183	136	74
West Baton Rouge	165	93	56
Lafourche Basin			
Assumption	595	396	67
Lafourche	473	298	63
Terrebonne	301	224	74
Prairie Parishes			
Calcasieu	84	23	27
Cameron	55	24	44
Iberia	153	91	59
Lafayette	691	272	39
St. Landry	407	295	72
St. Martin	313	185	59
St. Mary	100	88	88
Vermilion	289	105	36

Table 6.
Acadian Small Farmers, 1870

PARISH	TOTAL HOUSE-HOLDS	FARMS VALUED AT $1 TO $1,499	PERCENT
Acadian Coast/River Parishes			
Ascension	192	12	6
Iberville	213	14	7
St. James	183	3	2
West Baton Rouge	165	27	16
Lafourche Basin			
Assumption	596	65	11
Lafourche	473	54	11
Terrebonne	301	7	2
Prairie Parishes			
Calcasieu	84	44	52
Cameron	55	22	40
Iberia	153	10	7
Lafayette	691	41	6
St. Landry	407	47	12
St. Martin	313	2	0
St. Mary	100	3	3
Vermilion	289	64	22

Table 7.
Acadian Agricultural Work Force, 1870

PARISH	FARMERS	LABORERS	FARMERS AS PERCENTAGE OF ACADIAN AGRICULTURAL WORK FORCE*
Acadian Coast/River Parishes			
Ascension	45	10	82
Iberville	61	28	69
St. James	31	39	44
West Baton Rouge	62	47	57
Lafourche Basin			
Assumption	136	177	43
Lafourche	144	311	32
Terrebonne	90	233	28
Prairie Parishes			
Calcasieu	44	40	52
Cameron	39	13	75
Iberia	57	94	39
Lafayette	353	374	49
St. Landry	117	87	57
St. Martin	88	167	35
St. Mary	20	61	25
Vermilion	132	91	59

*Though legitimately constituting another component of the agricultural work force, overseers and farm/plantation managers, were not included because of their negligible numbers: Ascension Parish, 17; Assumption Parish, 15; Calcasieu Parish, 0; Cameron Parish, 0; Iberia Parish, 1; Iberville Parish, 14; Lafayette Parish, 12; Lafourche Parish, 11; St. James Parish, 19; St. Martin Parish, 0; St. Mary Parish, 4.

Table 8.
A Comparison of Real Wealth Controlled by
Acadians and Anglos, 1870

PARISH	ACADIANS		ANGLOS	
	APRAISED VALUE	PERCENT OF PARISH TOTAL	APPRAISED VALUE	PERCENT OF PARISH TOTAL
Acadian Coast/River Parishes				
Ascension	$186,510	20	$263,720	29
Iberville	389,605	17	1,263,375	54
St. James	142,800	11	332,750	26
West Baton Rouge	90,340	12	453,800	59
Lafourche Basin				
Assumption	$451,950	19	$1,330,900	57
Lafourche	288,614	16	711,615	40
Terrebonne	181,600	15	830,750	67
Prairie Parishes				
Calcasieu	$15,650	7	$145,580	63
Cameron	6,645	9	53,925	77
Iberia	101,260	8	735,690	55
Lafayette	631,035	50	253,800	20
St. Landry	182,635	7	1,340,070	53
St. Martin	335,000	22	204,400	14
St. Mary	14,100	0	2,340,865	70
Vermilion	55,220	16	145,825	43

Table 9.
A Comparison of Personal Property Controlled by
Acadians and Anglos, 1870

PARISH	ACADIANS		ANGLOS	
	APPRAISED VALUE	PERCENT OF PARISH TOTAL	APPRAISED VALUE	PERCENT OF PARISH TOTAL
Acadian Coast/River Parishes				
Ascension	$43,815	14	$57,659	18
Iberville	28,915	8	212,600	61
St. James	44,440	11	40,075	10
West Baton Rouge	19,610	9	85,920	41
Lafourche Basin				
Assumption	$253,775	24	$504,675	48
Lafourche	82,610	16	201,260	40
Terrebonne	51,825	10	285,500	55
Prairie Parishes				
Calcasieu	$53,780	18	$125,640	43
Cameron	20,900	20	57,275	55
Iberia	26,625	11	90,350	38
Lafayette	331,115	44	113,760	18
St. Landry	102,020	8	604,145	46
St. Martin	103,300	19	43,250	8
St. Mary	3,550	0	440,390	70
Vermilion	55,220	16	145,825	43

Table 10.
Acadians and Anglo-Americans in Acadiana, 1870

PARISH	ACADIANS		ANGLOS	
	NUMBER	PERCENT OF TOTAL POPU-LATION	NUMBER	PERCENT OF TOTAL POPU-LATION
Acadian Coast/River Parishes				
Ascension	921	11	721	8
Iberville	762	6	1,323	11
St. James	740	7	559	6
West Baton Rouge	681	13	434	8
Lafourche Basin				
Assumption	2,762	23	889	7
Lafourche	2,314	16	1,955	13
Terrebonne	1,452	13	2,257	20
Prairie Parishes				
Calcasieu	421	6	3,433	51
Cameron	206	1	787	49
Iberia	742	13	725	13
Lafayette	3,015	29	911	9
St. Landry	1,653	7	5,647	22
St. Martin	1,344	14	500	5
St. Mary	414	3	2,157	16
Vermilion	1,299	29	1,049	24

Table 11.
Creole and Foreign French Planters in the
Acadian Parishes, 1870

PARISH	CREOLES	FOREIGN FRENCH
Acadian Coast/River Parishes		
Ascension	1	0
Iberville	15	5
St. James	15	4
West Baton Rouge	3	1
Lafourche Basin		
Assumption	2	1
Lafourche	5	2
Terrebonne	2	0
Prairie Parishes		
Calcasieu	0	0
Cameron	0	0
Iberia	5	3
Lafayette	4	2
St. Landry	9	3
St. Martin	19	1
St. Mary	15	1
Vermilion	1	0

Table 12.

Landholdings of Creoles and Nineteenth-Century
French Immigrants in Acadiana, 1870

PARISH	CREOLES		FOREIGN FRENCH	
	NUMBER	PERCENT OF ALL LOCAL REAL ESTATE	NUMBER	PERCENT OF ALL LOCAL REAL ESTATE
Acadian Coast/River Parishes				
Ascension	357,050	39	24,800	3
Iberville	391,650	17	132,705	6
St. James	482,710	38	171,950	14
West Baton Rouge	93,900	12	18,450	2
Lafourche Basin				
Assumption	471,870	20	35,850	2
Lafourche	450,630	25	208,380	12
Terrebonne	183,400	15	25,500	2
Prairie Parishes				
Calcasieu	18,800	8	16,600	7
Cameron	4,450	6	100	0
Iberia	315,350	23	83,000	6
Lafayette	252,030	20	82,100	6
St. Landry	581,435	23	117,750	5
St. Martin	748,660	50	138,000	9
St. Mary	626,250	19	57,900	2
Vermilion	94,100	28	20,950	6

Table 13.
Landless Whites in the Acadian Parishes, 1870

PARISH	ACADIANS	CREOLES	ANGLOS	FOREIGN FRENCH	TOTAL WHITE HOUSE-HOLDS	PERCEN' OF ALL WHITE HOUSE-HOLDS
Acadian Coast/River Parishes						
Ascension	93	0	0	23	631	18
Iberville	145	126	268	57	864	69
St. James	136	301	230	80	932	80
W. Baton Rouge	93	72	67	7	396	60
Lafourche Basin						
Assumption	396	240	72	64	1,313	59
Lafourche	298	388	290	48	1,626	63
Terrebonne	224	251	401	62	1,177	79
Prairie Parishes						
Calcasieu	23	31	93	15	783	21
Cameron	24	9	75	1	243	45
Iberia	91	88	104	46	570	58
Lafayette	272	147	125	52	1,334	45
St. Landry	295	620	740	78	2,884	60
St. Martin	185	262	107	55	965	63
St. Mary	88	102	294	54	824	65
Vermilion	105	42	68	8	769	29

Table 14.
Acadians and White Creoles in Acadiana, 1870

PARISH	ACADIANS		CREOLES	
	NUMBER	PERCENT OF TOTAL POPU- LATION	NUMBER	PERCENT OF TOTAL POPU- LATION
Acadian Coast/River Parishes				
Ascension	921	11	733	9
Iberville	762	6	762	6
St. James	740	7	1,560	15
West Baton Rouge	681	13	433	8
Lafourche Basin				
Assumption	2,762	23	1,911	16
Lafourche	2,314	16	3,124	21
Terrebonne	1,452	13	1,493	13
Prairie Parishes				
Calcasieu	421	6	442	7
Cameron	206	1	141	9
Iberia	742	13	894	16
Lafayette	3,015	29	1,275	12
St. Landry	1,653	7	5,162	20
St. Martin	1,344	14	2,031	22
St. Mary	414	3	692	5
Vermilion	1,299	29	975	22

Table 15.
Acadians and Nineteenth-Century French Immigrants in Acadiana, 1870

PARISH	ACADIANS		FOREIGN FRENCH	
	NUMBER	PERCENT OF TOTAL POPU- LATION	NUMBER	PERCENT OF TOTAL POPU- LATION
Acadian Coast/River Parishes				
Ascension	921	11	143	2
Iberville	762	6	272	2
St. James	740	7	275	3
West Baton Rouge	681	13	86	2
Lafourche Basin				
Assumption	2,762	23	306	3
Lafourche	2,314	16	251	2
Terrebonne	1,452	13	273	2
Prairie Parishes				
Calcasieu	421	6	64	0
Cameron	206	1	11	0
Iberia	742	13	230	4
Lafayette	3,015	29	349	3
St. Landry	1,653	7	423	2
St. Martin	1,344	14	300	3
St. Mary	414	3	261	2
Vermilion	1,299	29	118	3

Table 16.
Spouses of Acadian Brides, Southwestern Louisiana, 1865 to 1876

	ACADIANS	ANGLOS	CREOLES	FOREIGN FRENCH	OTHERS
Total	719	288	397	272	25
Percent	42	17	23	16	1
1866–68	178	71	100	73	5
1869–70	160	61	85	61	5
1871–72	139	59	80	59	5
1873–74	91	33	53	17	5
1875–76	151	64	79	62	5

Spouses of Acadian Grooms, Southwestern Louisiana, 1865 to 1876

Total	668	236	319	225	23
Percent	45	16	22	15	2
1866–68	153	55	88	48	6
1869–70	139	55	62	42	2
1871–72	140	52	61	45	3
1873–74	102	35	46	25	4
1875–76	134	39	62	65	8

Spouses of Acadian Brides, Lafourche Basin, 1866 to 1870

Total	143	61	77	100	7
Percent	37	16	20	26	2
1866–70	143	61	77	100	7

Spouses of Acadian Grooms, Lafourche Basin, 1866 to 1870

Total	150	43	71	79	12
Percent	42	12	20	22	3
1866–70	150	43	71	79	12

Table 17.
Acadian Urbanites, 1870

TOWN	NUMBER	PERCENTAGE OF ALL ACADIANS IN THAT MUNICIPALITY
Abbeville	82	6
Baton Rouge	92	45
Brashear City	36	9
Donaldsonville	165	18
Grand Coteau	33	2
Houma	4	0
New Iberia	34	5
New Orleans	306	100
Opelousas	31	2
Plaquemine	41	5
St. Martinville	22	2
Thibodaux	159	7
Vermilionville	81	3
Washington	49	3

Table 18.

Occupations of Acadians in New Orleans, 1870

OCCUPATION	NUMBER	PERCENT
Mercantile clerk	16	22
Carpenter	15	20
Hosteler	6	8
Merchant	6	8
Day laborer	4	6
Policeman	3	4
Railroad agent	3	4
Attorney	2	3
Steamboat captain	2	3
Deputy clerk of court	2	3
Engineer	2	3
Baggage master	1	1
Bookkeeper	1	1
Bricklayer	1	1
Cigarmaker	1	1
Bank clerk	1	1
Bill collector	1	1
Doctor	1	1
Cotton factor	1	1
Farmer	1	1
Gunsmith	1	1
Machinist	1	1
Pilot	1	1
Professor of languages	1	1
Salesman	1	1
Speculator	1	1

Source: 1870 census, Orleans Parish.

Table 19.
Given Names of Acadian children in Households Owning
Less Than $2,500 in Real Estate, 1870
(Biblical names are not indicated)

PARISH	DOMINANT CULTURE	FRENCH PERCENT	ANGLO PERCENT
Peripheral Parishes			
Jefferson	Anglo	0	93
Orleans	Anglo	37	52
Plaquemines	Creole	75	15
Pointe Coupée	Creole	74	9
St. Charles	Creole	54	38
St. John	Creole	75	15
A Sampling of Traditional Settlement Areas			
St. James	Acadian	58	32
St. Landry	Anglo	75	13
St. Martin	Creole	72	18
St. Mary	Anglo	47	14
Terrebonne	Acadian	28	56
West Baton Rouge	Acadian	47	35

Table 20.
Vigilante Committees of South Louisiana, 1859

COMMITTEES	ORGANIZED
Côte Gelée	February 2, 1859
Vermilionville	March 15, 1859
St. Martinville	April 30, 1859
La Pointe	ca. April 30, 1859
Fausse Pointe	ca. April 30, 1859
Anse Lyon	(?)
Lac Simonet	(?)
Pont Perry	(?)
Anse-la-Butte	(?)
Marksville	(?)
Grande Pointe	(?)
Calcasieu	(?)
Jeanerette	(?)
Carencro	(?)
Vermilion Parish	(?)
Prairie Robert	(?)
Faquetaique	(?)
Foreman (Lafayette Parish)	(?)

Table 21.

Identity of All Known Vigilantes and Ethnic Composition
of Attakapas Vigilante Groups, 1859

NAME	ETHNIC BACKGROUND	VIGILANTE GROUP
Andrews, Hiram	Anglo	Calcasieu
Beguenaud	Creole	Pont Breaux
Beraud, Desire	Foreign French	Côte Gelée
Bernard, Alexandre	Acadian	Côte Gelée
Bernard, Gerassin	Acadian	Vermilionville
Bernard, L. F. Tréville	Acadian	Carencro
Bernard, Tréville	Acadian	Vermilionville
Bernard, Ursin	Acadian	Vermilionville
Bertrand, Octave	Creole	Vermilionville
Billaut, Martial	Creole	Côte Gelée
Boudreau, A. D.	Acadian	Vermilionville
Braux, Donat	Acadian	Vermilionville
Breaux, Valéry	Acadian	Vermilionville
Broussard, Don Louis	Acadian	Côte Gelée
Broussard, Jean B.	Acadian	Vermilionville
Broussard, Sarrazin	Acadian	Vermilion Parish
Broussard, Valsin	Acadian	Côte Gelée
Comeau, Adolphe	Acadian	Côte Gelée
Comeau, Charles Duclize	Acadian	Côte Gelée
Domengeaux, Louis	Creole	Grande Pointe
Doucet, Pierre Z.	Acadian	Vermilionville
Dugat, Jules	Acadian	Vermilionville
Dugat, Rosemond	Acadian	Vermilionville
Eastin, Hazard	Anglo	Vermilionville
Foreman, Asa	Anglo	Vermilion Parish
Guidry, D.	Acadian	Côte Gelée
Guidry, Eloi	Acadian	Côte Gelée
Guidry, Joseph	Acadian	Côte Gelée
Guidry, Joseph V.	Acadian	Vermilionville
Guidry, Lessin	Acadian	Vermilionville
Guidry, Treville	Acadian	Vermilionville
Guilbeaux, Edmond	Acadian	Vermilionville
Guilbeaux, Lucien	Acadian	Vermilionville

continued

Table 21. *continued*
Identity of All Known Vigilantes and Ethnic Composition
of Attakapas Vigilante Groups, 1859

NAME	ETHNIC BACKGROUND	VIGILANTE GROUP
Guilbeaux, Placide	Acadian	Vermilionville
Hébert, Desire	Acadian	?
Judice, Alcée	Creole	St. Martinville
Judice, Desire	Creole	Vermilionville
Labbé, Césaire	Creole	Côte Gelée
Lachaussée, Raphael	Acadian	Côte Gelée
Landry, Desire	Acadian	Vermilionville
Latiolais, Alexandre	Creole	Vermilionville
Lebleu de Comarsac	Creole	Prairie Robert
Maggy, Capt.	Anglo	Calcasieu
Martin, André Valerien	Acadian	Vermilionville
Martin, Charles Z.	Acadian	Vermilionville
Mouton, A. E.	Acadian	Vermilionville
Mouton, Alc.	Acadian	Vermilionville
Mouton, Alexandre	Acadian	Vermilionville
Mouton, Alfred	Acadian	Vermilionville
Mouton, Ignace	Acadian	Vermilionville
Murr, Auguste	Foreign French	Vermilionville
Nunez, Numa	Creole	Calcasieu
Patin, Dupré	Creole	Anse de la Butte
Prévost, Paul	Creole	Jeanerette
Rigues, John A.	Anglo(?)	Vermilionville
Saint Julien, Aurelien	Creole	Côte Gelée
Saint Julien, Paul-Leon	Creole	Côte Gelée
Savoie, Louis	Acadian	La Pointe
Stanton, Capt.	Anglo	Calcasieu
Voorhies, Alfred	Anglo	La Pointe

Source: Alexandre Barde, *The Vigilante Committees of the Attakapas: An Eyewitness Account of Banditry and Backlash in Southwestern Louisiana,* trans. Henrietta Guilbeau Rogers, ed. David C. Edmonds and Dennis Gibson (Lafayette, La.: Acadiana Press, 1981).

Table 22.

Known Vigilante Victims before September 3, 1859

NAME	ETHNIC/RACIAL BACKGROUND	CRIME	PUNISHMENT
Abshire, Leufroi	Anglo	Theft	Banishment
Alfred	Negro slave	Theft	Incarceration in vigilante jail
Anita	Negro slave	Attempting to escape from bondage and marry a white man	Flogging
Armentor, Manuel de	Spanish immigrant	Theft	Incarceration
Bergeron, Pierre	Acadian	Torturing slaves	Banishment
Boudreaux, Clerville	Acadian	Rustling	Banishment
Braux, Oscar	Acadian	Theft and cohabitation with a free mulatress	Banishment
Broussard, Thertule	Acadian	Rustling	Banishment
Claus, George	German immigrant	Accessory to rustling	Banishment
Don Louis	Negro	Theft	Banishment
Emerente	Free person of color	Prostitution	Banishment
Esteve, F. P. C.	Free person of color	Arson, burglary	Incarceration

Name	Category	Crime	Punishment
Gadrate	Free person of color	Prostitution	Banishment
Grand, Prosper	Foreign French	Theft	Incarceration
Gudbeer, August	German-American, the son of immigrants	Theft	Banishment and flogging
Guidry *dit* Canada, Olivier	Acadian	Banditry	Banishment
Herpin, Aladin	Foreign French	Theft and arson	Banishment
Herpin, Dolzin	Foreign French	Theft and arson	Banishment
Herpin, Valsin	Foreign French	Theft and arson	Banishment
Hulin, Tiburse	Creole	Theft	Incarceration
Lacouture, B.	Foreign French	Theft/murder	Banishment*
Lacouture, Jean	Foreign French	Murder	Banishment
Landry, Emile	Acadian	Antivigilante sympathies	Flogging, banishment
Marie the Pole	Mulatress	Theft	Banishment
Maux, Dosithée	Creole	Rustling	Banishment
Maux, Aurelien	Creole	Rustling	Banishment, flogging
"Picards"	Foreign French	Theft	Incarceration
Primo, Hervilien	Creole	Theft	Banishment
Primo, Euclide	Creole	Theft	Banishment

*He subsequently returned and was shot to death by vigilantes.

Table 22. (continued)
Known Vigilante Victims before September 3, 1859

NAME	ETHNIC/RACIAL BACKGROUND	CRIME	PUNISHMENT
Reed, Thomas	Anglo	Burglary	Banishment
Romero, Bernard	Creole	Harboring a "convicted" (by vigilantes) criminal	Banishment
Rouly, Maximin	St. Domingue Creole	Theft	Incarceration
Santa-Maria de la Plata	Spanish immigrant	Seducing and then abandoning white women and masquerading as a physician	Banishment
Unidentified slave	Negro	Theft	Flogging
Vital, Aristide	Foreign French	Theft	Incarceration
W(illiams?), John	Anglo	Attempting to kidnap and marry a slave	Flogging, banishment
Zozette	Free person of color	Prostitution	Banishment

Table 23.
Personal Violence Unrelated to Vigilante Activities,
1866–1877

ACADIANS		NEGROES	
killed by Acadians	4	killed by Acadians	1
killed by Creoles	2	killed by Creoles	0
killed by Anglos	1	killed by Anglos	1
killed by other whites	0	killed by other whites	0
killed by blacks	0	killed by blacks	3
assailant unknown	0	assailant unknown	4
CREOLES		OTHER WHITES	
killed by Acadians	1	killed by Acadians	1
killed by Creoles	0	killed by Creoles	1
killed by Anglos	0	killed by Anglos	2
killed by other whites	1	killed by other whites	1
killed by blacks	0	killed by blacks	0
assailant unknown	0	assailant unknown	0
ANGLOS			
killed by Acadians	4		
killed by Creoles	0		
killed by Anglos	3		
killed by other whites	0		
killed by blacks	1		
assailant unknown	2		

Source: Random issues of the *Lafayette Advertiser, Opelousas Courier, Opelousas Journal, Plaquemine Iberville South,* and *Thibodaux Sentinel.*

Table 24.

Acadian and Black Populations of the Acadian Parishes, 1870

PARISH	ACADIANS		BLACKS	
	NUMBER	PERCENT	NUMBER	PERCENT
Acadian Coast/River Parishes				
Ascension	921	11	5,506	64
Iberville	762	6	8,265	70
St. James	740	7	6,878	68
East Baton Rouge	206	1	11,078	63
West Baton Rouge	681	13	3,368	66
Lafourche Basin				
Assumption	2,762	23	6,027	50
Lafourche	2,314	16	6,550	45
Terrebonne	1,452	13	5,437	48
Prairie Parishes				
Calcasieu	421	6	1,303	19
Cameron	206	1	267	16
Iberia	742	13	2,954	52
Lafayette	3,015	29	4,627	45
St. Landry	1,653	7	10,647	42
St. Martin	1,344	14	5,018	54
St. Mary	414	3	9,459	69
Vermilion	1,299	29	952	21

Table 25.
Illiteracy and School Attendance in the
Acadian Parishes, 1870 (percent)

PARISH	ILLITERACY	SCHOOL ATTENDANCE
Ascension	14	16
Assumption	32	11
Calcasieu	43	8
Cameron	5	3
Iberia	37	11
Iberville	8	12
Lafayette	39	23
Lafourche	34	17
St. James	10	26
St. Landry	44	13
St. Martin	20	13
St. Mary	23	4
Terrebonne	16	37
Vermilion	58	5
West Baton Rouge	12	14

Table 26.
Returns of the 1868 Presidential Election in the Acadian Parishes

PARISH	SEYMOUR (Democrat)	GRANT (Republican)
Acadian Coast/River Parishes		
Ascension	1,125	1,491
Iberville	704	2,088
St. James	775	2,161
East Baton Rouge	1,350	1,247
West Baton Rouge	433	585
Lafourche Basin		
Assumption	1,375	1,387
Lafourche	1,796	1,617
Terrebonne	1,296	1,541
Prairie Parishes		
Calcasieu	782	9
Lafayette	1422	0
St. Landry	4787	0
St. Martin	1456	28
St. Mary	1819	1,142
Vermilion	958	0

Source: W. Dean Burnham, *Presidential Ballots, 1836–92* (Baltimore, 1955), pp. 486–501.

Table 27.
Ethnic Backgrounds of
White League Presidents,
Lafayette Parish, 1874

CLUB	PRESIDENT	ETHNIC BACKGROUND
Beaubassin	P. D. Guilbeau	Acadian
Begueneau (Begnaud)	A. D. Boudreaux	Acadian
Lafayette #1	J. E. Mouton	Acadian
Lafayette #2	Valéry Breaux	Acadian
Lafayette #3	Joachim Dugas	Acadian
Caruthers	John Caruthers	Anglo
Royville	Ed. Comeau	Acadian
White Man's	C. T. Patin	Creole
Old Côte Gelée	Norbert Landry	Acadian
Vermilionville	John Creighton	Anglo
Isle des Cannes	Marcel Broussard	Acadian
Carencro	Neuville Broussard	Acadian
Charles Hebert's	Dosité Hébert	Acadian
J. R. Creighton's	J. R. Creighton	Anglo
St. Julien's	J. G. St. Julien	Creole

Source: White League materials in the Paul DeBaillon Papers, Collection 7, Southwestern Archives, University of Southwestern Louisiana, Lafayette, Louisiana.

Table 28.
Ethnic Composition of Three White League Chapters,
Lafayette Parish, 1874

ETHNIC GROUP	BEAU-BASSIN	BEGNAUD	CARENCRO CENTRAL	TOTAL	PERCENT
Officers					
Acadians	10	3	9	22	88
Creoles	0	2	0	2	8
Foreign French	0	0	0	0	0
Anglos	1	0	0	1	4
Others	0	0	0	0	0
General Membership					
Acadians	43	25	48	116	65.91
Creoles	5	14	7	26	14.77
Foreign French	10	2	8	20	11.36
Anglos	7	2	2	11	6.00
Others	2	0	1	3	1.70

Source: White League materials in the Paul DeBaillon Papers, Collection 7, Southwestern Archives, University of Southwestern Louisiana, Lafayette, Louisiana.

Notes

CHAPTER ONE

1. Dudley J. LeBlanc, *The Acadian Miracle* (Lafayette, La.: Privately published, 1966); and LeBlanc, *The True Story of the Acadians* (Lafayette, La.: Privately published; 1932). On the body of mythology clouding Acadian history, see Glenn R. Conrad, "The Acadians: Myths and Realities," in Conrad, ed., *The Cajuns: Essays on Their History and Culture* (Lafayette, La.: Center for Louisiana Studies, 1978), pp. 1–20. On the changing view of the nineteenth-century Acadians in recent historiography see, among others, Vaughan B. Baker, "The Acadians in Antebellum Louisiana: A Study in Acculturation," in Conrad, ed., *Cajuns,* pp. 115–28; Carl A. Brasseaux, "The Founding of New Acadia: Reconstruction and Transformation of Acadian Society in Louisiana," 2 vols. (Ph.D. dissertation, University of Paris, 1982), vol. 2; James H. Dormon, *The People Called Cajuns: An Introduction to an Ethnohistory* (Lafayette, La.: Center for Louisiana Studies, 1983); Lawrence E. Estaville, Jr., "Changeless Cajuns: Nineteenth-Century Reality or Myth?" *Louisiana History* 28 (1987): 117–40; Estaville, "Were the Nineteenth-Century Cajuns Geographically Isolated?" *Geoscience and Man* 25 (1988): 85–96.

2. Carl A. Brasseaux, *The Founding of New Acadia: The Beginnings of Acadian Life in Louisiana, 1765–1803* (Baton Rouge: Louisiana State University Press, 1987), pp. 3, 16, 124, 131, 132, 188.

The Acadian worldview resulted in part from the failure of the French colonists to duplicate in the New World the feudalistic trappings of the Old. See William J. Eccles, *France in America* (New York: Harper & Row, 1972); Eccles, *The Canadian Frontier, 1534–1760* (Albuquerque: University of New Mexico Press, 1969); and R. C. Harris, *The Seigneurial System in Early Canada* (Madison: University of Wisconsin Press, 1966).

3. Brasseaux, *Founding of New Acadia,* pp. 188–97.

4. Mathé Allain, *Not Worth a Straw: French Colonial Policy and the Early Years of Louisiana* (Lafayette, La.: Center for Louisiana Studies, 1988), pp. 70–88; Lilian Creté, *Daily Life in Louisiana, 1815–1830,* trans. Patrick Gregory (Baton Rouge: Louisiana State University Press, 1981), pp. 68–77, 88–91, 96–116; Sidney Louis Villeré, *Jacques Philippe Villeré: First Native-Born Governor of Louisiana, 1816–1820* (New Orleans: Historic New Orleans Collection, 1981).

5. Brasseaux, *Founding of New Acadia,* pp. 35–54, 188–97.

6. Ibid., pp. 128, 196–97; Walter Prichard, Fred B. Kniffen, and Clair A. Brown, eds., "Southern Louisiana and Southern Alabama in 1819: The Journal of James Leander Cathcart," *Louisiana Historical Quarterly* 28 (1945): 823–24; Joseph Landry Estate, February 1809, St. Landry Parish Probate Records, St. Landry Parish Courthouse, Opelousas, Louisiana (hereafter cited as St. Landry Probate Records); Anaclet Cormier Estate, January 27, 1810, ibid.; Elizabeth Godin Estate, July 5, 1810, Ascension Parish Original Acts, Book J, p. 195, Ascension Parish Courthouse, Donaldsonville, Louisiana; Pierre-Louis Berquin-Duvallon, *Vue de la colonie du Mississippi, ou des provinces de Louisiane et Floride occidentale, en l'année 1802* (Paris: Imprimerie Expeditive, 1803), p. 118.

7. Jehu Wilkinson, "Judge Jehu Wilkinson's Reminiscences," *Attakapas Gazette* 11 (1976): 141; J. Carlyle Sitterson, *Sugar Country: The Cane Sugar Industry in the South, 1753–1950* (Lexington: University of Kentucky Press, 1953), pp. 100–150. Louisiana's sugar output increased significantly in the early 1830s, when the plantation system emerged in the Acadian river parishes. See Mark Schmitz, *Economic Analysis of Antebellum Sugar Plantations in Louisiana* (New York: Arno Press, 1977), p. 15; André LeBlanc, "The Parish of Assumption," *De Bow's Review* 9 (1850): 289; Pierre A. Delegos, *Statement of the Sugar Made in 1828 and 1829* (New Orleans: Privately published, 1829), copy on deposit at the Historic New Orleans Collection.

8. In this chapter, the term *sugar grower* signifies anyone engaged in sugar cultivation. Delegos, *Statement;* P. A. Champomier, *Statement of the Sugar Crop Made in Louisiana, 1849–1859* (New Orleans: Magne and Weisse, 1860), 1849, pp. 9–50.

9. Delegos, *Statement;* Fifth U.S. Census, 1830, Iberville Parish (hereafter cited as 1830 census, with parish name); Seventh U.S. Census, 1850, agricultural schedules, Iberville Parish (hereafter cited as 1850 agricultural census, with parish name); 1850 agricultural census, West Baton Rouge, Iberville, Ascension, St. James, Assumption, Lafourche, Terre-

bonne, St. Mary, St. Martin, Lafayette, St. Landry, Vermilion, and Calcasieu parishes.

10. Third U.S. Census, 1810 (hereafter cited as 1810 census, with parish name), West Baton Rouge, Iberville, Ascension, Assumption, St. James, Lafourche, St. Martin, and St. Landry parishes; Eighth U.S. Census, 1860 (hereafter cited as 1860 census, with parish name), population schedules, West Baton Rouge, Iberville, Ascension, St. James, Assumption, Lafourche, Terrebonne, St. Mary, St. Martin, Lafayette, St. Landry, Vermilion, and Calcasieu parishes; Sitterson, *Sugar Country*, pp. 100–150.

11. 1860 census, West Baton Rouge, Iberville, Ascension, St. James, Assumption, Lafourche, Terrebonne, St. Mary, St. Martin, Lafayette, St. Landry, Vermilion, and Calcasieu parishes. Louisiana boasted a total of 1,640 large slaveholders (those holding 50 or more slaves) in 1860. See Karl Joseph Menn, comp., *Large Slaveholders of Louisiana* (New Orleans: Pelican, 1964), pp. iii–iv, 1.

12. Small farmers constituted the following percentages of all gainfully employed Acadians in the Acadian Coast and Lafourche Valley parishes in 1860: Ascension 35; St. James, 29; Assumption, 34; and Lafourche, 38 (1860 census, Ascension, St. James, Assumption, and Lafourche parishes).

13. For an excellent study of this phenomenon, see Vaughan B. Baker, "The Acadian in Antebellum Louisiana: A Study of Acculturation," in Conrad, ed., *Cajuns*, pp. 115–28. See also Joseph C. Tregle, Jr., "Early New Orleans Society: A Reappraisal," *Journal of Southern History* 18 (1952): 20–36; W. H. Sparks, *The Memories of Fifty Years: Containing Brief Biographical Notices of Distinguished Americans and Anecdotes of Remarkable Men; Interspersed with Scenes and Events Occurring during a Long Life Chiefly Spent in the Southwest*, 4th ed. (Macon, Ga.: J. W. Burke, 1882), pp. 380–81; *Houma Ceres*, August 16, 23, 30, 1856; *Opelousas Courier*, August 7, 1858; *New Orleans Daily Picayune*, August 14, 15, 16, 1856; Leonard V. Huber, *Creole Collage: Reflections on the Colorful Customs of Latter-Day New Orleans Creoles* (Lafayette, La.: Center for Louisiana Studies, 1980); Zelia Rousseau Mouton to Alexandre Mouton, January 12, 1830, Alexandre Mouton Papers, Collection 40, folio 1-i, Southwestern Archives, University of Southwestern Louisiana, Lafayette, Louisiana; Desirée Martin, *Les veillées d'une soeur ou le destin d'un brin de mousse* (New Orleans: Imprimerie Cosmopolite, 1877), pp. 12–14; George F. Reinecke, trans. and ed., "Early Louisiana French Life and Folklore: From the Anonymous Breaux Manuscript, as Edited by Professor Jay K. Ditchy," *Louisiana Folklore Miscellany* 2 (1966): 7.

14. Amos Webb to Alexandre Mouton, May 17, 1834, Mouton Papers, Box 1, folio 1-s; Sidney A. Marchand, *The Flight of a Century (1800–1900)*

in Ascension Parish, Louisiana (Donaldsonville, La.: Privately published, 1936), p. 103; Alexander Mouton (grandson of the governor) Memoirs, Lucile Meredith Griffin Papers, Collection 26, Tablet 1, p. 7, Southwestern Archives, University of Southwestern Louisiana, Lafayette, Louisiana.

15. Newspaper advertisement quoted in Marchand, *Flight of a Century,* p. 58; William Henry Perrin, *Southwest Louisiana Biographical and Historical,* 2 parts (1891; rpt. Baton Rouge: Claitor's Publishing, 1971), pt. 2, pp. 15, 62, 68, 94–95, 99, 121, 158, 166, 206, 209–11, 228–30, 242, 244, 246, 315, 320; Goodspeed Publishing Company, *Goodspeed's History of Southeast Missouri* (1888; rpt. Cape Girardeau, Mo.: Ramfire Reprints, 1964), pp. 419–20; Harry Lewis Griffin, *Attakapas Country: A History of Lafayette Parish* (1959; rpt. Gretna, La.: Pelican, 1974), p. 44; Goodspeed Publishing Company, *Biographical and Historical Memoirs of Louisiana,* 2 vols. (1892; rpt. Baton Rouge: Claitor's Publishing, 1975), 2:418; "A Condensed Autobiography of Louis Hébert," photostatic copy in the author's possession; *Napoleonville Pioneer of Assumption,* November 24, 1877.

16. In 1860, for example, Assumption Parish's work force boasted thirty-three carpenters, five apprentice carpenters, seven masons, and four apprentice masons (1860 census, Assumption Parish).

17. 1860 census, West Baton Rouge, Iberville, Ascension, and St. James parishes.

18. The composite wealth of the Ascension planter caste was 91 percent of the Acadian total. Though individual amounts varied, the pattern of property ownership exhibited in Ascension Parish appears also in West Baton Rouge, Iberville, St. James, and Assumption parishes. In Iberville Parish, for example, planters owned 49.8 percent of all real wealth and 56 percent of all personal property. Acadian, Creole, and American planters possessed 12, 10, and 30 percent respectively of the local wealth. See 1860 census, West Baton Rouge, Iberville, Ascension, St. James, Assumption, Lafourche, Terrebonne, St. Mary, St. Martin, Lafayette, St. Landry, Vermilion, and Calcasieu parishes.

19. Frederick Law Olmsted, *A Journey in the Seaboard Slave States, in the Years 1853–1854, with Remarks on Their Economy,* 2 vols. (1856; rpt. New York: G. P. Putnam's Sons, 1904), 2:332–33; G. W. Pierce, "Terrebonne," *De Bow's Review* 11 (1851): 606.

20. William F. Rushton, *The Cajuns: From Acadia to Louisiana* (New York: Farrar, Straus, Giroux, 1979), p. 89; Dormon, *People Called Cajuns,* p. 27. For a refutation of Rushton's findings, see Glenn R. Conrad, comp., *Land Records of the Attakapas,* vol. 1, *The Attakapas Domesday Book: Land Grants, Claims and Confirmations in the Attakapas District, 1764–1826* (Lafayette, La.: Center for Louisiana Studies, 1990), pp. ix–xxxviii.

21. Sparks, *Memories,* pp. 375–77; LeBlanc, "Assumption," p. 292. For

the early nineteenth-century movement of Acadians from the river to other areas of south Louisiana, see, for example, Petition to Unzaga, March 2, 1772, Archivo General de Indias, Papeles Procedents de Cuba, legajo 189A, folio 358, Seville, Spain; U.S. Congress, *American State Papers: Public Lands,* 9 vols. (Washington, D.C.: Gales & Seaton/U.S. Government Printing Office, 1832–73), 2:263; Donald J. Hébert, comp., *Southwest Louisiana Records,* 35 vols. (Cecilia/Eunice, La.: Privately published, 1974–90), vol. 1. See also 1810 census, West Baton Rouge, Iberville, Ascension, St. James, and Lafourche parishes; 1830 census, St. James, Ascension, Assumption, Lafourche, and Terrebonne parishes; 1860 census, St. James, Ascension, Assumption, Lafourche, Terrebonne, and St. Mary parishes; *Franklin Planters' Banner,* September 24, 1847; Sparks, *Memories,* p. 379; Charles Lyell, *A Second Visit to the United States of North America,* 2 vols. (New York: Harper & Brothers, 1849), 2:112.

22. Examination of the 1840 and 1860 census reports for Terrebonne Parish indicates that 17 percent of all Acadian heads of households in 1860 had resided in other parishes, particularly Lafourche Parish, twenty years earlier. See also "Death of Joseph Adrien LeBlanc," *Thibodaux Minerva,* February 9, 1856.

23. Statistics for West Baton Rouge and Iberville parishes are unavailable, for census takers failed to differentiate between yeoman farmers and planters. 1860 census, Ascension, Assumption, Lafourche, St. James, and Terrebonne parishes; 1850 agricultural census, West Baton Rouge, Iberville, Ascension, Assumption, Lafourche, and Terrebonne parishes; Sam Bowers Hilliard, *Hog Meat and Hoecake: Food Supply in the Old South, 1840–1860* (Carbondale: Southern Illinois University Press, 1972), pp. 38–53.

24. Sparks, *Memories,* p. 375; Pierce, "Terrebonne," p. 606; 1860 census, West Baton Rouge, Iberville, Ascension, Assumption, St. James, Lafourche, and Terrebonne parishes.

25. Henry Marie Brackenridge, *Views of Louisiana, Together with a Journal of a Voyage Up the Mississippi River in 1811, 1814* (1818; rpt. Chicago: Quadrangle Books, 1962), p. 173; Berquin-Duvallon, *Vue de la colonie du Mississipi,* p. 51; Pierce, "Terrebonne," pp. 603–6; Sparks, *Memories,* pp. 373–78.

26. Pierce, "Terrebonne," p. 601; 1850 agricultural census, Lafourche and Terrebonne parishes. In Lafourche Parish, the typical Acadian landholder cleared 47.63 acres—46 percent of his property. See Sparks, *Memories,* p. 374; Pierce, "Terrebonne," p. 606.

27. Malcolm Comeaux, *Atchafalaya Swamp Life: Settlement and Folk Occupations* (Baton Rouge: Louisiana State University Press, 1972), p. 14. Swamp Acadians did shift from agriculture to hunting, fishing, lumbering, and other nonagrarian pursuits, but only in the postbellum period,

when severe floods inundated Acadian farmland along the eastern fringe of the Atchafalaya Basin, compelling the small farmers to seek their livelihood in the swamps (ibid., pp. 13–21). As late as 1900, less than 3 percent of all Louisiana Cajuns derived their livelihood from the marshes or swamps. See Lawrence E. Estaville, Jr., "The Louisiana French in 1900," *Journal of Historical Geography* 14 (1988): 351.

28. See Wilkinson, "Judge Jehu Wilkinson's Reminiscenses," p. 141; Delegos, *Statement.* Lafayette Parish's Acadian sugar growers constituted only 2 percent of the local Acadian community. See Delegos, *Statement;* 1830 census and 1850 agricultural census, Lafayette and St. Martin parishes.

29. *Opelousas Gazette,* August 31, 1844. In 1860, there were 333 Acadian residents in St. Mary Parish, most of whom were found in the Jeanerette area (1860 census, St. Mary Parish).

30. Seventy-five percent of St. Martin Parish's Acadian sugar growers resided at Grande Pointe (present-day Cecilia) and Fausse Pointe (present-day Loreauville). By 1860, the typical Acadian sugar planter in Lafayette Parish owned $31,023 in real property and $65,102 in personal wealth (1860 census, Lafayette Parish; 1850 agricultural census, St. Martin, Lafayette, and St. Landry parishes).

31. 1860 census, Lafayette Parish; 1850 agricultural census, St. Martin, Lafayette, and St. Landry parishes.

32. Menn, comp., *Large Slaveholders of Louisiana,* pp. 260–61; 1860 census and 1860 census, slave schedules, Lafayette Parish. For detailed studies of slavery in antebellum Lafayette Parish, consult Vaughan B. Baker, "Patterns of Acadian Slave Ownership in Lafayette Parish, 1850," *Attakapas Gazette* 9 (1974): 144–48; and Richard McGimsey, "Police and Slave Patrol Regulations, 1823–1857," *Attakapas Gazette* 10 (1975): 146–52; 1850 agricultural census, Lafayette Parish.

33. 1850 agricultural census, Lafayette Parish; Carl A. Brasseaux, "Prosperity and the Free Population of Lafayette Parish, 1850–1860," *Attakapas Gazette* 12 (1977): 105–6.

34. 1810 and 1830 censuses, St. Landry and St. Martin parishes.

35. Brackenridge, *Views,* p. 171; Frederick Law Olmsted, *A Journey through Texas,* 2 vols., 2d ed. (New York: G. P. Putnam's Sons, 1904), 2:395; Emily Caroline Douglas Autobiography, pp. 105–7, Department of Archives, Louisiana State University, Baton Rouge, Louisiana; 1860 census, Vermilion and Calcasieu parishes; 1850 agricultural census, Calcasieu, Vermilion, and St. Landry parishes.

36. Brackenridge, *Views,* p. 171; Olmsted, *Journey through Texas,* 2:393; Glenn R. Conrad, comp., *New Iberia: Essays on the Town and Its People* (Lafayette, La.: Center for Louisiana Studies, 1979), pp. 59–60; *Franklin Planters' Banner,* March 11, 1849; *Opelousas Gazette,* November 18, 1843; 1850 agricultural census, Calcasieu, Vermilion, and St. Landry parishes.

37. Median livestock production among Calcasieu's Acadian ranches totaled 589 head of cattle (1850 agricultural census, Calcasieu Parish). Frederick Law Olmsted described Creole ponies as being "descended from Norman and Arabian blood, and more valuable than the Spanish stock from Texas, being more intelligent, less vicious, better formed, but so small as to be suitable only for the saddle." In the mid-1850s, Creole ponies wee valued at "twenty to sixty dollars" (Olmsted, *Journey through Texas*, 2 : 393).

38. *Bousillage* is an insulating material composed of mud and Spanish moss and, occasionally, horsehair. The mixture had many of the same insulating properties as adobe, used in the American Southwest. It was used as an infill material in external walls.

39. Olmsted, *Journey through Texas,* 2 : 393–95, 402–3; Sylvère Thibodeau Estate, September 23, 1850, No. 1221, St. Landry Probate Records; R. Warren Robison, "Louisiana Acadian Domestic Architecture," pp. 64–68, and Carl A. Brasseaux, "Acadian Education: From Cultural Isolation to Mainstream America," pp. 212–14, both in Conrad, ed., *Cajuns.*

CHAPTER TWO

1. Alexandre Barde, *Histoire des comités de vigilance aux Attakapas* (Hahnville, La.: *Le Meschacebé,* 1861), p. 8; W. H. Sparks, *The Memories of Fifty Years . . . ,* 4th ed. (Macon Ga.: J. W. Burke, 1882), p. 377; Frederick Law Olmsted, *A Journey through Texas,* 2 vols., 2d ed. (New York: G. P. Putnam's Sons, 1904), 2 : 403–4; Emily Caroline Douglas Autobiography, pp. 105–7, Department of Archives, Louisiana State University, Baton Rouge, Louisiana; "A Trip to the Attakapas in Olden Times," *Attakapas Gazette* 8 (1973): 25; G. W. Pierce, "Terrebonne," *De Bow's Review* 11 (1851): 606.

2. Alcée Fortier, *Louisiana Studies, Literature, Customs and Dialects, History and Education* (New Orleans: F. F. Hansell & Brother, 1894), p. 175. George Lewis Prentiss echoed Fortier's sentiments, stating that "they [Louisiana Acadians] are the poorest, most ignorant set of beings you ever saw—without the least enterprise or industry. They raise a little corn and a few sweet potatoes—merely sufficient to support life; yet they seem perfectly contented and happy" (Prentiss, ed., *A Memoir of S. S. Prentiss,* 2 vols. [New York: Charles Scribner's Sons, 1855], 1 : 94–95).

3. Upland plovers, table birds formerly "much prized" in French Louisiana. They were the featured dish at several leading nineteenth-century New Orleans restaurants (William A. Read, *Louisiana French* [Baton Rouge: Louisiana State University Press, 1931], p. 55).

4. Charles Dudley Warner, "The Acadian Land," ed. James H. Dormon, *Attakapas Gazette* 7 (1972): 168–69; Carl A. Brasseaux, "Petition of the *Habitants* for the Destruction of Stray Cattle," *Attakapas Gazette*" (1976): 78–79; "An Act Relative to Roads, Levees, and Police of Cattle,"

Acts of Louisiana, 1807; St. Landry Parish Police Jury Minute Books, 1:152, St. Landry Parish Courthouse, Opelousas, Louisiana; Olmsted, *Journey through Texas,* 2:402, 404; Claude C. Robin, *Voyage to Louisiana,* trans. Stuart O. Landry (New Orleans: Pelican, 1966), 192–93; Malcolm Comeaux, *Atchafalaya Swamp Life: Settlement and Folk Occupations* (Baton Rouge: Louisiana State University Press, 1972), pp. 17–18; Sparks, *Memories,* p. 374; Philippine Duchesne to Madeline Sophie Barat, September 8, 1821, in Louise Calan, *Philippine Duchesne: Frontier Missionary of the Sacred Heart* (Westminster, Md.: Neuman Press, 1957), p. 364; interview with Cléobule LeJeune, June 19, 1976, Church Point, Louisiana; *Franklin Planters' Banner,* March 23, 30, 1870.

5. Acadian cattlemen devoted only minimal attention to their herds, branding calves in late spring and allowing the herds to roam the open range at will. Even in winter, ranchers devoted little attention to their cattle. Because the cotton harvest coincided with the hay-cutting season, most *petits habitants* failed to provide their cattle with an alternate food source during the winter months. The indigenous grasses were usually killed by the first frost, and starvation frequently decimated the prairie Acadians' herds, particularly calves. See Olmsted, *Journey through Texas,* 2:404; Robin, *Voyage to Louisiana,* p. 193; George F. Reinecke, trans. and ed., "Early Louisiana French Life and Folklore: From the Anonymous Breaux Manuscript, as Edited by Professor Jay K. Ditchy," *Louisiana Folklore Miscellany* 2 (1966): 27 (hereafter cited as "Breaux Manuscript").

6. 1850 agricultural census, West Baton Rouge, Iberville, Ascension, Assumption, St. James, Lafourche, Terrebonne, St. Landry, St. Mary, St. Martin, Lafayette, Vermilion, and Calcasieu parishes; Olmsted, *Journey through Texas,* 2:401–5; Pierce, "Terrebonne," p. 606; André LeBlanc, "The Parish of Assumption," *De Bow's Review* 9 (1850): 289–90; Sparks, *Memories,* passim; Frederick Law Olmsted, *A Journey in the Seaboard Slave States, in the Years 1853–1854, with Remarks on Their Economy,* 2 vols. (1856; rpt. New York: G. P. Putnam's Sons, 1904), 2:332.

7. Antebellum Southerners usually consumed salt pork or wild game, corn bread, and "rarely a vegetable of any description." As in the prairie parishes, where cattle were abundant, milk was rarely consumed domestically and butter was unknown. Sam Bowers Hilliard, *Hog Meat and Hoecake: Food Supply in the Old South, 1840–1860* (Carbondale: Southern Illinois University Press, 1972), 38–39. Olmsted noted that immediately before supper, he asked to wash his hands, and "a shallow cake-pan was brought and set upon the window-seat, and a mere rag offered us for a towel" (Olmsted, *Journey through Texas,* 2:405).

8. "Trip to the Attakapas in Olden Times," p. 25.

9. "Breaux Manuscript," p. 28; Sparks, *Memories,* p. 374; Robin, *Voyage to Louisiana,* p. 115; Pierce, "Terrebonne," p. 606; LeBlanc, "Assumption," p. 289.

10. "Breaux Manuscript," p. 28; Sparks, *Memories,* p. 379; interview with Duma Melançon, July 3, 1978; Comeaux, *Atchafalaya Swamp Life,* p. 66; Phillip Pittman, *Present State of the European Settlements on the Mississippi* (1770; rpt. Gainesville, Fla.: University Press of Florida, 1973), p. 5; Warner, "Acadian Land," p. 168; Pierce, "Terrebonne," p. 604; Henry Marie Brackenridge, *Views of Louisiana, Together with a Journal of a Voyage Up the Mississippi River in 1811, 1814* (1818; rpt. Chicago: Quadrangle Books, 1962), p. 172; Marielle Boudreau and Melvin Gallant, *La cuisine traditionelle en Acadie* (Moncton, N.B.: Editions d'Acadie, 1975), pp. 85–87.

11. Acadian probate records indicate that the typical household contained one to three large cast-iron kettles. Frying pans were rare, appearing in only three of eighteen representative antebellum Acadian successions in the St. Landry Parish Probate Records. On the geographic distribution of the earthen outdoor ovens, see Fred B. Kniffen, "The Outdoor Oven in Louisiana," *Louisiana History* 1 (1960): 25–35.

12. Fortier, *Louisiana Studies,* p. 175; Warner, "Acadian Land," 169; Pierre-Clément Laussat, *Memoirs of My Life to My Son during the Years 1803 and after Which I Spent in Public Service in Louisiana as Commissioner of the French Government for the Retrocession to France of That Colony and for Its Transfer to the United States* (Baton Rouge: Louisiana State University for the Historic New Orleans Collection, 1978), p. 97; Daniel H. Thomas, "Pre-Whitney Cotton Gins in French Louisiana," *Journal of Southern History* 31 (1965): 135–48; François Savoy Succession, December 28, 1780, St. Martin Parish Original Acts, St. Martin Parish Courthouse, St. Martinville, Louisiana; W. W. Pugh, "Bayou Lafourche from 1820 to 1825: Its Inhabitants, Customs and Pursuits," *Louisiana Planter and Sugar Manufacturer,* October 29, 1888, p. 143; "Breaux Manuscript," p. 21; Douglas Autobiography, pp. 105–7. Most Acadian homes boasted looms and spinning wheels. See, for example, antebellum probate records, such as Fabien Richard Estate, April 12, 1812, No. 37, St. Landry Probate Records.

13. "Breaux Manuscript," pp. 21–22; Pugh, "Bayou Lafourche," p. 143; Sparks, *Memories,* p. 374; Fortier, *Louisiana Studies,* p. 178. See also the illustrations in R. L. Daniels, "The Acadians of Louisiana," *Scribner's Monthly* 14 (1879): 383–92.

14. "Breaux Manuscript," pp. 21–22; Alfred Duperier, "A Narrative of Events Connected with the Early Settlement of New Iberia," in Glenn R. Conrad, comp., *New Iberia: Essays on the Town and Its People* (Lafayette, La.: Center for Louisiana Studies, 1979), p. 59; Sparks, *Memories,* pp. 374, 377.

15. Sparks, *Memories,* pp. 374–75; Duperier, "Narrative," p. 59; Pugh, "Bayou Lafourche," p. 143; Pierre-Louis Berquin-Duvallon, *Vue de la colonie du Mississipi, ou des provinces de Louisiane et Floride occidentale, en l'année*

1802 (Paris: Imprimerie Expéditive, 1803), p. 51; Barde, *Comités de vigilance,* p. 47.

16. 1850 agricultural census, West Baton Rouge, Iberville, Ascension, Assumption, St. James, Lafourche, Terrebonne, St. Mary, St. Martin, St. Landry, Lafayette, Vermilion, and Calcasieu parishes; Sparks, *Memories,* p. 375; Joseph Landry Estate, February 1809, No. 10, St. Landry Probate Records; Armand Gotreau Estate, 1811, Ascension Parish Original Acts, Book J, p. 143, Ascension Parish Courthouse, Donaldsonville, Louisiana; "Breaux Manuscript," p. 27; Duperier, "Narrative," p. 59; Daniels, "Acadians of Louisiana," p. 384.

17. R. Warren Robison, "Louisiana Acadian Domestic Architecture," in Glenn R. Conrad, ed., *The Cajuns: Essays on Their History and Culture* (Lafayette, La.: Center for Louisiana Studies, 1978), pp. 64–66. Robison says mule teams were the typical means of transporting logs to building sites, but the overwhelming majority of *petits habitants* owned no mules, relying instead on oxen and other draft animals. See 1850 agricultural census. Construction methods differed drastically on the prairies, where Acadians recycled "hereditary logs" or purchased lumber from sawmills along the Mermentau River. By the Reconstruction era, these mills began selling prefabricated frame homes in the Acadian design. When purchased by prairie settlers, these structures were mounted on *rances,* "long pieces of wood," which were set "on the axles of large wagons." The house was then pulled by ox team to the home site (Olmsted, *Journey through Texas,* p. 394; "Breaux Manuscript," p. 26; Sparks, *Memories,* p. 373; Pugh, "Bayou Lafourche," p. 143).

18. Paul Foret Estate, January 16, 1800, Vol. F, p. 813, Ascension Parish Original Acts; consistent style Pugh, "Bayou Lafourche," p. 143; "Breaux Manuscript," pp. 25–26; Joseph Landry Estate, February 1809, No. 10, St. Landry Parish Probate Records; Elizabeth Godin Estate, July 5, 1810, Book J, p. 143, Ascension Parish Probate Records; Daniels, "Acadians of Louisiana," p. 390; Carl A. Brasseaux, "Acadian Village, Lafayette, Louisiana," *Gulf Coast Historical Review* 3 (1988): 62–65.

19. Pierre Hébert Estate, n.d., Iberville Parish Conveyance Book A-7, Iberville Parish Courthouse, Plaquemine, Louisiana; Joseph Landry Estate, February 1809, No. 10, St. Landry Parish Probate Records; Elizabeth Godin Estate, Ascension Parish Original Acts, July 5, 1810, Book J, p. 195; Amand Gotreau Estate, 1811, ibid., p. 143; Estate of J. Pierre Doucet, September 1812, No. 44, St. Landry Parish Probate Records; Anaclet Cormier Estate, January 7, 1811, No. 27, ibid.; Fabien Richard Estate, April 12, 1812, No. 37, ibid.; Widow Joseph Bourque Estate, December 1815, No. 71, ibid.; Ele[a]nor Comeau Estate, September 1821, ibid.; Sylvain Sonnier Estate, October 1821, No. 236, ibid.; David Guidry Estate, February 18, 1822, No. 257, ibid.; Rosemond Landry Estate, April 14, 1825, Book P, Ascension Parish Original Acts; Gurcy Bourque

Estate (Auction), February 1837, St. Landry Parish Probate Records; Alexandre Blaize Brasseur (Brasseux) Estate, July 20, 1838, No. 870, ibid.; Mrs. Alexandre Castille Estate, July 2, 1844, No. 1130, ibid.; Azelia Breaux Estate, September 18, 1845, No. 1201, ibid.; Dominique Préjean Estate, September 24, 1849, No. 1220, ibid.

20. Lauren C. Post, *Cajun Sketches: From the Prairies of Southwest Louisiana* (Baton Rouge: Louisiana State University Press, 1962), pp. 91–93.

21. "Breaux Manuscript," p. 26; Daniels, "Acadians of Louisiana," p. 390.

22. See, for example, George Washington Cable, "Notes on Acadians in Louisiana," p. 158, Cable Collection, Manuscripts Division, Tulane University Library, New Orleans, Louisiana; photostatic copy on deposit at the Jefferson-Caffery Louisiana Room, Dupré Library, University of Southwestern Louisiana, Lafayette, Louisiana; and Fortier, *Louisiana Studies*, p. 176.

23. Sparks, *Memories*, p. 377; Pugh, "Bayou Lafourche," p. 143; Barde, *Comités de vigilance*, p. 47; Richard Taylor, *Destruction and Reconstruction: Personal Experiences of the Late War* (New York: D. Appleton, 1879), p. 106.

24. Fortier, *Louisiana Studies*, pp. 176–77.

25. Ibid., pp. 176–79; Sparks, *Memories*, p. 377; Pugh, "Bayou Lafourche," p. 143; Barde, *Comités de vigilance*, p. 47; Taylor, *Destruction and Reconstruction*, p. 106.

26. "Breaux Manuscript," p. 7; Daniels, "Acadians of Louisiana," p. 386; Sparks, *Memories*, p. 377; Cable, "Notes on Acadians," p. 158; *Abbeville Meridional*, March 23, April 6, 1878. For a dissenting view of violence at Acadian house dances, see Fortier, *Louisiana Studies*, p. 178.

27. Olmsted, *Journey in the Seaboard Slave States*, 1:648–50; Priscilla M. Bond Diary, December 7, 1864, Department of Archives, Louisiana State University, Baton Rouge, Louisiana. See also Proclamation of the parishioners of St. Bernard Catholic Church, August 28, 1834, Grady Estillette Papers, Southwestern Archives, University of Southwestern Louisiana, Lafayette, Louisiana.

28. Fortier, *Louisiana Studies*, p. 179; see also the portraits of Acadian horsemen and races in Daniels, "Acadians of Louisiana."

29. "Breaux Manuscript," p. 47.

30. Ibid.; Daniels, "Acadians of Louisiana," p. 387. *Sabbats* and *feu-follets* are ghosts in Louisiana Acadian folklore. *Feu-follets* are believed to be the lost souls of children. See Barry Jean Ancelet, Jay D. Edwards, and Glen Pitre, *Cajun Country* (Jackson: University Press of Mississippi, 1991), pp. 49, 95–98, 100.

31. On Christmas Eve, families gathered at the patriarch's home for a holiday feast. In the French tradition, however, gifts were exchanged only on New Year's Day. Bands of mounted maskers gathered on Mardi Gras for boisterous merrymaking. This practice appears to have origi-

nated in the second Acadian Coast in the late antebellum period and to have spread into the western prairie parishes by the early twentieth century. See "Breaux Manuscript," pp. 29, 31, 36, 51; *West Baton Rouge Sugar Planter,* February 25, 1860.

32. Patricia Rickels, "The Folklore of Acadiana," in Steven L. Del Sesto and Jon L. Gibson, eds., *The Culture of Acadiana: Tradition and Change in South Louisiana* (Lafayette, La.: University of Southwestern Louisiana, 1975), pp. 144–70; interviews with Duma Melançon and Ozémae Bergeron, retired *traiteurs,* and with Evon LeJeune, July 19, 1978, Church Point, Louisiana; "Breaux Manuscript," pp. 56–57.

33. The practice of making a sign of the cross on the patient's forehead varied by region. In some areas *traiteurs* applied spittle to the forehead, while in others holy water was administered ("Breaux Manuscript," p. 56; interview with Duma Melançon and Ozémae Bergeron; Rickels, "Folklore," p. 152).

34. "Breaux Manuscript," pp. 56–57; Rickels, "Folklore," p. 152.

35. Alcée Fortier, *Louisiana, Comprising Sketches of Counties, Towns, Events, Institutions and Persons, Arranged in Cyclopedic Form,* 3 vols. (Atlanta: Southern Historical Association, 1909), 1 : 20–21.

36. Roger Baudier, *The Catholic Church in Louisiana* (1939; rpt. Baton Rouge: Louisiana Library Association, 1972), pp. 248–387, 392–93; quotations on p. 382.

37. Proclamation of the parishioners of St. Bernard Catholic Church, August 28, 1834, Grady Estillette Papers.

38. Baudier, *Catholic Church,* pp. 335, 345, 348, 383.

39. Carl A. Brasseaux, *Lafayette: Where Yesterday Meets Tomorrow, an Illustrated History* (Chatsworth, Calif.: Windsor Publications, 1990), p. 44. For other examples, see the correspondence of individual pastors at the Department of Archives, Archidocese of New Orleans.

40. Brasseaux, *Lafayette,* p. 44; Baudier, *Catholic Church,* pp. 347–48.

41. Baudier, *Catholic Church,* pp. 347–48.

42. Ibid.

43. Ibid., pp. 301, 339, 348; Margaret C. Jacob, *The Radical Enlightenment: Pantheists, Freemasons and Republicans* (London: George Allen & Unwin, 1981), p. 113.

44. Acadians constituted 30 percent of the charter members of the Vermilionville Masonic lodge. Among the more notable members were Charles Homer Mouton, André Martin, R. Dugas, Onézime Mouton, and Alexandre Mouton. See Harry Lewis Griffin, *The Attakapas Country: A History of Lafayette Parish, Louisiana* (1959; rpt. Gretna, La.: Pelican, 1974), pp. 168–69; Brasseaux, *Lafayette,* pp. 44–47.

45. Brasseaux, *Lafayette,* pp. 44–47; Baudier, *Catholic Church,* pp. 347–48; Griffin, *Attakapas Country,* pp. 76–78.

46. Ron Bodin, "The Cajun Woman as Unofficial Deacon of the Sacraments and Priest of the Sacramentals in Rural Louisiana, 1800–1930," *Attakapas Gazette* 25 (1990): 2–13; quotation p. 9.

47. Based on a sample of 105 Acadian marriages for the period 1841 to 1847. Donald J. Hébert, comp., *Southwest Louisiana Records*, 35 vols. (Cecelia/Eunice, La.: Privately published, 1974–90), vol. 4.

48. "Breaux Manuscript," p. 34.

49. The 1810 census, for example, indicates that in St. Landry Parish, females ten to twenty-six years of age outnumbered their male counterparts sixty-three to fifty-nine (Donald J. Hébert, comp., *South Louisiana Records*, 11 vols. [Eunice/Cecilia, La.: Privately published, 1978–83], vol. 1; 1810 census, Lafourche Interior Parish; 1830 census, Lafourche and Terrebonne parishes). Between 1810 and 1830, 27.3 percent of all Acadian brides in the prairie parishes married Creoles and only 11.4 percent married American men. Only 1.3 percent selected nineteenth-century French immigrants as spouses. During the 1830s, the following intercultural marriage patterns emerged: Creoles, 36.3 percent; Americans, 11.7 percent; Irishmen, 0.8 percent; French immigrants, 0.8 percent. In Lafourche and Terrebonne parishes, intercultural marriages constituted the following percentages of all marriages involving Acadian women: Creoles, 33.4 percent; Americans, 6.8; French immigrants, 2.0; Italians, 1.5; Irish, 0.6 (Hébert, comp., *Southwest Louisiana Records*, vols. 1–2; and *South Louisiana Records*, vol. 1).

50. "Breaux Manuscript," pp. 38–40; Daniels, "Acadians of Louisiana," pp. 386–89.

51. Barde, *Comités de vigilance*, p. 74; "Breaux Manuscript," p. 45. Cajun women carefully plotted the path of the smoke emanating from the burning straw, believing that "there will soon be a death among the families who live in that direction."

52. Grover Rees, *A Narrative History of Breaux Bridge, Once Called "La Pointe"* (Lafayette, La.: Attakapas Historical Association, 1976), p. 82.

53. Daniels, "Acadians of Louisiana," p. 384; "Breaux Manuscript," pp. 38–39.

54. Sparks, *Memories*, p. 377; *New Iberia Enterprise*, May 2, 1885.

55. LeBlanc, "Assumption," p. 289; Sparks, *Memories*, p. 374; Pierce, "Terrebonne," p. 606; Olmsted, *Journey through Texas*, 2:402–7; Alexander Mouton Memoirs, Lucile Meredith Mouton Griffin Papers, Collection 26, Tablet 1, pp. 1–2, Southwestern Archives, University of Southwestern Louisiana, Lafayette, Louisiana; "Breaux Manuscript," p. 28; Desirée Martin, *Les veillées d'une soeur ou le destin d'un brin de mousse* (New Orleans: Imprimerie Cosmopolite, 1877), pp. 17–18, 44–46; 1850 agricultural census, Calcasieu, Lafayette, St. Landry, and Vermilion parishes.

56. Sparks, *Memories*, p. 375.

57. Olmsted, *Journey through Texas*, 2:402. Pig pens traditionally occupied a corner of the small barnyards at the rear of the Acadian home, while wooden chicken coops were scattered about the yard (Sparks, *Memories*, p. 375).

58. "Breaux Manuscript," p. 21; Pugh, "Bayou Lafourche," p. 143; Douglas Autobiography, pp. 105—7.

59. Carl A. Brasseaux, "Acadian Education: From Cultural Isolation to Mainstream America," in Conrad, ed., *Cajuns*, pp. 212—14; Martin, *Veillées*, pp. 44—45.

60. Karl Joseph Menn, comp., *Large Slaveholders of Louisiana* (New Orleans: Pelican, 1964), p. 121; 1860 census, Slave Schedules, Ascension Parish.

61. Martin, *Veillées*, pp. 11—13, 16—19, 31, 44—45; 1860 census, Calcasieu and Vermilion parishes; Felix Voorhies, *Acadian Reminiscences, with the True Story of Evangeline* (Opelousas, La.: Jacobs News Depot, 1907), pp. 1—107.

CHAPTER THREE

1. See, for example, Carl A. Brasseaux, trans., "Election of a Sindic in the Attakapas, 1773," *Attakapas Gazette* 12 (1977): 43; Marc de Villiers du Terrage, *Les dernières années de la Louisiane française* (Paris: Guilmoto, 1904), pp. 404—6; Memorial from the Lafourche residents to Marquis de Casa Calvo, August 14, 1804. Archivo General de Indias, Papeles Procedentes de Cuba, legajo 220, folio 120, Seville, Spain (hereafter cited as PPC, with volume and folio numbers).

2. See Oscar W. Winzerling, *Acadian Odyssey* (Baton Rouge: Louisiana State University Press, 1955); Memoir on the transportation of 1,730 Acadians to Louisiana, 1792, PPC, 197:968; Pierre Clément Laussat, *Memoirs of My Life to My Son during the Years 1803 and after . . .* Baton Rouge: Louisiana State University for the Historic New Orleans Collection, 1978), pp. 36, 44.

3. Villiers du Terrage, *Derniéres années*, pp. 404—6; Memorial from the Lafourche residents to Marquis de Casa Calvo, August 14, 1804, PPC, 220:120.

4. Joseph T. Hatfield, *William Claiborne: Jeffersonian Centurion in the American Southwest* (Lafayette, La.: Center for Louisiana Studies, 1976), p. 131; Sidney A. Marchand, *The Flight of a Century (1800—1900) in Ascension Parish, Louisiana* (Donaldsonville, La.: Privately published, 1936), pp. 9, 18; Dunbar Rowland, ed., *Official Letter Books of W. C. C. Claiborne, 1801—1816*, 6 vols. (Jackson, Miss.: Mississippi Department of Archives and History, 1917), 1:367—68; Clarence Carter, ed., *The Territorial Papers of the United States*, vol. 9, *The Territory of Orleans, 1803—1812* (Washington, D.C.: U.S. Government Printing Office, 1940), pp. 499—636, 650.

5. Carter, ed., *Territorial Papers,* 9:643–50, 668.

6. Amant Hébert of Acadia County (present-day Ascension and St. James parishes) was the sole Acadian representative at the 1812 state constitutional convention. See *Constitution or Form of Government for the State of Louisiana* (New Orleans: J. B. Baird, 1812.), pp. 1–17, 31; 1860 census, Terrebonne Parish; Roger W. Shugg, "Suffrage and Representation in Ante-Bellum Louisiana," *Louisiana Historical Quarterly* 19 (1936): 390–406; William H. Adams, *The Whig Party of Louisiana* (Lafayette, La.: Center for Louisiana Studies, 1973), p. 10.

7. Adams, *Whig Party,* pp. 2–3; *Journal of the Louisiana House of Representatives,* 1812–24 (New Orleans, 1812–24); *Journal of the Louisiana Senate,* 1812–24 (New Orleans, 1812–24); Joseph G. Tregle, Jr., "Henry S. Thibodaux," in Joseph G. Dawson III, *The Louisiana Governors: From Iberville to Edwards* (Baton Rouge: Louisiana State University Press, 1990), pp. 96–98.

8. *Journal of the House of Representatives,* 1816 (New Orleans, 1817), pp. 4–5. The 1820 census of Lafourche Parish lists 420 white adult males over the age of twenty-seven and 271 between the ages of sixteen and twenty-six.

9. Adams, *Whig Party,* pp. 17–18; Joseph G. Tregle, Jr., "Louisiana in the Age of Jackson" (Ph.D. dissertation, University of Pennsylvania, 1954), pp. 230–36; Perry H. Howard, *Political Tendencies in Louisiana,* 2d ed. (Baton Rouge: Louisiana State University Press, 1971), p. 29; Democratic Committee for Arrangements (Lafayette Parish) to Alexandre Mouton, December 15, 1828, Alexandre Mouton Papers, folio 1-i, Southwestern Archives, University of Southwestern Louisiana, Lafayette, Louisiana.

Strong anti-British sentiment apparently persisted in the Acadian parishes throughout the early antebellum period, for Acadian participation in the Battle of New Orleans was certainly not prompted by attachment to the new Anglo-American regime. Indeed, on the fifteenth anniversary of the American victory on the Plains of Chalmette, Alexandre Mouton experienced "very strong feelings of gratitude to Divine Providence which delivered us from hands of an enemy as barbaric and tyrannical as the English" (Alexandre Mouton to Zelia Rousseau Mouton, January 8, 1830, Mouton Papers).

10. Roger W. Shugg, *Origins of Class Struggle in Louisiana: A Social History of White Farmers and Laborers during Slavery and After, 1840–1875* (Baton Rouge: Louisiana State University Press, 1939), pp. 126, 128–29, 134, 148, 155–56; Vaughan B. Baker, "The Acadians in Antebellum Louisiana," in Glenn R. Conrad, ed., *The Cajuns: Essays on Their History and Culture* (Lafayette, La.: Center for Louisiana Studies, 1978), pp. 121–22; *Louisiana Courier* (New Orleans), November 8, 1828; *New Orleans Bee,* November 3, 28, 1832, November 16, 1836, November 7, 1840; *New Or-*

leans Daily Picayune, November 6, 7, 1840; *Opelousas St. Landry Whig,* September 19, 1844. Whig candidate DeClouet carried the overwhelmingly Acadian Pont Breaux (Breaux Bridge) precinct of St. Martin Parish despite rumors that "Mr. DeClouet has said two years ago that he could buy every vote about Breaux's Bridge with a few bottles of whiskey" (*St. Landry Whig,* September 19, 1844).

11. Adams, *Whig Party,* pp. 85−183, 191−92; Tregle, "Louisiana in the Age of Jackson," pp. 89−127; *Louisiana Courier,* November 8, 1828; *New Orleans Bee,* November 28, 1832, November 16, 1836, November 7, 1840; Shugg, *Origins of Class Struggle,* p. 130; *New Orleans Daily Picayune,* November 6, 7, 1840; Marguerite Watkins, "History of Terrebonne Parish to 1861" (M.A. thesis, Louisiana State University, 1939), pp. 50−51.

12. Adams, *Whig Party,* pp. 18−20, 41−269; *Journal of the House of Representatives,* 1812−52; *Journal of the Senate,* 1812−52.

13. *Opelousas Gazette,* June 4, 14, 1842, February 17, September 26, 1844, June 26, July 3, 10, August 28, 1845; *Opelousas Courier,* November 19, 1853, March 1, 8, 1856; St. Martin Parish Police Jury Minute Books, 1:1−95, St. Martin Parish Courthouse, St. Martinville, Louisiana; Ascension Parish Police Jury Minute Book, 1837−56, unpaginated; *Thibodaux Minerva,* July 16, 23, 30, August 6, 13, 27, September 24, October 1, 8, November 12, 1853, February 9, 1856.

14. *St. Martinville Creole,* quoted in *Baton Rouge Gazette,* October 25, November 15, 1845; *New Orleans Daily Picayune,* January 22, 1853; *Biographical Directory of the American Congress, 1774−1949* (Washington, D.C.: U.S. Government Printing Office, 1950), p. 1598; Adams, *Whig Party,* p. 247; Albert Leonce Dupont, "The Career of Paul Octave Hébert, Governor of Louisiana, 1853−1856," *Louisiana Historical Quarterly* 31 (1948): 505−14; 1860 census, Ascension, Assumption, St. James, Lafourche, and Terrebonne parishes; Howard, *Political Tendencies,* p. 46.

15. *Biographical Directory of the American Congress,* p. 1598; Adams, *Whig Party,* pp. 112−18.

16. *Opelousas Gazette,* July 9, 16, 1842; Adams, *Whig Party,* pp. 111−12.

17. Adams, *Whig Party,* pp. 117−18; Wendell H. Stephenson, *Alexander Porter: Whig Planter of Old Louisiana,* LSU Studies No. 16 (Baton Rouge: Louisiana State University, 1934), pp. 27−29; Shugg, "Suffrage and Representation," p. 396.

18. *Louisiana Courier,* November 7, 10, 14, 1845.

19. Adams, *Whig Party,* pp. 138, 153; *Opelousas Courier,* July 19, October 25, 1856; Carl A. Brasseaux, "The Secession Movement in St. Landry Parish, 1860−1861," *Louisiana Review/Revue de Louisiane* 7 (1978): 131, 151; *New Orleans Bee,* November 21, 1845; Alexandre Barde, *Histoire des comités de vigilance aux Attakapas* (Hahnville, La.: *Le Meschacebé,* 1861, p. 417.

20. *New Orleans Daily Picayune,* November 6–7, 1840, November 2, 8, 1852, November 6, 19, 1856; 1860 census, Ascension and Assumption parishes; *Louisiana Courier,* November 8, 1828; *New Orleans Bee,* July 29, 1836; Brasseaux, "Secession Movement," pp. 150–51.

21. Dupont, "Career of Paul Octave Hébert," pp. 505–14; Glenn R. Conrad, ed., *Dictionary of Louisiana Biography,* 2 vols. (New Orleans: Louisiana Historical Association; 1988), 1:392–93, 587–88. See also J. Franklin Mouton III, comp. and ed., *The Moutons: A Genealogy* (Lafayette, La.: Privately published, 1978).

22. Ascension Parish Police Jury Minute Book, 1837–56, unpaginated; 1860 census, Lafourche Parish.

23. Harry Lewis Griffin, *Attakapas Country: A History of Lafayette Parish* (1959; rpt. Gretna, La.: Pelican, 1974), pp. 245–47; 1860 census, St. Landry Parish; *Opelousas Courier,* March 8, 1856, March 30, May 9, 30, June 6, 13, 1857; Brasseaux, "Secession Movement," p. 146.

24. *Opelousas Courier,* July 19, October 25, 1856; Blanche DeClouet to Paul DeClouet, October 10, 1860, DeClouet Papers, Southwestern Archives, University of Southwestern Louisiana, Lafayette, Louisiana; *West Baton Rouge Sugar Planter,* November 24, 1860; *Plaquemine Gazette and Sentinel,* February 25, March 3, August 11, October 13, 1860; Barde, *Comités de vigilance,* p. 417; *Baton Rouge Gazette,* November 15, 1845; *New Orleans Bee,* November 21, 1845.

25. Joe Gray Taylor, *Negro Slavery in Louisiana* (Baton Rouge: Louisiana Historical Association, 1963), pp. 36–38, 215–17, 227–31; *Opelousas Courier,* July 19, 1856, March 3, 1860; Iona Weiland, "Typical Household: Lafayette Parish, 1825–1835," *Attakapas Gazette* 9 (1974): 4; Richard McGimsey, "Police and Slave Regulations, 1823–1857," *Attakapas Gazette* 10 (1975): 144–52; Vaughan B. Baker, "Patterns of Slave Ownership in Lafayette Parish, 1850," *Attakapas Gazette* 9 (1974): 144–48; J. Carlyle Sitterson, *Sugar Country: The Cane Sugar Industry in the South, 1753–1950* (Lexington: University of Kentucky Press, 1953), pp. 47–50, 60; Herbert Aptheker, *Nat Turner's Slave Rebellion: Together with the Full Text of the So-Called "Confessions" of Nat Turner, Made in Prison in 1831* (New York: Grove Press, 1968), p. 71; Lafayette Parish Police Jury Minute Book, 1:63, Lafayette Parish Courthouse; Lafayette, Louisiana; *Acts of Louisiana,* 1841, pp. 32–33.

26. *Alexandria American,* quoted in *New Orleans Daily Crescent,* October 29, 1859; Shugg, *Origins of Class Struggle,* p. 154; Brasseaux, "Secession Movement," p. 136; *West Baton Rouge Sugar Planter,* November 24, 1860; *Plaquemine Gazette and Sentinel,* February 25, September 29, October 13, 1860; *Baton Rouge Gazette,* October 25, November 15, 1845; *Louisiana Courier,* December 3, 1845.

27. In 1860, only 22 percent of the Acadian households in Vermilion

Parish and 16 percent of those in Calcasieu Parish owned slaves (1860 census, Vermilion and Calcasieu parishes; 1860 census, slave schedules, Vermilion and Calcasieu parishes). See also Richard Taylor, *Destruction and Reconstruction: Personal Experiences of the Late War* (New York: D. Appleton, 1879), p. 106; Frederick Law Olmsted, *A Journey through Texas*, 2 vols., 2d ed. (New York: G. P. Putnam's Sons, 1904), 2:393–405.

28. Barde, *Comités de vigilance*, pp. 27, 50, 57–58, 67–70, 125–38, 146, 159, 186, 199–206, 420; William Henry Perrin, *Southwest Louisiana Biographical and Historical*, 2 parts (1891; rpt. Baton Rouge: Claitor's Publishing, 1971), pt. 1, p. 72; Wayne Gard, *Frontier Justice* (Norman: University of Oklahoma Press, 1949), pp. 104–212.

29. *Opelousas Courier*, September 10, 17, 1859, April 21, 1860; Barde, *Comités de vigilance*, pp. 390–403, 422–28; Perrin, *Southwest Louisiana*, pt. 1, pp. 77–78.

30. Barde, *Comités de vigilance*, pp. 390–403, 422–28; Perrin, *Southwest Louisiana*, pt. 1, pp. 77–78.

31. Barde, *Comités de vigilance*, pp. 402–8, 417.

CHAPTER FOUR

This chapter was produced, in part, through financial assistance provided by Jean Lafitte National Park.

1. Interview with Cléobule LeJeune, July 15, 1975, Richard, Louisiana; interview with Duma Melançon, August 12, 1975, Church Point, Louisiana; interview with Lastie Bergeron, February 11, 1982, Lafayette, Louisiana. The three Acadian generals were Jean-Jacques Alfred Mouton, Louis Hébert, and Paul Octave Hébert.

2. Albert Leonce Dupont, "The Career of Paul Octave Hébert, Governor of Louisiana, 1853–1856," *Louisiana Historical Quarterly* 31 (1948): 505–14; Vaughan B. Baker, "The Acadians in Antebellum Louisiana: A Study in Acculturation," in Glenn R. Conrad, ed., *The Cajuns: Essays on Their History and Culture* (Lafayette, La.: Center for Louisiana Studies, 1978), pp. 115–28; Karl Joseph Menn, comp., *Large Slaveholders of Louisiana* (New Orleans: Pelican, 1964), pp. 242–49; 1860 census, slave schedules, St. James Parish.

3. Richard Taylor, *Destruction and Reconstruction: Personal Experiences of the Late War* (New York: D. Appleton, 1879), p. 108; *Opelousas Courier*, July 19, 1856, September 15, 1860.

4. Willie Malvin Caskey, *Secession and Restoration of Louisiana* (Baton Rouge: Louisiana State University Press, 1938), pp. 2–3; James K. Greer, *Louisiana Politics, 1845–1861* (Baton Rouge: Ramires-Jones Printing Company, 1930), pp. 223–30.

5. *Opelousas Courier*, September 15, 1860; Carl A. Brasseaux, "The Se-

cession Movement in St. Landry Parish, 1860–1861," *Louisiana Review/ Revue de Louisiane* 7 (1978): 150.

6. Taylor, *Destruction and Reconstruction,* p. 108; Charles B. Dew, "The Long Lost Returns: The Candidates and Their Totals in Louisiana's Secession Election," *Louisiana History* 10 (1969): 360–69; Brasseaux, "Secession Movement," pp. 129–55.

7. Greer, *Louisiana Politics,* p. 252; Caskey, *Secession and Restoration,* p. 22.

8. The cooperationist senatorial candidates in Ascension, Assumption, Iberville, Lafourche, St. James, and Terrebonne parishes garnered 51, 90, 45, 96, 89, and 53 percent of the popular vote respectively (Dew, "Long Lost Returns," pp. 358–59).

9. Caskey, *Secession and Restoration,* p. 29; Greer, *Louisiana Politics,* p. 274.

10. Caskey, *Secession and Restoration,* p. 41; Napier Bartlett, *Military Record of Louisiana* . . . (1875; rpt. Baton Rouge: Louisiana State University Press, 1964), pt. 1, pp. 58–59; 1860 census, Ascension Parish.

11. U.S. War Department, *The War of the Rebellion: A Compilation of the Official Records of the Union and Confederate Armies,* 70 vols. in 128 parts (Washington, D.C.: U.S. Government Printing Office, 1880–1901), Ser. 4, vol. 1, p. 475 (hereafter cited as *OR*).

12. W. H. Tunnard, *A Southern Record: The History of the Third Regiment, Louisiana Infantry* (Baton Rouge: Privately published, 1866), pp. 28–30; Bartlett, *Military Record,* pt. 2, p. 1.

13. William Arceneaux, *Acadian General: Alfred Mouton and the Civil War* (Lafayette, La.: Center for Louisiana Studies, 1972), pp. 28–37; Alexandre Barde, *Histoire des Comités de vigilance aux Attakapas* (Hahnville, La.: *Le Meschacebé,* 1861), pp. 388–402.

14. John D. Winters, *The Civil War in Louisiana* (Baton Rouge: Louisiana State University Press, 1963), p. 83. From 1862 to 1865, the Confederate enrollment officers at Opelousas were Colonel J. M. Porter (1862); Captain W. C. Morrell (1863–64), and Lieutenant John M. Taylor (1864–65) (Adjutant General's Orders, January 12, 1862, Washington, D.C., National Archives Microfilm Publications, Microcopy 359, Records of the Louisiana State Government, 1850–88, Roll 20: Orders of the Adjutant General's Office).

15. Arthur W. Bergeron, Jr., ed., "Prison Life at Camp Pratt," *Louisiana History* 14 (1973): 387; Vaughan Baker, ed., "Glimpses of New Iberia in the Civil War," *Attakapas Gazette* 6 (1971): 87.

16. Spanish Lake, formerly known as Lake Tasse and Lake Flammand, is located approximately two miles northwest of present-day New Iberia, Louisiana. At the time of the Civil War, it was in St. Martin Parish.

17. Bergeron, ed., "Prison Life," pp. 388–89. See also *Martha Ann*

Rayne v. *the United States,* Case 74, British and American Claims Commission Records, National Archives, Washington, D.C.

18. *OR,* Ser. 1, vol. 15, pp. 245, 872, 919.

19. Ibid., p. 245; *Franklin Attakapas Register,* quoted in the *New Orleans Daily Picayune,* November 21, 1862.

20. For accounts of this Union invasion of the Lafourche basin, see Morris Raphael, *The Battle in the Bayou Country* (Detroit: Harlo, 1975); and Taylor, *Destruction and Reconstruction,* pp. 111–28.

21. *OR,* Ser. 1, vol. 15, p. 393; Colonel W. W. Hyatt's Paymaster Records, Arthur Hyatt Papers, Department of Archives, Louisiana State University Archives, Baton Rouge, Louisiana.

22. *OR,* Ser. 1, vol. 15, pp. 872; Taylor, *Destruction and Reconstruction,* pp. 129–47; Winters, *Civil War,* pp. 284–97; L. Boyd Finch, "Surprise at Brashear City: Sherod Hunter's Sugar Cooler Cavalry," *Louisiana History* 25 (1984): 403–34; Michael James Foret, "Raising Cattle in the Attakapas, 1860–1883: Testimony from the French and American Claims Commission," *Attakapas Gazette* 20 (1985): 89–96.

23. *OR,* Ser. 1, vol. 15, p. 872; *Richmond* (Ind., *Palladium,* November [8?], 1863, clipping in the Walter J. Burke Papers, Southwestern Archives, University of Southwestern Louisiana, Lafayette, Louisiana. As early as November 1862, Richard Taylor had reported that "the parishes in which it has been found most difficult to execute the conscript law are the river parishes from Carroll down and the Gulf parishes from New Orleans to the Sabine River. . . . In many instances it becomes necessary to scour the country with cavalry to bring the conscripts to the camps of instruction" (*OR,* Ser. 1, vol. 15, p. 872; vol. 34, p. 966; Winters, *Civil War,* p. 306).

24. *OR,* Ser. 1, vol. 34, pp. 901–2; *Opelousas Courier,* November 12, 1864; Compiled Service Records of Volunteer Confederate Soldiers, Consolidated Eighteenth Louisiana Infantry and Yellow Jacket Battalion, National Archives Microfilm Publications, Microcopy 320, Rolls 1–3.

25. *OR,* Ser. 1, vol. 34, pp. 962–67; *Opelousas Courier,* August 15, December 12, 1863, February 20, March 5, September 10, October 22, 1864; Winters, *Civil War,* p. 306. For the best account of Acadian Louisiana at this time see David C. Edmonds, *Yankee Autumn in Acadiana: A Narrative of the Great Texas Overland Expedition through Southwest Louisiana, October–December 1863* (Lafayette, La.: Acadiana Press, 1979).

26. *Richmond Palladium* (quote); *OR,* Ser. 1, vol. 26, p. 382. Extant records indicate that, the correspondent's claims notwithstanding, not a single Acadian enlisted in the First Battalion, Cavalry Scouts, U.S. Army (Compiled Service Records of Volunteer Union Soldiers, Louisiana, First Battalion, Cavalry Scouts, National Archives Microfilm Publications, Microcopy 396, Roll 11).

27. *OR,* Ser. 1, vol. 26, p. 778.

28. W. W. Hyatt Diary, vol. 2, September 22, October 8, 1863, Hyatt Papers; *OR*, Ser. 1, vol. 26, p. 532.

29. *S. A. Sorrel* v. *the United States*, Claim 594, pp. 596–683, French and American Claims Commission Records, National Archives, Washington, D.C.; James Franklin Fitts, "The Yankee Officer and the Partisan," *Ballou's Monthly Magazine*, July 1869, p. 54; Richard B. Irwin, *History of the Nineteenth Army Corps* (New York: G. P. Putnam's Sons, 1892), p. 131; Henry P. Whipple, *The Diary of a Private Soldier* (Waterloo, Wisc.: Privately published, 1906), p. 29. According to Fitts, more than three thousand head of cattle were taken from the prairies immediately north of Vermilionville. The remainder were taken from St. Landry Parish *vacheries*. The Acadians had grown so resentful of Confederate foraging raids that in January 1864 they drove their few remaining cattle "to the enemy," even though the Union army had decimated the prairie herds during the preceding months. By selling their livestock to the Yankees, the Acadians not only kept their cattle out of rebel hands, but they also exchanged their beef for valuable greenbacks (*OR*, Ser. 1, vol. 34, p. 903. See also Henry Watkins Allen, *Message of Gov. Henry W. Allen to the Legislature of the State of Louisiana* [Shreveport, La.: *Caddo Gazette*, 1863], p. 2). As early as June 1862, Confederate General J. G. Pratt had been authorized to "impress into the service of the State" as many horses as necessary. Large numbers of prairie cattle were also subsequently confiscated by the Confederacy for shipment to states east of the Mississippi River (Orders for J. G. Pratt, June 4, 1862, Adjutant General's Reports; Orders for E. W. Fuller, June 8, 1862, Adjutant General's Reports; Whipple, *Diary*, pp. 29–30).

30. Whipple, *Diary*, p. 30; *Official Report Relative to the Conduct of Federal Troops in Western Louisiana during the Invasions of 1863 and 1864* (Shreveport, La.: *Caddo Gazette*, 1865), p. 41; Irwin, *History of the Nineteenth Army Corps*, pp. 127–28; *OR*, Ser. 1, vol. 26, p. 382.

31. *Official Report*, p. 41. For other accounts, see, for example, *Sarah Arnaud* v. *the United States*, Claim 251; *S. A. Sorrel* v. *the United States*, Claim 594; *Victor Route* v. *the United States*, Claim 307, French and American Claims Commission Records.

32. Edmonds, *Yankee Autumn in Acadiana*, pp. 136–42.

33. *Official Report*, p. 41. On the attitude of Union soldiers to persons of French descent, see Edmonds, *Yankee Autumn in Acadiana*, pp. 136, 306.

34. Ibid., pp. 24–25; *Opelousas Courier*, December 12, 1863; *OR*, Ser. 1, vol. 26, pp. 763, 855.

35. *OR*, Ser. 1, vol. 26, p. 889; vol. 34, p. 831.

36. *Opelousas Courier*, December 12, 1863.

37. Louis Bringier to Stella Bringier, May 13, 1864, Bringier Papers, Department of Archives, Louisiana State University Archives, Baton Rouge, Louisiana.

38. Priscilla M. Bond Diary, May 13, 1864, Department of Archives,

Louisiana State University, Baton Rouge; proclamation by Richard Taylor, May 18, 1864, Bringier Papers; Hyatt Diary, vol. 2, August 23, 1863.

39. Hyatt Diary, vol. 2, October 8, 1863; *OR*, Ser. 1, vol. 34, p. 901.

40. Louis A. Bringier to Stella Bringier, June 12, July 25, 1864, Bringier Papers.

41. *OR*, Ser. 1, vol. 48, p. 625.

42. Ibid., p. 101; Louis A. Bringier to Stella Bringier, January 18, 1865, Bringier Papers.

43. Edward C. Bearss, ed., *A Louisiana Confederate: Diary of Felix Pierre Poché*, trans. Eugénie Watson Somdal (Natchitoches, La.: Louisiana Studies Institute, 1972), p. 17; Hélène Dupuy Diary, May 22, 1863, Department of Archives, Louisiana State University, Baton Rouge. See also "Reminiscences," *Thibodaux Sentinel*, December 24, 1870.

44. *Honoré Gueymard v. the United States*, Claim 480, French and American Claims Commission Records; *OR*, Ser. 1, vol. 15, pp. 795–96; vol. 34, p. 136; Carl A. Brasseaux, ed., "The Glory Days: E. T. King Recalls the Civil War," *Attakapas Gazette* 11 (1976): 24–27. Michel Gaudet, a committee member, owned eighty-four slaves and $83,000 in real and movable property in 1860, and J. Adam Gaudet, who called the meeting to order, owned sixty-four slaves and $219,000 in property (Menn, comp., *Large Slaveholders of Louisiana*, pp. 120–24, 353–58).

45. *OR*, Ser. 1, vol. 47, pp. 151–52, 246–49, 558, 755; Dupuy Diary, August 11, 1864. Of the twenty-eight Lafourche and Terrebonne Parish Acadians conscripted into the First Louisiana Cavalry (Union) in 1864, fourteen subsequently deserted (Compiled Service Records of Volunteer Union Soldiers, First Louisiana Cavalry, National Archives Microfilm Publications, Microcopy 396, rolls 1–9).

46. Dupuy Diary, May 10, 1865.

47. Ibid., April 4, 1862–May 22, 1865.

CHAPTER FIVE

1. Joe Gray Taylor, *Louisiana Reconstructed, 1863–1877* (Baton Rouge: Louisiana State University Press, 1974), pp. 314–63, quotation p. 358; Glenn R. Conrad, comp., *Land Records of the Attakapas*, vol. 1, *The Attakapas Domesday Book: Land Grants, Claims and Confirmations in the Attakapas District, 1764–1826* (Lafayette, La.: Center for Louisiana Studies, 1990), pp. xxvi–xxvii. For a comparison of postbellum and Depression-era illustrations, see Leonard V. Huber, *Louisiana: A Pictorial History* (New York: Charles Scribner's Sons, 1975), pp. 166–217, 232, 258–67; Glenn R. Conrad and Vaughan B. Baker, eds. *Louisiana Gothic: Recollections of the 1930s* (Lafayette, La.: Center for Louisiana Studies, 1984), pp. 18–25.

2. Taylor, *Louisiana Reconstructed*, pp. 317–18.

3. Mark Schmitz, "The Transformation of the Southern Cane Sugar Sector, 1860–1930," *Agricultural History* 53 (1979): 272.

4. Taylor, *Louisiana Reconstructed*, pp. 314–63; U.S. Senate, *Executive Document* 2, 39th Cong., 1st sess., p. 39; Captain James A. Payne to Mrs. Sterrett, September 3, 1865, in John D. Barnhart, ed., "Reconstruction on the Lower Mississippi," *Mississippi Valley Historical Review* 21 (1934): 387–96; *Napoleonville Pioneer of Assumption*, August 4, 1877; *Thibodaux Sentinel*, October 7, November 18, 1865.

5. Schmitz, "Transformation," pp. 272–73; Taylor, *Louisiana Reconstructed*, p. 345; Walter Prichard, "The Effects of the Civil War on the Louisiana Sugar Industry," *Journal of Southern History* 5 (1939): 318–21.

6. Taylor, *Louisiana Reconstructed*, p. 345; Michael G. Wade, "Justice Delayed: *Appoline Patout* v. *the United States,*" *Louisiana History* 31 (1990): 144, 148.

7. In 1870, the wage scale in Lafayette Parish for agricultural laborers was $15 per month (*Franklin Planters' Banner*, January 19, 1870).

8. Taylor, *Louisiana Reconstructed*, pp. 314–17; Carl A. Brasseaux and Glenn R. Conrad, "Historical Research," in *Schematic Interpretive Plan, Longfellow-Evangeline State Commemorative Area: Analysis of Site and Existing Resources* (St. Martinville, La.: Al J. Landry and Associates, 1984), pp. 92–148. Information regarding the accumulation of personal debts by small planters in St. Martin Parish, included in "Historical Research," is complemented by information on their counterparts in Louisiana's southwestern sugar and cotton belts by consulting the late antebellum conveyance records of St. Landry Parish, a huge local political unit then encompassing much of south-central Louisiana.

9. Three crops are taken from one field before replanting. See Allen Begnaud, "The Louisiana Sugar Cane Industry: An Overview," in *Green Fields: Two Hundreds Years of Louisiana Sugar* (Lafayette, La.: Center for Louisiana Studies, 1980), p. 32.

10. Schmitz, "Transformation," pp. 272–73; Taylor, *Louisiana Reconstructed*, p. 365; *Franklin Planters' Banner*, January 19, 1870; William E. Highsmith, "Some Aspects of Reconstruction in the Heart of Louisiana," *Journal of Southern History* 13 (1947): 468–69.

11. Prichard, "Effects of the Civil War," p. 324; Schmitz, "Transformation," p. 272; *Opelousas Courier*, April 14, 21, 1866, June 1, 1867, March 27, May 15, July 3, 1869, January 22, August 20, October 22, November 5, 1870, July 15, 1871; *Opelousas Journal*, June 20, August 15, 1868, October 23, November 13, 1869.

12. Taylor, *Louisiana Reconstructed*, pp. 344–45; William E. Highsmith, "Social and Economic Conditions in Rapides Parish during Reconstruction" (M.A. thesis, Louisiana State University, 1947), pp. 31–32.

13. Quoted in Schmitz, "Transformation," p. 272. See also *Thibodaux*

Sentinel, April 28, August 25, 1866; *Plaquemine Iberville South,* September 29, 1866.

14. Howard A. White, *The Freedmen's Bureau in Louisiana* (Baton Rouge: Louisiana State University Press, 1970), pp. 67–68.

15. See, for example, Carl A. Brasseaux, ed., "The Glory Days: E. T. King Recalls the Civil War," *Attakapas Gazette* 11 (1976): 29–30; *Thibodaux Sentinel,* March 30, 1867, April 1, 1876.

16. Taylor, *Louisiana Reconstructed,* pp. 345–48; *Opelousas Courier,* October 8, 1870. During the 1867 flood, the *Thibodaux Sentinel* reported that "we have never seen business so dull in Thibodaux as it is at present. People are afraid to expend a dollar as they fear the overflow will cause the loss of their crops. Every one is anxious and uneasy, and knows not what to do" (*Thibodaux Sentinel,* March 30, 1867; *Plaquemine Iberville South,* November 23, 1867; *Franklin Planters' Banner,* January 19, 1870).

17. *Franklin Planters' Banner,* January 19, July 27, 1870, April 5, 1871; *Opelousas Journal,* August 15, 1868; *Opelousas Courier,* August 12, 19, September 16, 1871. At the end of the war, the state legislature had postponed payment of back taxes for the years 1860 through 1864 until 1868. In 1867, the legislature extended the suspension until 1870. In 1870, however, plantations were offered for sale to pay back taxes (Taylor, *Louisiana Reconstructed,* pp. 344–45).

18. *Plaquemine Iberville South,* August 26, 1865. See also Highsmith, "Some Aspects of Reconstruction," p. 476; Goodspeed Publishing Company, *Biographical and Historical Memoirs of Louisiana,* 2 vols. (1892; rpt. Baton Rouge: Claitor's Publishing, 1975), 1:238; Ronald Vern Jackson, ed., *Louisiana, 1870* (Salt Lake City: Accelerated Indexing Systems International, 1987), p. 877.

19. This trend is reflective of the South as a whole. Forrest McDonald and Grady McWhiney have noted that "the deposed and discredited [Anglo-American] planter class continued after the war to own a disproportionate share of the land: in 1870 the wealthiest 5 percent owned over two-fifths of the land and the wealthiest 20 percent owned nearly three-quarters of the land" ("The South from Self-Sufficiency to Peonage: An Interpretation," *American Historical Review* 85 [1980]: 1115).

20. 1870 census, Ascension, Assumption, Calcasieu, Cameron, Iberia, Iberville, Lafayette, Lafourche, St. James, St. Landry, St. Martin, St. Mary, Terrebonne, Vermilion, and West Baton Rouge parishes.

21. Ibid.

22. Taylor, *Louisiana Reconstructed,* p. 382.

23. 1860 census, West Baton Rouge, Iberville, Ascension, St. James, Assumption, Lafourche, Terrebonne, St. Mary, St. Martin, Lafayette, St. Landry, and Vermilion parishes.

24. *Franklin Planters' Banner,* January 19, 1870. Whites also reported

accounted for approximately one-half of the agricultural labor in St. Landry Parish in 1870. See ibid., March 23, 1870.

25. Taylor, *Louisiana Reconstructed*, pp. 368–75.

26. Ibid., p. 376; *Franklin Planters' Banner*, January 19, 1870; *Thibodaux Sentinel*, April 4, 1874. Forrest McDonald and Grady McWhiney maintain that Celtic yeomen in the southeastern states followed a different path to peonage ("The South from Self-Sufficiency to Peonage," pp. 1115–18).

27. Taylor, *Louisiana Reconstructed*, pp. 374–76; *Franklin Planters' Banner*, January 19, 1870. On November 22, 1873, the *Thibodaux Sentinel* reported, "The hard times are bringing down prices rapidly. Everything classed among delicacies and luxuries are a drug on the market, substantials only are in demand."

28. Frederick Law Olmsted, *The Cotton Kingdom: A Traveller's Observations on Cotton and Slavery in the American Slave States*, 2 vols. (New York: Mason Brothers 1861), 1:22.

29. McDonald and McWhiney, "The South from Self-Sufficiency to Peonage," pp. 1102–3; Ted Ownby, "The Defeated Generation at Work: White Farmers in the Deep South, 1865–1890," *Southern Studies* 23 (1984): 327. For its relevance to the Louisiana Acadians, see the *Thibodaux Sentinel*, February 25, 1871.

30. McDonald and McWhiney, "The South from Self-Sufficiency to Peonage," pp. 1095–1118. For Joe Gray Taylor's misconceptions regarding the postbellum Acadian diet, see *Louisiana Reconstructed*, p. 408.

31. Alcée Fortier, *Louisiana Studies, Literature, Customs and Dialects, History and Education* (New Orleans: F. F. Hansell & Brother, 1894), p. 179.

32. J. Carlyle Sitterson, *Sugar Country: The Cane Sugar Industry in the South, 1753–1950* (Lexington: University of Kentucky Press, 1953), p. 221.

33. Ownby, "Defeated Generation," p. 328; *Thibodaux Sentinel*, January 23, February 6, July 17, 1869, February 25, 1871, November 16, 1872; Richard J. Amundson, "Oakley Plantation: A Post–Civil War Venture in Louisiana Sugar," *Louisiana History* 9 (1968): 27–28; *Opelousas Journal*, April 18, May 9, 1868, September 25, December 4, 1869, November 26, 1870; *Opelousas Courier*, August 10, 1872; C. Peter Ripley, *Slaves and Freedmen in Civil War Louisiana* (Baton Rouge: Louisiana State University Press, 1976), p. 101.

European recruits came from throughout the Continent. In addition, approximately 1,500 Chinese laborers were introduced between 1865 and 1877, but only 372 remained in Louisiana in 1890. See Taylor, *Louisiana Reconstructed*, p. 391; *Thibodaux Sentinel*, November 6, 27, December 9, 1865, March 3, May 5, 1866, October 29, December 10, 1870, April 22, September 23, 30, 1871, November 11, 25, 1871.

34. In May 1869, for instance, parts of the Lafourche country were

inundated by a flood caused by a crevasse at the Roman Plantation along the Mississippi River (*Thibodaux Sentinel,* May 29, 1869).

35. O. V. Wells, "The Depression of 1873–79," *Agricultural History* 11 (1937): 237–39; H. C. Taylor, "Historical Aspects of Agricultural Adjustment: The Historical Approach to the Economic Problems of Agriculture," *Agricultural History* 11 (1937): 221–51.

36. Taylor, *Louisiana Reconstructed,* p. 359.

37. Ibid., p. 361.

38. Ibid., pp. 360–61; *Napoleonville Pioneer of Assumption,* June 16, 1877; Barnhart, ed., "Reconstruction on the Lower Mississippi," p. 396.

CHAPTER SIX

1. See, for example, Philip Mason, *Patterns of Dominance* (New York: Oxford University Press, 1970); and Chester L. Hunt and Lewis Walker, *Ethnic Dynamics: Patterns of Intergroup Relations in Various Societies* (Homewood, Ill.: Dorsey Press, 1974); Richard Alonzo Schermerhorn, *Comparative Ethnic Relations: A Framework for Theory and Research* (New York: Random House, 1970); Raymond N. Morris and C. Michael Lamphier, *Three Scales of Inequality: Perspectives on French-English Relations* (Don Mills, Ont.: Longmans Canada, 1977), p. 46.

2. See, for example, Morris and Lamphier, *Three Scales of Inequality;* Jean-Claude Vernex, *Les Francophones du Nouveau-Brunswick: Géographie d'un groupe ethnoculturel minoritaire,* 2 vols. (Paris: Librairie Honoré Champion, 1978); Leon Theriault, *La question du pouvoir en Acadie,* 2d ed. (Moncton, N.B.: Editions d'Acadie, 1982); Nanciellen Davis, *Ethnicity and Ethnic Group Persistence in an Acadian Village in Maritime Canada* (New York: AMS Press, 1985); Stanley Lieberson, *Language and Ethnic Relations in Canada* (New York: Wiley, 1970); 1870 census, Ascension, Assumption, Calcasieu, Cameron, Iberia, Iberville, Lafayette, Lafourche, St. James, St. Landry, St. Martin, St. Mary, Terrebonne, Vermilion, and West Baton Rouge parishes.

3. Morris and Lamphier, *Three Scales of Inequality,* pp. 46–47.

4. Ibid., pp. 47–48.

5. Ibid.

6. Ibid., p. 9; Lieberson, *Language and Ethnic Relations in Canada,* p. 84.

7. Nanciellen Davis notes, "Many Acadians consider Quebeckers political extremists and interpret their behavior towards Acadians as condescending, if not insulting. Many Quebeckers, on the other hand, seem to consider the poorer, less well-educated, and largely rural-dwelling Acadians as something of an embarrassment to French Canada" (*Ethnicity and Ethnic Group Persistence,* pp. 14–18). In the western portion of New Brunswick, the resulting hybrid people are called "Brayons," an epithet

used by their Acadian neighbors to the east and north. See Vernex, *Francophones du Nouveau-Brunswick*, 1:292.

8. Clement Eaton, *The Civilization of the Old South: Writings of Clement Eaton*, ed. Albert D. Kirwan (Lexington: University of Kentucky Press, 1968), p. 90; Susan Cole Doré, *The Pelican Guide to Plantation Homes of Louisiana* (Gretna, La.: Pelican, 1989); Philip D. Uzee, *The Lafourche Country: The People and the Land* (Lafayette, La.: Center for Louisiana Studies, 1985), pp. 228–39; Paul F. Stahls, Jr., *Plantation Homes of the Lafourche Country* (Gretna, La.: Pelican, 1976), pp. 12, 22–25; Louis Hébert, Autobiography, Louis Hébert Papers, Hill Memorial Library, Louisiana State University, Baton Rouge, Louisiana; 1870 census, Ascension, Assumption, Calcasieu, Cameron, Iberia, Iberville, Lafayette, Lafourche, St. James, St. Landry, St. Martin, St. Mary, Terrebonne, Vermilion, and West Baton Rouge parishes; Timothy F. Reilly, "Early Acadiana through Anglo-American Eyes," *Attakapas Gazette* 13 (1978): 58.

9. In discussing the eventual preeminence of class distinctions in antebellum Louisiana, Roger W. Shugg notes that "class distinctions were in the air: to accept them unconsciously was as natural as to breathe, because they were implicit in the economic and social order of the Old South" (Shugg, *Origins of Class Struggle in Louisiana: A Social History of White Farmers and Laborers during Slavery and After, 1840–1875* [Baton Rouge: Louisiana State University Press, 1953], p. 29 and passim).

10. Glenn R. Conrad, "Friend or Foe? Religious Exiles at the Opelousas Post in the American Revolution," *Attakapas Gazette* 12 (1977): 137–40.

11. Lawrence E. Estaville, Jr., "The Louisiana French Language in the Nineteenth Century," *Southeastern Geographer* 30 (1990): 110; Lewis W. Newton, "Creoles and Anglo-Americans in Old Louisiana: A Study in Cultural Conflicts," *Southwestern Social Science Quarterly* 14 (1933): 33, n. 8; Eaton, *Civilization of the Old South*, pp. 77–106. On the continuing nineteenth-century French immigration, see Carl A. Brasseaux, *The "Foreign French": Nineteenth-Century French Immigration into Louisiana*, vol. 1, *1820–1839* (Lafayette, La.: Center for Louisiana Studies, 1990).

12. 1870 census, Ascension, Assumption, Calcasieu, Cameron, Iberia, Iberville, Lafayette, Lafourche, St. James, St. Landry, St. Martin, St. Mary, Terrebonne, Vermilion, and West Baton Rouge parishes. Riverine lands remained at least five times more expensive than lands in the prairies and piny hills throughout the nineteenth century. According to the *Franklin Planters' Banner*, March 23, 1870, "land [in St. Landry Parish] near the navigable streams . . . can be purchased at from $10 to $15 per acre . . . in the western [prairie] portion of the parish, at $2.50 and $1.25."

13. Forrest McDonald and Grady McWhiney have estimated that approximately 70 percent of all whites in the antebellum southeastern states

were of Celtic extraction. Most of these individuals were small farmers and herdsmen. Whites in the "tidewater plantation country of the Atlantic seaboard" were typically of English descent ("The South from Self-Sufficiency to Peonage: An Interpretation," *American Historical Review* 85 [1980]: 1107). See also Grady McWhiney, *Cracker Culture: Celtic Ways in the Old South* (University, Ala.: University of Alabama Press, 1988); Conrad, "Friend or Foe?" pp. 137–40; Clement Eaton, *A History of the Old South: Emergence of a Reluctant Nation,* 3d ed. (New York: Macmillan, 1975); Frank Lawrence Owsley, *Plain Folk of the Old South* (Baton Rouge: Louisiana State University Press, 1949).

14. *Baton Rouge Gazette,* November 24, 1843; Gabriel Audisio, "Crisis in Baton Rouge, 1840–1860: Foreshadowing the Demise of Louisiana's French Language?" *Louisiana History* 29 (1988): 343–63; Francis Leon Gassler, *History of St. Joseph's Church, Baton Rouge, La., from 1789 to Date* (Marrero, La.: New Hope Press, 1943), pp. 47–62.

15. Audisio, "Crisis in Baton Rouge," pp. 343–51.

16. T. N. McMullan, comp., *Louisiana Newspapers, 1794–1961: A Union List of Louisiana Newspaper Files Available in Public, College and University Libraries in Louisiana* (Baton Rouge: Louisiana State University Library in cooperation with the Louisiana Library Association; 1965); Winifred Gregory, ed., *American Newspapers, 1821–1936: A Union List of Files Available in the United States and Canada* (New York: H. W. Wilson, 1937). See also the *Napoleonville Pioneer of Assumption,* June 16, 1877.

17. Alexandre Barde, *The Vigilante Committees of the Attakapas: An Eyewitness Account of Banditry and Backlash in Southwestern Louisiana,* trans. Henrietta Guilbeau Rogers, ed. David C. Edmonds and Dennis Gibson (Lafayette, La.: Acadiana Press, 1981), p. 95.

18. Victor Tixier, *Tixier's Travels on the Osage Prairies,* trans. Albert J. Salvan, ed. John Francis McDermott (1940; rpt. Norman: University of Oklahoma Press, 1968), p. 39.

19. See Estaville, "Louisiana French Language," pp. 107–20; Estaville, "The Louisiana French in 1900," *Journal of Historical Geography* 14 (1988): 342–59; Carl A. Brasseaux, "Four Hundred Years of Acadian Life in North America," *Journal of Popular Culture* 23 (1989): 3–23.

20. George E. Harris to William B. Benson, Plaquemine, La., March 5, 1867, no. 2426, microfilm copy in Hill Memorial Library, Louisiana State University, Baton Rouge, Louisiana.

21. See, for example, Louis Hébert, Autobiography; Frederick Law Olmsted, *A Journey through Texas,* 2 vols., 2d ed. (New York: G. P. Putnam's Sons, 1904), 2:396; Estaville, "Louisiana French in 1900," p. 346; quote from Audisio, "Crisis in Baton Rouge," p. 360.

22. Article VI, Section 15, of the Louisiana constitution of 1812 had "established English as the language of Louisiana law" (Warren M. Bil-

lings, ed., *The Historic Rules of the Supreme Court of Louisiana, 1813—1879* [Lafayette, La.: Center for Louisiana Studies, 1985], p. 6, n. 15). For patterns of language usage, as well as references to Alfred Mouton's nickname, see Alexandre Mouton to Zelia Rousseau Mouton, January 30, 1830, Alexandre Mouton Papers, Personal Correspondence, Collection 40, folder 1-j, Southwestern Archives, University of Southwestern Louisiana, Lafayette, Louisiana. All of the following references in this note are taken from this collection: Alexandre Mouton to Zelia Rousseau Mouton, January 27, February 3, 1830, folder 1-j; Zelia Rousseau Mouton to Alexandre Mouton, February 6, 1829 [actually 1830], February 16, 20, 1830, folder 1-j; Zelia Rousseau Mouton to Alexandre Mouton, February 22, 1830, folder 1-k. See also Odeide Mouton to an unidentified sister, August 23, 1863, folder 1-ff; Alexandre Mouton to Emma Gardner, July 27, 1848, folder 1-ee.

23. Louis Hébert, Autobiography; Arthur W. Bergeron, Jr., "Hébert, Louis," in Glenn R. Conrad, ed., *Dictionary of Louisiana Biography,* 2 vols. (New Orleans: Louisiana Historical Association, 1988), 1:392.

24. Louis Hébert, Autobiography; Bergeron, "Hébert."

25. George E. Harris to William B. Benson, Plaquemine, La., March 5, 1867.

26. *Plaquemine Iberville South,* August 26, 1865; *Opelousas Courier,* April 17, 24, May 22, 29, 1869.

27. William Charles Cole Claiborne, *Official Letter Books of W. C. C. Claiborne, 1801—1816,* ed. Dunbar Rowland, 6 vols. (Jackson: Mississippi Department of Archives and History, 1917); Joseph T. Hatfield, *William Claiborne: Jeffersonian Centurion in the American Southwest* (Lafayette, La.: Center for Louisiana Studies, 1976).

28. *Baton Rouge Gazette,* quoted in Audisio, "Crisis in Baton Rouge," p. 358.

29. Leon C. Soulé, "Know-Nothing Party," in David C. Roller and Robert W. Twyman, eds., *The Encyclopedia of Southern History* (Baton Rouge: Louisiana State University Press, 1979), pp. 692—93; Marius M. Carrière, Jr., "The Know Nothing Movement in Louisiana" (Ph.D. dissertation, Louisiana State University, 1977); Leon C. Soulé, *The Know Nothing Party in New Orleans: A Reappraisal* (Baton Rouge: Louisiana State University Press, 1961); W. Darrell Overdyke, *The Know-Nothing Party in the South* (Baton Rouge: Louisiana State University Press, 1950).

30. Carrière, "Know Nothing Movement," pp. 91, 100, 109—12, 115, 138, 139, 144—46, 154—55, 162; *Baton Rouge Weekly Comet,* April 16, 1856; *Thibodaux Minerva,* May 10, 1856.

31. Timothy F. Reilly, "Early Acadiana through Anglo-American Eyes," *Attakapas Gazette* 12 (1977): 159.

32. Ibid., pp. 159—76.

33. Albert Rhoads, "The Louisiana Creoles," *Galaxy* 14 (July 1873): 253.

34. Reilly, "Early Acadiana," pp. 159–60.

35. A. R. Waud, "Acadians of Louisiana," *Harper's Weekly*, October 20, 1866, p. 670.

36. Rhoads, "Louisiana Creoles," p. 154.

37. See, for example, the letter from "Improve" in the *Thibodaux Sentinel*, February 25, 1871.

38. Frederick Law Olmsted, *A Journey in the Seaboard Slave States in the Years 1853–1854, with Remarks on Their Economy*, 2 vols. (1856; rpt. New York: G. P. Putnam's Sons, 1904), 2:332–33.

39. R. L. Daniels, "The Acadians of Louisiana," *Scribner's Monthly* 19 (1879–80): 384; letter from "Louisianais" in the *Thibodaux Sentinel*, January 30, 1875; George Washington Cable, "Notes on Acadians in Louisiana," p. 111, Cable Collection, Manuscripts Division, Tulane University Library, New Orleans, Louisiana; photostatic copy on deposit at the Jefferson-Caffery Louisiana Room, Dupré Library, University of Southwestern Louisiana, Lafayette, Louisiana.

40. See the letter from "Louisianais" in the *Thibodaux Sentinel*, January 30, 1875.

41. See Charles Nordhoff, *The Cotton States in the Spring and Summer of 1875*, 2d ed. (New York: D. Appleton, 1876), p. 73; Alcée Fortier, *Louisiana Studies, Literature, Customs and Dialects, History and Education* (New Orleans: F. F. Hansell & Brother, 1894), pp. 163, 168–97.

42. See, for example, *Thibodaux Sentinel*, February 25, 1871.

43. The number of Acadian households in random Acadian parishes containing Creole and Anglo residents respectively were as follows: Lafayette Parish, 30, 24; St. Landry Parish, 61, 36; St. Martin Parish, 87, 13; Terrebonne Parish, 18, 21; West Baton Rouge Parish, 38, 19.

44. Cable, "Notes on Acadians," p. 130.

45. The data presented in this and the following four paragraphs regarding marital patterns are taken from Donald J. Hébert, comp., *Southwest Louisiana Records*, 35 vols. (Eunice/Cecilia, La.: Privately Published, 1974–80), vols. 8–12; Hébert, comp., *South Louisiana Records*, 11 vols. (Eunice/Cecilia, La.: Privately published, 1978–83), vol. 4.

46. 1870 census, Avoyelles, Jefferson, Livingston, Plaquemines, Pointe Coupee, St. Bernard, St. Charles, and St. John parishes.

47. 1870 census, Lafayette Parish. See also *New Orleans Republican*, March 10, 1870; *Lafayette Advertiser*, January 2, 16, July 17, 1869, April 24, 1870, March 15, 1873; *Thibodaux Sentinel*, September 9, 1865, January 13, 20, May 5, August 11, 1866, April 13, 1867, April 17, 24, 1869; *New Orleans Republican*, March 10, 1870; *Opelousas Courier*, April 26, December 10, 1865, May 12, 1866, March 10, April 2, 1870,

January 27, 1872, June 17, 1876; *Opelousas Journal,* June 10, 1871; U.S. House of Representatives; *House Report 261,* 43d Cong., 2d sess., p. 130; Estaville, "Louisiana French in 1900," p. 347.

48. *New Orleans Republican,* March 10, 1870; *Lafayette Advertiser,* January 2, 16, 1869, July 17, 1869, April 24, 1870, March 15, 1873; *Thibodaux Sentinel,* September 9, 1865, January 13, 20, May 5, August 11, 1866, April 13, 1867, April 17, 24, 1869; *Opelousas Courier,* April 26, December 10, 1865, May 12, 1866, March 10, April 2, 1870, January 27, 1872, June 17, 1876; *Opelousas Journal,* June 10, 1871; 1870 census, East Baton Rouge, Jefferson, and Orleans parishes.

49. Céline Fremaux Garcia, *Céline: Remembering Louisiana, 1850–1871,* ed. Patrick J. Geary (Athens, Ga.: University of Georgia Press, 1987); Whitelaw Reid, *After the War: A Tour of the Southern States, 1865–1866,* ed. C. Vann Woodward (New York: Harper & Row, 1965), p. 240.

50. 1870 census, Ascension, Assumption, Calcasieu, Cameron, Iberia, Iberville, Lafayette, Lafourche, St. James, St. Landry, St. Martin, St. Mary, Terrebonne, Vermilion, and West Baton Rouge parishes; Hébert, comp., *Southwest Louisiana Records,* vols. 8–12; Hébert, comp., *South Louisiana Records,* vol. 4.

51. 1870 census, Ascension, Assumption, Calcasieu, Cameron, Iberia, Iberville, Lafayette, Lafourche, St. James, St. Landry, St. Martin, St. Mary, Terrebonne, Vermilion, and St. Mary parishes.

52. 1870 census, Jefferson, Orleans, Plaquemines, Pointe Coupée, St. Charles, St. James, St. John, St. Landry, St. Martin, St. Mary, Terrebonne, and West Baton Rouge parishes.

53. Included in Cajun French are such Creole terms as *breme* for eggplant and such English words as *flask* and *though.* See Colette Guidry Leistner, "French and Acadian Influences upon the Cajun Cuisine of Southwest Louisiana" (M.A. thesis, University of Southwestern Louisiana, 1986), pp. 33–46, 78; John J. Guilbeau, "The French Spoken in Lafourche Parish, Louisiana" (Ph.D. dissertation, Universtiy of North Carolina at Chapel Hill, 1950), p. 20; William A. Read, *Louisiana French,* rev. ed. (Baton Rouge: Louisiana State University Press, 1963), pp. xvii–xviii; Jay K. Ditchy, *Les Acadiens Louisianais et leur parler* (Paris: Librairie E. Droz, 1932); Barry Jean Ancelet and Elemore Morgan, Jr., *The Makers of Cajun Music/Musiciens cadiens et creoles* (Austin: University of Texas Press, 1984), pp. 20–25; A. David Barry, "Biculturalism and Bilingualism: The Cajun Experience," in Jean Lafitte National Park, *The Cajuns: Their History and Culture,* 5 vols. in 13 parts (Opelousas, La.: Hamilton and Associates, 1987), vol. 3, pt. 9, pp. 257–67; Barry Jean Ancelet, "Louisiana French Oral Tradition: An Overview," ibid., vol. 3, pt. 9, pp. 277–342; "Français, Cadien, Cajin, Kahjan?" ibid., vol. 3, pt. 9, pp. 347–68; Ancelet, "Louisiana French Folklife," ibid., vol. 2, pt. 5, pp. 51–78. I am deeply indebted

to Ancelet for his assistance in preparing this discussion of postbellum south Louisiana's linguistic development.

54. Tixier, *Tixier's Travels,* pp. 39, 53; Olmsted, *Journey through Texas,* 2:403; Cable, "Notes on Acadians," p. 125; Rhoads, "Louisiana Creoles," p. 154; Harris to Benson, March 5, 1867; letter from "Louisianais" in the *Thibodaux Sentinel,* January 30, 1875. Alcée Fortier mistakenly viewed the Acadian community as monolithic in *Louisiana, Comprising Sketches of Counties, Towns, Events, Institutions and Persons, Arranged in Cyclopedic Form,* 3 vols. (Atlanta: Southern Historical Association, 1909), 1:20–21. This confusion has persisted. For a more recent example, see "Creoles Acadiens," *Amitiés Catholiques Françaises,* February 15, 1930.

55. Samuel H. Lockett, *Louisiana as It is: A Geographical and Topographical Description of the State,* ed. Lauren C. Post (Baton Rouge: Louisiana State University Press, 1969), pp. 51–52.

56. Carl A. Brasseaux et al. *The Courthouses of Louisiana,* USL Architecture Series 1 (Lafayette, La.: Center for Louisiana Studies, 1977), pp. 75–78.

CHAPTER SEVEN

1. George Washington Cable, "Notes on Acadians in Louisiana," p. 147, Cable Collection, Manuscripts Division, Tulane University Library, New Orleans, Louisiana. See also Victor Tixier, *Tixier's Travels on the Osage Prairies,* trans. Albert J. Salvan, ed. John Francis McDermott (1940; rpt. Norman: University of Oklahoma Press, 1968), p. 40.

2. Cable, "Notes on Acadians," p. 147.

3. Richard Maxwell Brown, *Strain of Violence: Historical Studies of American Violence and Vigilantism* (New York: Oxford University Press, 1975), p. 4.

4. Ibid., pp. 96–143.

5. Ibid., pp. 97–98.

6. Ibid., p. 100.

7. Cable, "Notes on Acadians," pp. 133, 167; Harry Lewis Griffin, *The Attakapas Country: A History of Lafayette Parish* (1959; rpt. Gretna, La.: Pelican, 1974), pp. 131–32; Alexandre Barde, *The Vigilante Committees of the Attakapas: An Eyewitness Account of Banditry and Backlash in Southwestern Louisiana,* trans. Henrietta Guilbeau Rogers, ed. David C. Edmonds and Dennis Gibson (Lafayette, La.: Acadiana Press, 1981), pp. 35, 39, 42, 43, 55, 105.

8. Carl A. Brasseaux, *The Founding of New Acadia: The Beginning of Acadian Life in Louisiana, 1765–1803* (Baton Rouge: Louisiana State University Press, 1987), pp. 8, 144.

9. Brown, *Strain of Violence,* p. 150.

10. *Napoleonville Pioneer of Assumption,* December 14, 1856, quoted in *Houma Ceres,* December 20, 1856; *Houme Ceres,* December 27, 1856, January 3, 1857.

11. Brown, *Strain of Violence,* pp. 100–101, 134–43, 305–19.

12. Barde, *Vigilante Committees,* pp. 6–90, 198–99.

13. Ibid.

14. Ibid., pp. 19–251.

15. Creoles constituted 23.34 percent of all known vigilantes, Anglos, 11.67 percent, and French Immigrants, 3.34 percent.

16. Barde, *Vigilante Committees,* pp. 197–99.

17. Ibid., pp. 120–34.

18. Ibid., pp. 197–251.

19. Though identified by Barde as "Don Louis F. J. Broussard," this person was probably Don Louis Broussard, a founder of the Cote Gelée committee (ibid., p. 203).

20. Ibid., pp. 13, 202–3.

21. Ibid., pp. 208–13, 228, 249.

22. Ibid., pp. 212–22.

23. Ibid., pp. 212–27.

24. Ibid., pp. 233–39.

25. Ibid., pp. 236–41, 254. A contemporary news article, however, places the total at between 121 and 136 persons—40 of whom fled upon the approach of the vigilantes, 71 who surrendered to vigilante forces, and 10 to 15 who managed to escape. See unidentified news clippings, Paul DeBaillon Papers, Collection 7, Box 4, folder 4–5, Southwestern Archives, University of Southwestern Louisiana, Lafayette, Louisiana.

26. Barde, *Vigilante Committees,* pp. 233–51.

27. Ibid., pp. 240–46.

28. The number of prisoners is based on an estimate by a contemporary journalist, who indicated that seventy-one antivigilantes surrendered when ordered to lay down their arms and that an additional ten to fifteen persons had escaped. Alexandre Barde does not give the total number of prisoners taken at Bayou Queue de Tortue. The number reported by the contemporary press and secondary sources varies widely. Historian Harry Lewis Griffin, who does not cite his sources, has maintained that "two hundred prisoners" were taken but that "all but eighty were released on their solemn pledge never again to molest the peace of the district" (Griffin, *Attakapas Country,* p. 136). For a contemporary report, see unidentified news clippings, DeBaillon Papers.

29. Vigilantes claimed that Geneus Guidry died of self-inflicted gunshot wounds to the head *and* self-inflicted multiple stab wounds. The nature of Guidry's wounds, however, suggests that he was murdered by vigilantes (Barde, *Vigilante Committees,* pp. 246–50).

The translation of Barde's book omits his discussion of unfavorable press coverage of the September 3, 1859, incident. For excerpts of the major local news articles, see Barde, *Histoire des comités de vigilance aux Attakapas* (Hahnville, La.: *Le Meschacebé* 1861), pp. 402–12. See ibid., p. 400, regarding the number of lashes given to the prisoners. Newspaper sources identify Jean-Baptiste Chiasson, Joseph Dédé Istre, James Jankins, and Emilien Lagrange as being among those receiving 120 lashes (unidentified news clippings, DeBaillon Papers).

30. See Barde, *Comités de vigilance*, pp. 402–12.

31. Ibid.; *Opelousas Courier*, April 21, 1860.

32. *OR*, Ser. 1, vol. 15, pp. 245, 393; *Opelousas Courier*, August 15, 1863; General Order No. 55, Bureau of Conscription, Trans-Mississippi Department, ibid., August 20, 1864; 1860 census, St. Landry Parish, p. 130.

33. *Opelousas Courier*, April 21, 1860; Carl A. Brasseaux, "Ozémé Carrière and the St. Landry Jayhawkers," *Attakapas Gazette* 13 (1978): 186.

34. *Opelousas Courier*, August 15, 1863.

35. Ibid., February 20, March 5, 1864, January 28, 1865; *OR*, Ser. 1, vol. 34, p. 599, 962–77; John D. Winters, *The Civil War in Louisiana* (Baton Rouge: Louisiana State University Press, 1963), p. 306.

36. *OR*, Ser. 1, vol. 34, pp. 966 (quotation), 962–68.

37. Ibid., p. 966.

38. Ibid., Ser. 1, vol. 26, p. 978; vol. 34, p. 599; *New Orleans Tribune* quoted in *Opelousas Courier*, August 12, 1865.

39. *OR*, Ser. 1, vol. 34, pp. 962, 965–67; Proclamation by Major-General Richard Taylor, May 18, 1864, Louis Amédée Bringier Papers, Department of Archives, Louisiana State University, Baton Rouge, Louisiana.

40. *Opelousas Courier*, March 5, September 10, October 10, 29, 1864; Louis Amédée Bringier to Stella Bringier, April 21, 1864, Bringier to his son, November 26, 1864, Bringier to Headquarters, January 1, 3, 1865, Bringier Papers.

41. Brasseaux, "Ozémé Carrière," pp. 188–89.

42. *New Orleans Republican* quoted in *Opelousas Courier*, August 12, 1865; *Opelousas Courier*, December 18, 1865, January 20, February 3, 1866; C. Peter Ripley, *Slaves and Freedmen in Civil War Louisiana* (Baton Rouge: Louisiana State University Press, 1976), pp. 96–99.

43. Cable, "Notes on Acadians," pp. 147, 158.

44. *Opelousas Courier*, December 4, 1869; U.S. House of Representatives, *Miscellaneous Document 211*, 42d Cong., 2d sess., pp. 165–74, 347–48.

45. On the racial dimension of vigilante activities, see Claude Oubre and Roscoe Leonard, "Free and Proud: St. Landry's *Gens de Couleur*," in Vaughan B. Baker and Jean T. Kreamer, eds., *Louisiana Tapestry: The Eth-*

nic Weave of St. Landry Parish (Lafayette, La.: Center for Louisiana Studies, 1982), pp. 70–81; and Claude Oubre, "St. Landry's *Gens de Couleur Libre:* The Impact of War and Reconstruction," ibid., pp. 82–90.

46. *Acts Passed at the First Session of the Fifteenth Legislature of the State of Louisiana, 1841* (New Orleans, 1841), pp. 32–33; *Opelousas Gazette,* May 28, July 9, 1842; *Houma Ceres,* December 20, 27, 1856.

47. 1870 census, Ascension, Assumption, Calcasieu, Cameron, Iberia, Iberville, Lafayette, Lafourche, St. James, St. Landry, St. Martin, St. Mary, Terrebonne, Vermilion, and West Baton Rouge parishes.

48. Comparative studies of cross-cultural borrowing are limited by the absence of works delineating the impact of local Francophone cultures on Acadiana's immense African-American population. See Barry Jean Ancelet, Jay D. Edwards, and Glen Pitre, *Cajun Country* (Jackson: University Press of Mississippi, 1991), pp. 149–51, 156, 158, 170, 183, 185; James H. Dormon, *The People Called Cajuns: An Introduction to an Ethnihistory* (Lafayette, La.: Center for Louisiana Studies, 1983), pp. 38–39.

49. *Thibodaux Sentinel,* October 14, November 11, 18, 1865, August 14, October 30, 1869; *Opelousas Courier,* December 26, 1868, April 24, 1869.

50. Geraldine Mary McTigue has found that "freedmen became most restless in counties [parishes] policed by colored soldiers" ("Forms of Racial Interaction in Louisiana, 1860–1880" [Ph.D. dissertation, Yale University, 1975], p. 142; see also pp. 124–41).

51. *Renaissance Louisianaise* (New Orleans), quoted in *Opelousas Courier,* August 5, 1865; my translation. See also *Opelousas Courier,* December 2, 1865.

52. *Opelousas Courier,* January 25, 1868. See also ibid., May 25, 1867, December 26, 1868, April 24, 1869; and articles regarding the arrest of Charles Davis, "the notorious robber, house burner and murderer, who . . . was the captain of the band of outlaws who infested the Attakapas country a few years ago," in the *Lafayette Advertiser,* January 11–25, 1873. See also ibid., September 25, 1869.

53. *Thibodaux Sentinel,* October 14, November 11, 18, 1865, August 14, October 30, 1869; *Opelousas Courier,* December 2, 1865, December 8, 1866, June 1, 1867.

54. Joe Gray Taylor, *Louisiana Reconstructed, 1863–1877* (Baton Rouge: Louisiana State University Press, 1974), p. 98; Henry Clay Warmoth, *War, Politics and Reconstruction: Stormy Days in Louisiana* (New York: Macmillan, 1930), p. 42.

55. Leon F. Litwack, *Been in the Storm So Long: The Aftermath of Slavery* (New York: Knopf, 1979), p. 428; see p. 368 for a detailed description of the punishment specified for offenders. For the storm of controversy that it precipitated between Colonel R. F. Atkins, the local military commander who approved the code, and Thomas W. Conway, head of the

Freedmen's Bureau in Louisiana, see Howard A. White, *The Freedmen's Bureau in Louisiana* (Baton Rouge: Louisiana State University Press, 1970), pp. 20–21. For a discussion of West Baton Rouge Parish's black code, see Ripley, *Slaves and Freedmen*, p. 191; see p. 193 for a discussion of the patrols established to enforce the code in St. James Parish.

56. *Opelousas Courier,* May 25, 1867. On other contemporary attempts to increase Louisiana's white electorate, see Taylor, *Louisiana Reconstructed,* p. 165.

57. *Opelousas Courier,* April 3, November 11, 1865, March 31, May 12, 1866; James G. Dauphine, "The Knights of the White Camelia and the Election of 1868: Louisiana's White Terrorists, a Benighting Legacy," *Louisiana History* 30 (1989): 181.

58. Taylor, *Louisiana Reconstructed,* pp. 129–37, 143–44; Allen W. Trelease, *White Terror: The Ku Klux Klan Conspiracy and Southern Reconstruction* (New York: Harper & Row, 1971), p. 51.

59. John D. Barnhart, ed., "Reconstruction on the Lower Mississippi," *Mississippi Valley Historical Review* 21 (1934): 394.

60. Taylor, *Louisiana Reconstructed,* p. 145. For the use of intimidation by military authorities, see Joseph G. Dawson III, *Army Generals and Reconstruction: Louisiana, 1862–1877* (Baton Rouge: Louisiana State University Press, 1982), pp. 200–215.

61. R. L. Daniels, "The Acadians of Louisiana," *Scribner's Monthly* 19 (1879–80): 386.

62. Taylor, *Louisiana Reconstructed,* p. 145; Dauphine, "Knights of the White Camelia," 173.

63. Testimony of Thomas Conway, February 22, 1866, *Report of the Joint Committee on Reconstruction, at the First Session, Thirty-Ninth Congress,* 4 parts (Washington, D.C.: U.S. Government Printing Office, 1966), pt. 4, p. 82; Lawrence E. Estaville, Jr., "The Louisiana French Language in the Nineteenth Century," *Southeastern Geographer* 30 (1990): 111; McTigue, "Forms of Racial Interaction," pp. 149–54; Ripley, *Slaves and Freedmen,* p. 139; Alcée Fortier, *Louisiana Studies, Literature, Customs and Dialects, History and Education* (New Orleans: F. F. Hansell & Brother, 1894), p. 175.

64. James G. Dauphine, "The Knights of the White Camelia in Louisiana, 1867 to 1869" (M.A. thesis, University of Southwestern Louisiana, 1983), pp. 34–36; U.S. House of Representatives, *Report 261,* 43d Cong., 2d sess., p. 109.

65. Trelease, *White Terror,* pp. 92–93; John Rose Ficklen, *History of Reconstruction in Louisiana (through 1868)* (1910; rpt. Gloucester, Mass.: Peter Smith, 1966), pp. 218–19. Other contemporary sources, compiled by congressional investigators, maintained that organization of the White League was also, in part, a response to prevailing lawlessness. "It was

proven that crime and lawlessness were rampant; that robberies and burglaries were of almost daily occurrence; that citizens, and even ladies of the highest position and respectability, were assaulted and robbed on the most public streets in broad daylight; and that, finally, the very best class of the citizens—merchants, bankers, professional men, and others—organized under the name of the White League for protective purposes" (House of Representatives, *Report 261*, 43d Cong., 2d sess., p. 4).

66. Trelease, *White Terror*, pp. 92–95, 128; Dauphine, "Knights of the White Camelia in Louisiana, 1867 to 1868," p. 50; Taylor, *Louisiana Reconstructed*, pp. 151–55.

67. See Charles Homer Mouton's speech, in English, in the DeBaillon Papers, Collection 7, box 4, folder 4-8; *Opelousas Courier*, August 1, September 5, 1868; Dauphine, "Knights of the White Camelia in Louisiana, 1867 to 1869," pp. 50–51.

68. Dauphine, "Knights of the White Camelia in Louisiana, 1867 to 1869," pp. 54–55.

69. Claude F. Oubre, "The Opelousas Riot of 1868," *Attakapas Gazette* 8 (1973): 139–52; R. A. Littell and James M. Thompson were the leaders of the St. Landry Knights of the White Camelia during the so-called Opelousas Riot. See Dauphine, "Knights of the White Camelia," p. 184. There is considerable scholarly disagreement over the spelling of Bentley's name. The spelling used here is taken from U.S. House of Representatives, *Miscellaneous Document 211*, 42d Cong., 2d sess., p. 311, which was derived from the journalist-educator's signature.

70. Oubre, "Opelousas Riot," pp. 139–52; Carolyn E. DeLatte, "The St. Landry Riot: A Forgotten Incident of Reconstruction Violence," *Louisiana History* 17 (1976): 41–49.

71. Oubre, "Opelousas Riot," pp. 139–52; DeLatte, "St. Landry Riot," pp. 41–49; Dauphine, "Knights of the White Camelia in Louisiana, 1867 to 1869," pp. 53–54; U.S. House of Representatives, *Miscellaneous Document 154*, 41st Cong., 2d sess., pt. 1, pp. 406–16; U.S. House of Representatives, *Executive Document 30*, 44th Cong., 2d sess., pp. 183–84; U.S. Senate, *Report 41*, 42d Cong., 2d sess., pt. 1, pp. 251–52; McTigue, "Forms of Racial Interaction," pp. 293–98; Ted Tunnell, *Crucible of Reconstruction: War, Radicalism and Race in Louisiana, 1862–1877* (Baton Rouge: Louisiana State University Press, 1984), pp. 156–57.

72. Testimony by Oscar A. Rice in the case of *C. B. Darrall* v. *Adolphe Baily*, before E. C. Warton, U.S. commissioner in New Orleans, quoted in *Lafayette Advertiser*, July 3, 1869. For additional information regarding Rice, see U.S. House of Representatives, *Miscellaneous Document 211*, 42d Cong., 2d sess., pp. 206–7.

73. Dauphine, "Knights of the White Camelia in Louisiana, 1867 to

1869," pp. 53–54; *Opelousas Courier*, April 25, 1868; Taylor, *Louisiana Reconstructed*, p. 169; Frank Joseph Wetta, "The Louisiana Scalawags" (Ph.D. dissertation, Louisiana State University, 1977), p. 280.

74. Trelease, *White Terror*, pp. 51, 82, 447, n. 1; Tunnell, *Crucible of Reconstruction*, pp. 156–57.

75. Trelease, *White Terror*, p. 136; W. Dean Burnham, *Presidential Ballots, 1836–1892* (Baltimore: Johns Hopkins University Press, 1955), pp. 486–501; Taylor, *Louisiana Reconstructed*, pp. 180–82; Tunnell, *Crucible of Reconstruction*, pp. 156–57.

76. Taylor, *Louisiana Reconstructed*, pp. 227–46.

77. Ibid., pp. 183, 237–39.

78. Ibid., pp. 227–49.

79. Ibid., pp. 239–52.

80. Quoted ibid., pp. 281–82.

81. Ibid., pp. 281–85. The August 8, 1874, issue of the *Opelousas Courier* mistakenly asserts that there were only fourteen White League chapters in Lafayette Parish. For materials relating to the organization and early activities of the Franklin, Opelousas, and Lafayette chapters of the White League, see U.S. House of Representatives, *Miscellaneous Document 211*, 42d Cong., 2d sess., pp. 874–77.

82. Taylor, *Louisiana Reconstructed*, p. 285. Scalawags were native-born Republicans and Republican sympathizers. Acadians Gilbert Labauve of Vermilion Parish, Ernest P. Broussard of Vermilion(?) Parish, Judge Theogene Castille of St. Martin Parish, and V. Trahan of Vermilion Parish were reputed scalawags. As Wetta has noted, these scalawags were lower-priority targets than their carpetbagger cohorts, and they thus appear to have avoided much of the Reconstruction violence directed at the transplanted Northerners. See House of Representatives, *Miscellaneous Document 211*, 42d Cong., 2d sess., pp. 211, 270, 345, 794; *Lafayette Advertiser*, June 28, 1873; Wetta, "Louisiana Scalawags," p. 283.

Pierre Landry, a prominent Reconstruction-era Republican in Ascension Parish, was a former free man of color of Acadian and African-American parentage. See Charles Vincent, *Black Legislators in Louisiana during Reconstruction* (Baton Rouge: Louisiana State University Press, 1976), p. 144; House of Representatives, *Report 261*, 43d Cong., 2d sess., p. 26.

83. *Lafayette Advertiser*, March 29, April 5, 12, 1873.

84. Ibid., June 28, 1873; Taylor, *Louisiana Reconstructed*, pp. 274–75; Suzy Shea and Gertrude Taylor, "A Man for the People: Alcibiades DeBlanc and the St. Martinville Insurrection of 1873," *Attakapas Gazette* 14 (1979): 3–10; *New York Times*, May 11, 1873; *New Orleans Daily Picayune*, May 10, 11, 1873.

85. Taylor, *Louisiana Reconstructed*, pp. 274–75.

86. *New Iberia Louisiana Sugar Bowl,* August 1874; *New Orleans Daily Picayune,* August 18, 1874; H. Oscar Lestage, Jr., "The White League in Louisiana and Its Participation in Reconstruction," *Louisiana Historical Quarterly* 18 (1935): 656; Stuart O. Landry, *The Battle of Liberty Place: The Overthrow of Carpet-bag Rule in New Orleans, September 14, 1874* (New Orleans: Pelican, 1955), p. 48; Taylor, *Louisiana Reconstructed,* pp. 284–86; U.S. House of Representatives, *Report 261,* 43d Cong., 2d sess., pp. 27, 33–34, 123–24, 346, 348, 793, 876.

87. Taylor, *Louisiana Reconstructed,* pp. 286, 291–96.

88. U.S. House of Representatives, *Report 261,* 43d Cong., 2d sess., pp. 168, 171, 786–87. O. Delahoussaye, Jr., assistant supervisor of voter registration at St. Martinville, testified in 1874: "I understand in 1873, when the metropolitans were there, they [White Leaguers] had called on a certain founderyman, of [New] Iberia, and got him to get out two cannon, which had belonged to Fuller's battery [during the Civil War] and had been sunk in the bayou during the war, and paid him forty or fifty dollars to raise them and fix them." This cannon apparently helped intimidate the Federal occupation forces before the 1874 election (U.S. House of Representatives, *Miscellaneous Document 211,* 42d Cong., 2d sess., p. 351).

89. Taylor, *Louisiana Reconstructed,* pp. 297–313; U.S. House of Representatives, *Report 261,* 43d Cong., 2d sess., p. 93.

90. U.S. House of Representatives, *Report 261,* 43d Cong., 2d sess., p. 168.

91. Ibid., pp. 166, 347.

92. Taylor, *Louisiana Reconstructed,* pp. 480–505.

93. Ibid., pp. 194–97, 495–96.

94. Ibid., pp. 497–505.

95. William Lynwood Montell, *Killings: Folk Justice in the Upper South* (Lexington: University Press of Kentucky, 1986), pp. xiii–64.

CONCLUSION

1. W. H. Sparks, *The Memories of Fifty Years . . . ,* 4th ed. (Macon, Ga.: J. W. Burke, 1882), pp. 379–80.

2. Cajuns had customarily consumed far less potent alcoholic beverages before the Civil War. See George Washington Cable, "Notes on Acadians in Louisiana," pp. 126, 164, Cable Collection, Manuscripts Division, Tulane University Library, New Orleans, Louisiana.

Bibliography

Primary Sources

MANUSCRIPTS

Archivo General de Indias. Papeles Procedentes de Cuba, legajos 189A, 220, Seville, Spain.
Ascension Parish Original Acts, Books F through J, Ascension Parish Courthouse, Donaldsonville, Louisiana.
Ascension Parish Police Jury Minute Book, 1837–56, unpaginated. Ascension Parish Courthouse, Donaldsonville, Louisiana.
Bond, Priscilla "Mittie" Munnikhuysen. Diary. Department of Archives, Louisiana State University, Baton Rouge, Louisiana.
Bringier Papers. Department of Archives, Louisiana State University, Baton Rouge, Louisiana.
Bringier, Louis Amédée. Papers. Department of Archives, Louisiana State University, Baton Rouge, Louisiana.
British and American Claims Commission Records. Case 74, National Archives, Washington, D.C.
Burke, Walter J. Papers. Southwestern Archives, University of Southwestern Louisiana, Lafayette, Louisiana.
Cable, George Washington. "Notes on Acadians in Louisiana." Cable Collection, Manuscripts Division, Tulane University Library, New Orleans, Louisiana; photostatic copy on deposit at the Jefferson-Caffery Louisiana Room, Dupré Library, University of Southwestern Louisiana, Lafayette, Louisiana.

DeBaillon, Paul. Papers. Southwestern Archives, University of Southwestern Louisiana, Lafayette, Louisiana.

DeClouet Papers. Southwestern Archives, University of Southwestern Louisiana, Lafayette, Louisiana.

Douglas, Emily Caroline. Autobiography. Department of Archives, Louisiana State University, Baton Rouge, Louisiana.

Dupuy, Hélène. Diary. Department of Archives, Louisiana State University, Baton Rouge, Louisiana.

French and American Claims Commission Records. Claim 251, 307, 480, and 594, National Archives, Washington, D.C.

Harris, George E., to William B. Benson, Plaquemine, La., March 5, 1867. No. 2426, George E. Harris Papers, microfilm copy in Hill Memorial Library, Louisiana State University, Baton Rouge, Louisiana.

Hébert, Louis. Autobiography. Louis Hébert Papers, Hill Memorial Library, Louisiana State University, Baton Rouge, Louisiana.

Hébert, Louis. "A Condensed Autobiography of Louis Hébert." Photostatic copy in the author's possession.

Hyatt, Arthur. Papers. Department of Archives, Louisiana State University, Baton Rouge, Louisiana.

Iberville Parish Conveyance Book A-7. Clerk of Court's Office, Iberville Parish Courthouse, Plaquemine, Louisiana.

Lafayette Parish Police Jury Minute Book. Vol. 1. Lafayette Parish Courthouse, Lafayette, Louisiana.

Mouton, Alexander (grandson of Alexandre Mouton). Memoirs, Lucile Meredith Griffin Papers, Collection 26, Tablet 1, Southwestern Archives, University of Southwestern Louisiana, Lafayette, Louisiana.

Mouton, Alexandre. Papers. Collection 40, Southwestern Archives, University of Southwestern Louisiana, Lafayette, Louisiana.

Proclamation of the parishioners of St. Bernard Catholic Church, August 28, 1834. Grady Estillette Papers, Southwestern Archives, University of Southwestern Louisiana, Lafayette, Louisiana.

St. Landry Parish Police Jury Minute Books. Vol. 1. St. Landry Parish Courthouse, Opelousas, Louisiana.

St. Landry Parish Probate Records, 1805–60. St. Landry Parish Courthouse, Opelousas, Louisiana.

St. Martin Parish Original Acts. St. Martinville Courthouse, St. Martinville, Louisiana.

St. Martin Parish Police Jury Minute Books. Vol. 1. St. Martin Parish Courthouse, St. Martinville, Louisiana.

FEDERAL CENSUS REPORTS

Third Census of the United States, 1810, Population Schedules, Louisiana, National Archives, Washington, D.C.

Fifth Census of the United States, 1830, Population Schedules, Louisiana, National Archives, Washington, D.C.
Seventh Census of the United States, 1850, Population Schedules, Louisiana, National Archives, Washington, D.C.
Seventh Census of the United States, 1850, Agricultural Schedules, Louisiana, National Archives, Washington, D.C.
Seventh Census of the United States, 1850, Slave Schedules, Louisiana, National Archives, Washington, D.C.
Eighth Census of the United States, 1860, Agricultural Schedules, Louisiana, National Archives, Washington, D.C.
Eighth Census of the United States, 1860, Population Schedules, Louisiana, National Archives, Washington, D.C.
Eighth Census of the United States, 1860, Slave Schedules, Louisiana, National Archives, Washington, D.C.
Ninth Census of the United States, 1870, Agricultural Schedules, Louisiana, National Archives, Washington, D.C.
Ninth Census of the United States, 1870, Population Schedules, Louisiana, National Archives, Washington, D.C.

INTERVIEWS

Bergeron, Lastie. February 11, 1982, Lafayette, Louisiana.
Bergeron, Ozémae. July 19, 1978, Church Point, Louisiana.
LeJeune, Cléobule. July 15, 1975, and June 19, 1976, Pointe Noire, Louisiana.
Melançon, Duma. July 19, 1978, Church Point, Louisiana.
Melançon, Evon LeJeune. July 19, 1978, Church Point, Louisiana.

NEWSPAPERS

Abbeville Meridional, 1877–78.
Alexandria American, 1859.
Baton Rouge Gazette, 1845.
Franklin Attakapas Register, 1862.
Franklin Planters' Banner, 1849–75.
Houma Ceres, 1856.
Napoleonville Pioneer of Assumption, 1877.
New Iberia Louisiana Sugar Bowl, 1873–77.
New Orleans Bee, 1832–45.
New Orleans Daily Crescent, 1859.
New Orleans Daily Picayune, 1837–77.
New Orleans Louisiana Courier, 1828–60.
Opelousas Courier, 1852–77.

Opelousas Gazette, 1842−45.
Opelousas Journal, 1865−68.
Opelousas St. Landry Whig, 1844.
Plaquemine Gazette and Sentinel, 1860.
Plaquemine Iberville South, August 26, 1865−February 9, 1867.
Richmond (Ind.) *Palladium,* 1863.
St. Martinville Creole, 1845.
Thibodaux Minerva, 1853−56.
Thibodaux Sentinel, 1865−77.
West Baton Rouge Sugar Planter, 1860.

MICROFILM PUBLICATIONS OF THE NATIONAL ARCHIVES

Compiled Service Records of Volunteer Confederate Soldiers, Consolidated Eighteenth Louisiana Infantry and Yellow Jacket Battalion, Microcopy 320, Rolls 1−3.
Compiled Service Records of Volunteer Union Soldiers, Louisiana, First Battalion, Cavalry Scouts, Microcopy 396, Roll 11.
Records of the Louisiana State Government, 1850−88, Orders of the Adjutant General's Office, Microcopy 359, Roll 20.

BOOKS

Acts of Louisiana, 1805−65.
Allen, Henry Watkins. *Message of Gov. Henry W. Allen to the Legislature of the State of Louisiana.* Shreveport, La.: *Caddo Gazette,* 1863.
Barde, Alexandre. *Histoire des comités de vigilance aux Attakapas.* Hahnville, La.: *Le Meschacebé,* 1861.
―――. *The Vigilante Committees of the Attakapas: An Eyewitness Account of Banditry and Backlash in Southwestern Louisiana.* Translated by Henrietta Guilbeau Rogers. Edited by David C. Edmonds and Dennis Gibson. Lafayette, La.: Acadiana Press, 1981.
Bartlett, Napier. *Military Record of Louisiana.* . . . 1875. Reprint. Baton Rouge: Louisiana State University Press, 1964.
Bearss, Edward C., ed. *A Louisiana Confederate: Diary of Felix Pierre Poché.* Translated by Eugénie Watson Somdal. Natchitoches, La.: Louisiana Studies Institute, 1972.
Berquin-Duvallon, Pierre-Louis. *Vue de la colonie du Mississipi, ou des province de Louisiane et Florida occidentale, en l'anne'e 1802.* Paris: Imprimerie Expeditive, 1803.
Billings, Warren M., ed. *The Historic Rules of the Supreme Court of Louisiana, 1813−1879.* Lafayette, La.: Center for Louisiana Studies, 1985.

Brackenridge, Henry Marie. *Views of Louisiana, Together with a Journal of a Voyage Up the Mississippi River in 1811, 1814.* 1818. Reprint. Chicago: Quadrangle Books, 1962.

Carter, Clarence, ed. *The Territorial Papers of the United States.* Vol. 9, *The Territory of Orleans, 1803–1812.* Washington, D.C.: U.S. Government Printing Office, 1940.

Champomier, P. A. *Statement of the Sugar Crop Made in Louisiana, 1849–1859.* New Orleans: Magne and Weisse, 1860.

Claiborne, William Charles Cole. *Official Letter Books of W. C. C. Claiborne, 1801–1816.* Edited by Dunbar Rowland. 6 vols. Jackson, Miss.: Mississippi Department of Archives and History, 1917.

Constitution or Form of Government for the State of Louisiana. New Orleans: J. B. Baird, 1812.

Delegos, Pierre A. *Statement of the Sugar Made in 1828 and 1829.* New Orleans: Privately published, 1829.

Fitts, James Franklin. "The Yankee Officer and the Partisan." *Ballou's Monthly Magazine,* July 1869, pp. 54–59.

Fortier, Alcée. *Louisiana, Comprising Sketches of Counties, Towns, Events, Institutions and Persons, Arranged in Cyclopedic Form.* 3 vols. Atlanta: Southern Historical Association, 1909.

———. *Louisiana Studies, Literature, Customs and Dialects, History and Education.* New Orleans: F. F. Hansell & Brother, 1894.

Garcia, Céline Fremaux. *Céline: Remembering Louisiana, 1850–1871.* Edited by Patrick J. Geary. Athens, Ga.: University of Georgia Press, 1987.

Goodspeed Publishing Company. *Biographical and Historical Memoirs of Louisiana.* 2 vols. 1892. Reprint. Baton Rouge: Claitor's Publishing, 1975.

———. *Goodspeed's History of Southeast Missouri.* 1888. Reprint. Cape Girardeau, Mo.: Ramfire Reprints, 1964.

Hébert, Donald J., comp. *South Louisiana Records.* 11 vols. Eunice/Cecilia, La.: Privately published, 1978–83.

———. *Southwest Louisiana Records.* 35 vols. Eunice/Cecilia, La.: Privately published, 1974–90.

Irwin, Richard B. *History of the Nineteenth Army Corps.* New York: G. P. Putnam's Sons, 1892.

Journal of the Louisiana House of Representatives, 1812–52.

Journal of the Louisiana Senate, 1812–52.

Laussat, Pierre Clément. *Memoirs of My Life to My Son during the Years 1803 and after Which I Spent in Public Service in Louisiana as Commissioner of the French Government for the Retrocession to France of That Colony and for Its Transfer to the United States.* Baton Rouge: Louisiana State University for the Historic New Orleans Collection, 1978.

Lockett, Samuel H. *Louisiana as It Is: A Geographical and Topographical Description of the State.* Edited by Lauren C. Post. Baton Rouge: Louisiana State University Press, 1969.

Lyell, Charles. *A Second Visit to the United States of North America.* 2 vols. New York: Harper & Brothers, 1849.

Martin, Desirée. *Les vielées d'une soeur ou le destin d'un brin de mousse.* New Orleans: Imprimerie Cosmopolite, 1877.

Nordhoff, Charles. *The Cotton States in the Spring and Summer of 1875.* 2d ed. New York: D. Appleton, 1876.

Official Report Relative to the Conduct of Federal Troops in Western Louisiana during the Invasions of 1863 and 1864. Shreveport, La.: Caddo Gazette, 1865.

Olmsted, Frederick Law. *The Cotton Kingdom: A Traveller's Observations on Cotton and Slavery in the American Slave States.* 2 vols. New York: Mason Brothers, 1861.

———. *A Journey in the Seaboard Slave States, in the Years 1853–1854, with Remarks on Their Economy.* 2 vols. 1856. Reprint. New York: G. P. Putnam's Sons, 1904.

———. *A Journey through Texas.* 2 vols. 2d ed. New York: G. P. Putnam's Sons, 1904.

Perrin, William Henry. *Southwest Louisiana Biographical and Historical.* 2 parts. 1891. Reprint. Baton Rouge: Claitor's Publishing, 1971.

Pittman, Phillip. *Present State of the European Settlements on the Mississippi.* 1770. Reprint. Gainesville, Fla.: University Press of Florida, 1973.

Prentiss, George Lewis, ed. *A Memoir of S. S. Prentiss.* 2 vols. New York: Charles Scribner's Sons, 1855.

Reid, Whitelaw. *After the War: A Tour of the Southern States, 1865–1866.* Edited by C. Vann Woodward. New York: Harper & Row, 1965.

Report of the Joint Committee on Reconstruction, at the First Session, Thirty-Ninth Congress. 4 parts. Washington, D.C.: U.S. Government Printing Office, 1866.

Robin, Claude C. *Voyage to Louisiana.* Translated by Stuart O. Landry. New Orleans: Pelican, 1966.

Rowland, Dunbar, ed. *Official Letter Books of W. C. C. Claiborne, 1801–1816.* 6 vols. Jackson: Mississippi Department of Archives and History, 1917.

Sparks, W. H. *The Memories of Fifty Years: Containing Brief Biographical Notices of Distinguished Americans and Anecdotes of Remarkable Men; Interspersed with Scenes and Events Occurring during a Long Life Chiefly Spent in the Southwest.* 4th ed. Macon, Ga.: J. W. Burke, 1882.

Taylor, Richard. *Destruction and Reconstruction: Personal Experiences of the Late War.* New York: D. Appleton, 1879.

Tixier, Victor. *Tixier's Travels on the Osage Prairies.* Translated by Albert J. Salvan. Edited by John Francis McDermott. 1940. Reprint. Norman: University of Oklahoma Press, 1968.

Tunnard, W. H. *A Southern Record: The History of the Third Regiment, Louisiana Infantry.* Baton Rouge: Privately published, 1866.

U.S. Congress. *American State Papers: Public Lands.* 9 vols. Washington, D.C.: Gales & Seaton/Government Printing Office, 1832–73.

U.S. House of Representatives. *Executive Document 30.* 44th Cong., 2d sess.

———. *Miscellaneous Document 154, Pt. 1.* 41st Cong., 2d sess.

———. *Miscellaneous Document 211.* 42d Cong., 2d sess.

———. *Report 261.* 43d Cong., 2d sess.

U.S. Senate. *Executive Document 2.* 39th Cong., 1st sess.

———. *Report 41, Pt. 1.* 42d Cong., 2d sess.

U.S. War Department. *The War of the Rebellion: A Compilation of the Official Records of the Union and Confederate Armies.* 128 parts in 170 vols. Washington, D.C.: U.S. Government Printing Office, 1880–1901.

Warmoth, Henry Clay. *War, Politics and Reconstruction: Stormy Days in Louisiana.* New York: Macmillan, 1930.

Whipple, Henry P. *The Diary of a Private Soldier.* Waterloo, Wisc.: Privately published, 1906.

ARTICLES

Baker, Vaughan, ed. "Glimpses of New Iberia in the Civil War." *Attakapas Gazette* 6 (1971): 87.

Barnhart, John D., ed., "Reconstruction on the Lower Mississippi." *Mississippi Valley Historical Review* 21 (1934): 387–96.

Brasseaux, Carl A., trans. "Election of a Sindic in the Attakapas, 1773." *Attakapas Gazette* 12 (1977): 43.

———, trans. "Petition of the *Habitants* for the Destruction of Stray Cattle." *Attakapas Gazette* 11 (1976): 78–79.

———, ed. "The Glory Days: E. T. King Recalls the Civil War." *Attakapas Gazette* 11 (1976): 3–34.

Daniels, R. L. "The Acadians of Louisiana." *Scribner's Monthly* 14 (1879–80): 383–92.

LeBlanc, André. "The Parish of Assumption." *De Bow's Review* 9 (1850): 286–93.

Pierce, G. W. "Terrebonne." *De Bow's Review* 11 (1851): 601–11.

Prichard, Walter, Fred B. Kniffen, and Clair A. Brown, eds. "Southern Louisiana and Southern Alabama in 1819: The Journal of James Leander Cathcart." *Louisiana Historical Quarterly* 28 (1943): 735–921.

Pugh, W. W. "Bayou Lafourche from 1820 to 1825: Its Inhabitants, Customs and Pursuits." *Louisiana Planter and Sugar Manufacturer,* October 29, 1888, p. 143.

Reinecke, George F., trans. and ed. "Early Louisiana French Life and Folklore: From the Anonymous Breaux Manuscript, as Edited by Professor Jay K. Ditchy." *Louisiana Folklore Miscellany* 2 (1966): 1–58.

Rhoads, Albert. "The Louisiana Creoles." *Galaxy* 14 (July 1873): 253.

"A Trip to the Attakapas in Olden Times." *Attakapas Gazette* 8 (1973): 25.

Warner, Charles Dudley. "The Acadian Land." Edited by James H. Dormon. *Attakapas Gazette* 7 (1972): 157–69.

Waud, A. R. "Acadians of Louisiana." *Harper's Weekly,* October 20, 1866, p. 670.

Wilkinson, Jehu. "Judge Jehu Wilkinson's Reminiscences." *Attakapas Gazette* 11 (1976): 141–42.

SECONDARY SOURCES

BOOKS

Adams, William H. *The Whig Party in Louisiana.* Lafayette, La.: Center for Louisiana Studies, 1973.

Allain, Mathé. *Not Worth a Straw: French Colonial Policy and the Early Years of Louisiana.* Lafayette, La.: Center for Louisiana Studies, 1988.

Ancelet, Barry Jean, Jay D. Edwards, and Glen Pitre. *Cajun Country.* Folklife in the South Series. Jackson: University Press of Mississippi, 1991.

Ancelet, Barry Jean, and Elemore Morgan, Jr. *The Makers of Cajun Music/ Musiciens cadiens et créoles.* Austin: University of Texas Press, 1984.

Aptheker, Herbert. *Nat Turner's Slave Rebellion: Together with the Full Text of the So-Called "Confessions" of Nat Turner, Made in Prison in 1831.* New York: Grove Press, 1968.

Arceneaux, William. *Acadian General: Alfred Mouton and the Civil War.* Lafayette, La.: Center for Louisiana Studies, 1972.

Baudier, Roger. *The Catholic Church in Louisiana.* 1939. Reprint. Baton Rouge: Louisiana Library Association, 1972.

Biographical Directory of the American Congress, 1774–1949. Washington, D.C.: U.S. Government Printing Office, 1950.

Boudreau, Marielle, and Melvin Gallant. *La cuisine traditionelle en Acadie.* Moncton, N.B.: Editions d'Acadie, 1975.

Brasseaux, Carl A. *The Founding of New Acadia: The Beginnings of Acadian Life in Louisiana, 1765–1803.* Baton Rouge: Louisiana State University Press, 1987.

————. *In Search of Evangeline: Birth and Evolution of the Evangeline Myth.* Thibodaux, La.: Blue Heron Press, 1988.

————. *Lafayette: Where Yesterday Meets Tomorrow, an Illustrated History.* Chatsworth, Calif.: Windsor Publications, 1990.

————, et al. *The Courthouses of Louisiana.* USL Architecture Series, No. 1. Lafayette, La.: Center for Louisiana Studies, 1977.

————, comp. *The "Foreign French: Nineteenth-Century French Immigration into Louisiana.* Vol. 1, *1820–1839.* Lafayette, La.: Center for Louisiana Studies, 1990.

Brown, Richard Maxwell. *Strain of Violence: Historical Studies of American Violence and Vigilantism.* New York: Oxford University Press, 1975.

Burnham, W. Dean. *Presidential Ballots, 1836–1892.* Baltimore: Johns Hopkins University Press, 1955.

Cable, George Washington. *The Creoles of Louisiana.* London: John C. Nimmo, 1885.

Calan, Louise. *Philippine Duchesne: Frontier Missionary of the Sacred Heart.* Westminster, Md.: Neuman Press, 1957.

Caskey, Willie Malvin. *Secession and Restoration of Louisiana.* Baton Rouge: Louisiana State University Press, 1938.

Comeaux, Malcolm. *Atchafalaya Swamp Life: Settlement and Folk Occupations.* Baton Rouge: Louisiana State University Press, 1972.

Conrad, Glenn R., ed. *The Cajuns: Essays on Their History and Culture.* Lafayette, La.: Center for Louisiana Studies, 1978.

————. *Dictionary of Louisiana Biography.* 2 vols. New Orleans: Louisiana Historical Association, 1988.

————, comp. *Land Records of the Attakapas District.* Vol. 1, *The Attakapas Domesday Book: Land Grants, Claims and Confirmations in the Attakapas District, 1764–1826.* Lafayette, La.: Center for Louisiana Studies, 1990.

————. *New Iberia: Essays on the Town and Its People.* Lafayette, La.: Center for Louisiana Studies, 1979.

Conrad, Glenn R., and Vaughan B. Baker, eds. *Louisiana Gothic: Recollections of the 1930s.* Lafayette, La.: Center for Louisiana Studies, 1984.

Creté, Lilian. *Daily Life in Louisiana, 1815–1830.* Translated by Patrick Gregory. Baton Rouge: Louisiana State University Press, 1981.

Davis, Nanciellen. *Ethnicity and Ethnic Group Persistence in an Acadian Village in Maritime Canada.* New York: AMS Press, 1985.

Dawson, Joseph G., III. *Army Generals and Reconstruction: Louisiana, 1862–1877.* Baton Rouge: Louisiana State University Press, 1982.

Del Sesto, Steven L., and Jon L. Gibson, eds. *The Culture of Acadiana: Tradition and Change in South Louisiana.* Lafayette, La.: University of Southwestern Louisiana, 1975.

De Ville, Winston. *Opelousas: The History of a French and Spanish Military Post in America, 1716–1803.* Cottonport, La.: Polyanthos, 1973.

Ditchy, Jay K. *Les Acadiens Louisianais et leur parler.* Paris: Librairie E. Droz, 1932.

Doré, Susan Cole. *The Pelican Guide to Plantation Homes of Louisiana.* Gretna, La.: Pelican, 1989.

Dormon, James H. *The People Called Cajuns: An Introduction to an Ethnihistory.* Lafayette, La.: Center for Louisiana Studies, 1983.

Eaton, Clement. *The Civilization of the Old South: Writings of Clement Eaton.* Edited by Albert D. Kirwan. Lexington, Ky.: University of Kentucky Press, 1968.

———. *A History of the Old South: Emergence of a Reluctant Nation.* 3d ed. New York: Macmillan, 1975.

Eccles, William J. *The Canadian Frontier, 1534–1760.* Albuquerque: University of New Mexico Press, 1969.

———. *France in America.* New York: Harper & Row, 1972.

Edmonds, David C. *Yankee Autumn in Acadiana: A Narrative of the Great Texas Overland Expedition through Southwest Louisiana, October–December 1863.* Lafayette, La.: Acadiana Press, 1979.

Ficklen, John Rose. *History of Reconstruction in Louisiana (through 1868).* 1910. Reprint. Gloucester, Mass.: Peter Smith, 1966.

Gahn, Robert. Sr. *A History of Evangeline: Its Land, Its Men and Its Women Who Made It a Beautiful Place to Live.* Baton Rouge: Claitor's Publishing, 1972.

Gard, Wayne. *Frontier Justice.* Norman: University of Oklahoma Press, 1949.

Gassler, Francis Leon. *History of St. Joseph's Church, Baton Rouge, La., from 1789 to Date.* Marrero, La.: New Hope Press, 1943.

Gates, Paul Wallace. *Agriculture and the Civil War.* New York: Knopf, 1965.

Greer, James K. *Louisiana Politics, 1845–1861.* Baton Rouge: Ramires-Jones Printing Company, 1930.

Gregory, Winifred, ed. *American Newspapers, 1821–1936: A Union List of Files Available in the United State and Canada.* New York: H. W. Wilson, 1937.

Griffin, Harry Lewis. *Attakapas Country: A History of Lafayette Parish.* 1959. Reprint. Gretna, La.: Pelican, 1974.

Harris, R. C. *The Seigneurial System in Early Canada.* Madison: University of Wisconsin Press, 1966.

Hatfield, Joseph T. *William Claiborne: Jeffersonian Centurion in the American Southwest.* Lafayette, La.: Center for Louisiana Studies, 1976.

Hilliard, Sam Bowers. *Hog Meat and Hoecake: Food Supply in the Old South, 1840–1860.* Carbondale: Southern Illinois University Press, 1972.

Howard, Perry. *Political Tendencies in Louisiana.* 2d ed. Baton Rouge: Louisiana State University Press, 1971.

Huber, Leonard V. *Creole Collage: Reflections on the Colorful Customs of Latter-Day New Orleans Creoles.* Lafayette, La.: Center for Louisiana Studies, 1980.

————. *Louisiana: A Pictorial History.* New York: Charles Scribner's Sons, 1975.

Hunt, Chester L., and Lewis Walker. *Ethnic Dynamics: Patterns of Intergroup Relations in Various Societies.* Homewood, Ill.: Dorsey Press, 1974.

Jackson, Ronald Vern, ed. *Louisiana, 1870.* Salt Lake City: Accelerated Indexing Systems International, 1987.

Jacob, Margaret C. *The Radical Enlightenment: Pantheists, Freemasons and Republicans.* London: George Allen & Unwin, 1981.

Jean Lafitte National Park. *The Cajuns: Their History and Culture.* 5 vols. in 13 parts. Opelousas, La.: Hamilton and Associates, 1987.

Landry, Stuart O. *The Battle of Liberty Place: The Overthrow of Carpet-bag Rule in New Orleans, September 14, 1874.* New Orleans: Pelican, 1955.

LeBlanc, Dudley J. *The Acadian Miracle.* Lafayette, La.: Privately published, 1966.

————. *The True Story of the Acadians.* Lafayette, La.: Privately published, 1932.

Lieberson, Stanley. *Language and Ethnic Relations in Canada.* New York: Wiley, 1970.

Litwack, Leon F. *Been in the Storm So Long: The Aftermath of Slavery.* New York: Knopf, 1979.

Lonn, Ella. *Reconstruction in Louisiana after 1868.* 1918. Reprint. New York: Russell & Russell, 1967.

McMullan, T. N., comp. *Louisiana Newspapers, 1794–1961: A Union List of Louisiana Newspaper Files Available in Public, College and University Libraries in Louisiana.* Baton Rouge: Louisiana State University Library in cooperation with the Louisiana Library Association, 1965.

McWhiney, Grady. *Cracker Culture: Celtic Ways in the Old South.* University, Ala.: University of Alabama Press, 1988.

Marchand, Sidney A. *The Flight of a Century (1800–1900) in Ascension Parish, Louisiana.* Donaldsonville, La.: Privately published, 1936.

Mason, Philip. *Patterns of Dominance.* New York: Oxford University Press, 1970.

Menn, Karl Joseph, comp. *Large Shareholders of Louisiana.* New Orleans: Pelican, 1964.

Montell, William Lynwood. *Killings: Folk Justice in the Upper South.* Lexington: University Press of Kentucky, 1986.

Morris, Raymond N., and C. Michael Lamphier. *Three Scales of Inequality: Perspectives on French-English Relations.* Don Mills, Ont.: Longmans Canada, 1977.

Mouton, J. Franklin III, comp. and ed. *The Moutons: A Genealogy.* Lafayette, La.: Privately published, 1978.

Oubre, Claude F. *Forty Acres and a Mule: The Freedmen's Bureau and Black Land Ownership.* Baton Rouge: Louisiana State University Press, 1978.

Overdyke, W. Darrell. *The Know-Nothing Party in the South.* Baton Rouge: Louisiana State University Press, 1950.

Owsley, Frank Lawrence. *Plain Folk of the Old South.* Baton Rouge: Louisiana State University Press, 1949.

Post, Lauren C. *Cajun Sketches: From the Prairies of Southwest Louisiana.* Baton Rouge: Louisiana State University Press, 1962.

Raphael, Morris. *The Battle in the Bayou Country.* Detroit: Harlo, 1975.

Read, William A. *Louisiana French.* 1931. Rev. ed. Baton Rouge: Louisiana State University Press, 1963.

Rees, Grover. *A Narrative History of Breaux Bridge, Once Called "La Pointe."* Lafayette, La.: Attakapas Historical Association, 1976.

Ripley, C. Peter. *Slaves and Freedmen in Civil War Louisiana.* Baton Rouge: Louisiana State University Press, 1976.

Roller, David C., and Robert W. Twyman, eds. *The Encyclopedia of Southern History.* Baton Rouge: Louisiana State University Press, 1979.

Rushton, William F. *The Cajuns: From Acadia to Louisiana.* New York: Farrar, Straus, Giroux, 1979.

Schermerhorn, Richard Alonzo. *Comparative Ethnic Relations: A Framework for Theory and Research.* New York: Random House, 1970.

Schmitz, Mark. *Economic Analysis of Antebellum Sugar Plantations in Louisiana.* New York: Arno Press, 1977.

Shugg, Roger W. *Origins of Class Struggle in Louisiana: A Social History of White Farmers and Laborers during Slavery and After, 1840–1875.* Baton Rouge: Louisiana State University Press, 1939.

Sitterson, J. Carlyle. *Sugar Country: The Cane Sugar Industry in the South, 1753–1950.* Lexington: University of Kentucky Press, 1953.

Soulé, Leon D. *The Know Nothing Party in New Orleans: A Reappraisal.* Baton Rouge: Louisiana State University Press, 1961.

Stahls, Paul F., Jr. *Plantation Homes of the Lafourche Country.* Gretna, La.: Pelican, 1976.

Stephenson, Wendell H. *Alexander Porter: Whig Planter of Old Louisiana.* LSU Studies No. 16. Baton Rouge: Louisiana State University, 1934.

Taylor, Joe Gray. *Louisiana Reconstructed, 1863–1877.* Baton Rouge: Louisiana State University Press, 1974.

————. *Negro Slavery in Louisiana.* Baton Rouge: Louisiana Historical Association, 1963.

Theriault, Léon. *La question du pouvoir en Acadie.* 2d ed. Moncton, N.B.: Editions d'Acadie, 1982.

Trelease, Allen W. *White Terror: The Ku Klux Klan Conspiracy and Southern Reconstruction.* New York: Harper & Row, 1971.

Tunnell, Ted. *Crucible of Reconstruction: War, Radicalism, and Race in Louisiana.* Baton Rouge: Louisiana State University Press, 1984.

Uzee, Philip D. *The Lafourche Country: The People and the Land.* Lafayette, La.: Center for Louisiana Studies, 1985.

Vernex, Jean-Claude. *Les Francophones du Nouveau-Brunswick: Geographie d'un groupe ethnoculturel minoritaire.* 2 vols. Paris: Librairie Honoré Champion, 1978.

Villeré, Sidney Louis. *Jacques Philippe Villeré: First Native-Born Governor of Louisiana, 1816–1820.* New Orleans: Historic New Orleans Collection, 1981.

Villiers du Terrage, Marc de. *Les dernières années de la Louisiane française.* Paris: Guilmoto, 1904.

Vincent, Charles. *Black Legislators in Louisiana during Reconstruction.* Baton Rouge: Louisiana State University Press, 1976.

Voorhies, Felix. *Acadian Reminiscences, with the True Story of Evengeline.* Opelousas, La.: Jacobs News Depot, 1907.

White, Howard A. *The Freedmen's Bureau in Louisiana.* Baton Rouge: Louisiana State University Press, 1970.

Winters, John D. *The Civil War in Louisiana.* Baton Rouge: Louisiana State University Press, 1963.

Winzerling, Oscar W. *Acadian Odyssey.* Baton Rouge: Louisiana State University Press, 1955.

ARTICLES

Amundson, Richard J. "Oakley Plantation: A Post–Civil War Venture in Louisiana Sugar." *Louisiana History* 9 (1968): 21–42.

Audisio, Gabriel. "Crisis in Baton Rouge, 1840–1860: Foreshadowing the Demise of Louisiana's French Language?" *Louisiana History* 29 (1988): 343–63.

Baker, Vaughan B. "Patterns of Acadian Slave Ownership in Lafayette Parish, 1850," *Attakapas Gazette* 9 (1974): 144–48.

Barry, A. David. "Biculturalism and Bilingualism: The Cajun Experience." In Jean Lafitte National Park, *The Cajuns: Their History and Culture.* 5 vols. in 13 parts. Opelousas, La.: Hamilton and Associates, 1987.

Begnaud, Allen. "The Louisiana Sugar Cane Industry: An Overview." In *Green Fields: Two Hundred Years of Louisiana Sugar,* pp. 29–50. Lafayette, La.: Center for Louisiana Studies, 1980.

Bergeron, Arthur W., Jr. "Prison Life at Camp Pratt." *Louisiana History* 14 (1973): 386–91.

Bodin, Ron. "The Cajun Woman as Unofficial Deacon of the Sacraments and Priest of the Sacramentals in Rural Louisiana, 1800–1930." *Attakapas Gazette* 25 (1990): 2–13.

Brasseaux, Carl A. "Acadian Village, Lafayette, Louisiana." *Gulf Coast Historical Review* 3 (1988): 62–65.

———. "Four Hundred Years of Acadian Life in North America." *Journal of Popular Culture* 23 (1989): 3–23.

———. "Ozémé Carrière and the St. Landry Jayhawkers." *Attakapas Gazette* 13 (1978): 185–89.

———. "Prosperity and the Free Population of Lafayette Parish, 1850–1860." *Attakapas Gazette* 12 (1977): 105–8.

———. "The Secession Movement in St. Landry Parish, 1860–1861." *Louisiana Review/Revue de Louisiane* 7 (1978): 129–54.

Brasseaux, Carl A., and Glenn R. Conrad. "Historical Research." In *Schematic Interpretive Plan, Longfellow-Evangeline State Commemorative Area: Analysis of Site and Existing Resources*, pp. 91–148. St. Martinville, La.: Al J. Landry and Associates, 1984.

Conrad, Glenn R. "Friend or Foe? Religious Exiles at the Opelousas Post in the American Revolution." *Attakapas Gazette* 12 (1977): 137–40.

Dauphine, James G. "The Knights of the White Camelia and the Election of 1868: Louisiana's White Terrorists, a Benighting Legacy." *Louisiana History* 30 (1989): 173–90.

DeLatte, Carolyn E. "The St. Landry Riot: A Forgotten Incident of Reconstruction Violence." *Louisiana History* 17 (1976): 41–49.

Dew, Charles B. "The Long Lost Returns: The Candidates and Their Totals in Louisiana's Secession Election." *Louisiana History* 10 (1969): 360–69.

Dupont, Albert Léonce. "The Career of Paul Octave Hébert, Governor of Louisiana, 1853–1856." *Louisiana Historical Quarterly* 31 (1948): 505–14.

Estaville, Lawrence E., Jr. "Changeless Cajuns: Nineteenth-Century Reality or Myth?" *Louisiana History* 28 (1987): 117–40.

———. "The Louisiana French in 1900." *Journal of Historical Geography* 14 (1988): 342–59.

———. "The Louisiana French Language in the Nineteenth Century." *Southeastern Geographer* 30 (1990): 107–20.

———. "Mapping the Cajuns." *Southern Studies* 25 (1986): 163–71.

———. "Mapping the Louisiana French." *Southeastern Geographer* 26 (1986): 90–113.

———. "Were the Nineteenth-Century Cajuns Geographically Isolated?" *Geoscience and Man* 25 (1988): 85–96.

Finch, L. Boyd. "Surprise at Brashear City: Sherod Hunter's Sugar Cooler Cavalry." *Louisiana History* 25 (1984): 403–34.

Fitts, James Franklin. "The Yankee Officer and the Partisan." *Ballou's Monthly Magazine,* July 1869, p. 54.

Foret, Michael James. "Raising Cattle in the Attakapas, 1860–1883: Testimony from the French and American Claims Commission." *Attakapas Gazette* 20 (1985): 89–96.

Highsmith, William E. "Some Aspects of Reconstruction in the Heart of Louisiana." *Journal of Southern History* 13 (1947): 460–91.

Hilliard, Sam Bowers. "Site Characteristics and Spatial Stability of the Louisiana Sugarcane Industry." *Agricultural History* 53 (1979): 254–67.

Kniffen, Fred B. "The Outdoor Oven in Louisiana." *Louisiana History* 1 (1960): 25–35.

Lack, Paul D. "Slavery and Vigilantism in Austin, Texas, 1840–1860." *Southwestern Historical Quarterly* 85 (July 1981): 1–20.

Lestage, H. Oscar, Jr. "The White League in Louisiana and Its Participation in Reconstruction." *Louisiana Historical Quarterly* 18 (1935): 617–95.

McDonald, Forrest, and Grady McWhiney. "The South from Self-Sufficiency to Peonage: An Interpretation." *American Historical Review* 85 (1980): 1095–1118.

McGimsey, Richard. "Police and Slave Patrol Regulations, 1823–1857." *Attakapas Gazette* 10 (1975): 146–52.

Newton, Lewis W. "Creoles and Anglo-Americans in Old Louisiana: A Study in Cultural Conflicts." *Southwestern Social Science Quarterly* 14 (1933): 31–48.

Oubre, Claude F. "The Opelousas Riot of 1868." *Attakapas Gazette* 8 (1973): 139–52.

———. "St. Landry's *Gens de Couleur Libre:* The Impact of War and Reconstruction." In Vaughan B. Baker and Jean T. Kreamer, eds., *Louisiana Tapestry: The Ethnic Weave of St. Landry Parish.* Lafayette, La.: Center for Louisiana Studies, 1982.

Oubre, Claude, and Roscoe Leonard. "Free and Proud: St. Landry's *Gens de Couleur.*" In Vaughan B. Baker and Jean T. Kreamer, eds., *Louisiana Tapestry: The Ethnic Weave of St. Landry Parish.* Lafayette, La.: Center for Louisiana Studies, 1982.

Ownby, Ted. "The Defeated Generation at Work: White Farmers in the Deep South, 1865–1890." *Southern Studies* 23 (1984): 325–47.

Pecquet, Gary M. "Public Finance in Confederate Louisiana." *Louisiana History* 29 (1988): 253–97.

Prichard, Walter. "The Effects of the Civil War on the Louisiana Sugar Industry." *Journal of Southern History* 5 (1939): 315–32.

Reilly, Timothy F. "Early Acadiana through Anglo-American Eyes." *Attakapas Gazette* 12 (1977): 3–20, 159–76, 185–94; 13 (1978): 53–71.

Schlomowitz, Ralph. "The Origins of Southern Sharecropping." *Agricultural History* 53 (1979): 557–75.

Schmitz, Mark. "The Transformation of the Southern Cane Sugar Sector, 1860–1930." *Agricultural History* 53 (1979): 270–85.

Shea, Suzy, and Gertrude Taylor. "A Man for the People: Alcibiades DeBlanc and the St. Martinville Insurrection of 1873." *Attakapas Gazette* 14 (1979): 3–10.

Shugg, Roger W. "Suffrage and Representation in Ante-Bellum Louisiana." *Louisiana Historical Quarterly* 19 (1936): 390–406.

Taylor, H. C. "Historical Aspects of Agricultural Adjustment: The Historical Approach to the Economic Problems of Agriculture." *Agricultural History* 11 (1937): 221–51.

Thomas, Daniel H. "Pre-Whitney Cotton Gins in French Louisiana." *Journal of Southern History* 31 (1965): 135–48.

Tregle, Joseph G., Jr. "Early New Orleans Society: A Reappraisal." *Journal of Southern History* 18 (1952): 20–36.

———. "Henry S. Thibodaux." In Joseph G. Dawson III, *The Louisiana Governors: From Iberville to Edwards,* pp. 96–98. Baton Rouge: Louisiana State University Press, 1990.

Wade, Michael G. "Justice Delayed: *Appoline Patout* v. *the United States.*" *Louisiana History* 31 (1990): 141–59.

Weiland, Iona. "Typical Household: Lafayette Parish, 1825–1835." *Attakapas Gazette* 9 (1974): 3–8.

Wells, O. V. "The Depression of 1873–79." *Agricultural History* 11 (1937): 237–49.

THESES AND DISSERTATIONS

Brasseaux, Carl A. "The Founding of New Acadia: Reconstruction and Transformation of Acadian Society in Louisiana." 2 vols. Ph.D. dissertation, University of Paris, 1982.

Carrière, Marius M., Jr. "The Know-Nothing Movement in Louisiana." Ph.D. dissertation, Louisiana State University, 1977.

Dauphine, James G. "The Knights of the White Camelia in Louisiana, 1867 to 1869." M.A. thesis, University of Southwestern Louisiana, 1983.

Guilbeau, John J. "The French Spoken in Lafourche Parish, Louisiana." Ph.D. dissertation, University of North Carolina at Chapel Hill, 1950.

Highsmith, William E. "Social and Economic Conditions in Rapides Parish during Reconstruction." M.A. thesis, Louisiana State University, 1947.

Leistner, Colette Guidry. "French and Acadian Influences upon the Cajun Cuisine of Southwest Louisiana." M.A. thesis, University of Southwestern Louisiana, 1986.

McTigue, Geraldine Mary. "Forms of Racial Interaction in Louisiana, 1860–1880." Ph.D. dissertation, Yale University, 1975.

Tregle, Joseph G., Jr. "Louisiana in the Age of Jackson." Ph.D. dissertation, University of Pennsylvania, 1954.

Watkins, Marguerite. "History of Terrebonne Parish to 1861." M.A. thesis, Louisiana State University, 1939.

Wetta, Frank Joseph. "The Louisiana Scalawags." Ph.D. dissertation, Louisiana State University, 1977.

Index

Abbeville, La., 30, 33, 70, 144, 170
Abshire family, exogamy in, 106
Abshire, Leufroy, 176
Acadia Parish, 16, 66
Acadia, pre-dispersal, 4, 46
Acadian Coast, 46, 47, 80, 81, 95, 97, 103, 135
Acadian Village, 27
Acadians, Anglo-Americans and, 8–10, 38, 41, 44, 47, 49, 56, 65, 69, 92–105, 108–11, 169
Acadians, anticlericalism of, 33–37; antivigilantes among, 56, 122–23; architectural styles of, 9, 18, 26–28; artisans among, 9, 103; assimilation of other groups by, 43, 151–52; attitude toward outsiders, 21; Civil War's impact on, 58–73; communal harvests by, 22; Confederate army and the, 61–67, 71–73, 76; confused with Creoles, 101–02, 104, 110; conscription and, 58, 63–67, 71–73, 127; consumption of alcoholic beverages by, 22; corn production by, 17; costume of, 24–25, 42; cotton production by, 6, 15, 18,

77, 79, 82, 83, 87; courtship among, 39; Creoles and, 4, 8–10, 13, 38, 43–45, 50, 56, 59, 92, 94–97, 99, 104–06, 108–09, 120, 128, 151; crops grown by, 12, 13; cuisine of, 22–24, 29; cultural transformation of, 89–112; day laborers among, 12, 18, 82, 86; demographic movements of, 11–13; diet of, 12, 13, 17, 22–24, 41, 85; during Reconstruction, 74–112, 127–49; economic classes in, 3–19; egalitarianism of, 4; elite among, 8, 50, 51, 53–57, 59–62, 72, 73, 80–81, 91, 95, 96, 98–99, 153; endogamy among, 38–39; English and French language usage by, 89–112; exogamy among, 38–39, 105–06, 109, 169; female roles among, 42–43; folk beliefs of, 31; folk life of, 20–44; folk medicine, 31–32; footwear of, 25, 26; Freemasons among, 34, 36, 37; funerary traditions, 40; gambling among, 28; hog production by, 17; holidays of, 31; horse racing and, 30; horses raised by,

243

Acadians, (*continued*)
17; house dances (*bals de maison*), 28–30, 39, 129; hunting and, 21, 22, 85; illiteracy among, 95; Jay-hawkers and, 66, 71, 72, 76, 115, 124–28, 131, 132; large families among, 13; male roles among, 42; music of, 22, 28, 29; naming prac-tices among, 108, 172; *petits habi-tants* among, 10, 11, 20–22, 29, 31, 40, 41, 50, 57, 59, 104–05; planters, 8; political officeholders among, 45, 47–53, 152; politics of, 45–57; postbellum economic crisis, 74–88; ranching by, 12, 13, 15–18, 21, 22, 41, 55, 59, 68, 82, 84; religious beliefs of, 31–32, 37–38; rice production by, 16; Second Expulsion of, 11; share-croppers among, 83, 84, 151; slav-ery and, 4, 5, 7, 10, 15, 17, 54, 55, 57, 60, 61, 73, 75, 77, 131, 133; social classes in, 3–19; stereo-types, 3, 99–105; sugar produc-tion by, 6–8, 10, 14, 15, 50, 54, 76, 77, 82, 83, 99, 103; swamp-related activities and the, 14; tex-tiles of, 24–25, 42; urban, 107, 108, 170; urban occupations of, 171; values of, 4–5, 17, 18, 21, 40, 41, 58, 82; vigilantes among, 55–57, 63, 113–24, 130, 136–44, 173, 175–79; violence among, 30, 112–49; wartime property losses, 68–69
Alexandria Caucasian, 143, 144
Alexandria, La., 72
American (Know-Nothing) Party, 53, 99
Andrews, Hiram, 174
Anglo-Americans, 8–10, 38, 41, 44, 47, 49, 56, 65, 69, 92–105, 108–11, 169
Anse Charpentier, 15
Anse Lyon, 173

Anse-la-Butte, 118, 121, 173
Anti-vigilantes, 56
Architecture, 9
Armentor, Manuel de, 176
Ascension Parish, 6, 8, 10, 12, 13, 47, 48, 50, 52, 53, 55, 62, 72, 73, 82, 155–56, 158–68, 180–82
Assumption Parish, 5–8, 10, 12–14, 28, 49, 50, 82, 128, 131, 155, 158–68, 180–82
Atchafalaya Basin, 6, 14, 21, 49, 65, 73, 78, 93, 151
Atchafalaya River, 7, 8, 10, 11, 14, 40, 62, 82, 107, 151
Attakapas district, 11, 46, 92, 110, 117, 123, 130
Attakapas Prairie, 70
Attakapas Register, 139
Audisio, Gabriel, 93
Avoyelles Parish, 107, 110, 111, 118

Back Country Regulators, 113
Baltimore, Md., 59
Banks, Nathaniel P., 65–67
Barde, Alexandre, 26, 117, 122
Barras family, exogamy in, 106
Bartlett, Napier, 62
Baton Rouge Gazette, 94, 95
Baton Rouge, La., 61, 78, 87, 93, 107, 135, 170,
Baton Rouge (La.) *Advocate,* 123
Battle of Bisland, 65
Battle of Irish Bend, 65
Battle of Labadieville, 64–65
Battle of Liberty Place, 146
Battle of New Orleans (1815), 49
Battle of Pleasant Hill, 70
Battle of Shiloh, 64
Battle of the Cabildo, 143
Bayou Black, 12, 13
Bayou Blue, 13
Bayou Boeuf, 73
Bayou Chemise, 73
Bayou Du Large, 13
Bayou Lafourche, 4, 5, 7–9, 12, 46,

48, 50, 54, 61, 64, 65, 70, 73, 82,
  107, 110, 115, 131, 136, 146, 151
Bayou Little Caillou, 13
Bayou Little Terrebonne, 13
Bayou Mallet, 66
Bayou Queue de Tortue, 16, 56,
  120, 121
Bayou Rapides, 72
Bayou Teche, 4–9, 15, 23, 33, 48–
  51, 53, 54, 57, 64, 65, 67, 78, 83,
  110, 126, 136, 148
Bayou Terrebonne, 7, 13, 48, 49
Beaubassin area, 183–84
Beauprez, Francis P., 34
Begnaud family, 39
Bentley, Emerson, 139
Beraud, Desire, 174
Bergeron, Pierre, 176
Bernard, Alexandre, 116, 174
Bernard, Felix, 47
Bernard, Gerassin, 119, 174
Bernard, Tréville, 174
Bernard, L. F. Tréville, 174
Bertrand, Octave, 174
Billaut, Martial, 174
Billon, Joseph, 34
Black Codes, 133, 134
Blacks, 4, 5, 7, 10, 15, 17, 54, 55, 57,
  60, 61, 73, 75, 77, 78, 85, 131,
  132, 134–47; demographic im-
  pact of, 131, 180; denigration of
  Cajuns by, 101
Blakewood, B. W., 62
Blanc, Antoine, 36
Bodin, Ron, 37
Bois Mallet area, 57, 123, 126
Bond, Priscilla M., 70
Boucheries, 24, 28, 43
Boudreaux, 69
Boudreaux, A. D., 118, 174, 183
Boudreaux, Clerville, 176
Boudreaux, Omar, 73
Boussillage, 18, 26–27
Braux, Donat, 174
Braux, Oscar, 176

Breaux Bridge, La., 15, 33, 65, 69,
  73, 121, 144, 146, 170, 173
Breaux, Joseph A., 25, 60, 62, 152
Breaux, Pierre R., 119
Breaux, Valéry, 118, 174, 183
Breckinridge, John C., 60
Bringier, Louis Amédée, 70–72,
  216
Brogard, J. N., 93, 96
Broussard, Don Louis F. J., 119
Broussard, Don Louis, 116, 174
Broussard, Edwin, 152
Broussard, Jean B., 174
Broussard, La., 110
Broussard, Marcel, 183
Broussard, Neuville, 183
Broussard, Robert, 152
Broussard, Sarrazan, 95, 174
Broussard, Thertule, 176
Broussard, Valsin, 116, 174
Brown, Richard Maxwell, 113, 116
Bruslée St. Martin, La., 128
Brusly, La., 34
Burleigh family, 39
Bush, Louis, 70, 126
Bush, Marie Clarisse, 97

Cable, George Washington, 104,
  105, 112, 115, 129
Cajuns: Anglos vilify, 99–105;
  blacks vilify, 101; creation of cultural group, 89–111; definition
  of, 105, 150; relations with blacks,
  4, 5, 7, 10, 15, 17, 54, 55, 57, 60,
  61, 73, 75, 77, 78, 85, 131, 132,
  134–47; vilify Anglos, 104. *See
  also* Acadians
Calcasieu Parish, 6, 13, 16–18, 41,
  51, 60, 83, 84, 93, 117, 121, 137,
  141, 155, 158–68, 173, 180–82
Calcasieu River, 66
California, 101
Cameron Parish, 84, 93, 180–82
Camp Pratt, 63–65
Camp Vicocq, 133

Cantrelle family, 152
Carencro, La., 173, 183–84
Carrière, Ozémé, 66, 124–26
Caruthers family, exogamy in, 106
Caruthers, John, 183
Cecilia, La., 15
Charleston, S.C., 59, 61
Chauvin family, 152
Cheevers, John A., 129
Chiasson, Jean-Baptiste, 120, 121
Choate family, exogamy in, 106
Church Point, La., 33, 125. *See also*
   Plaquemine Brulée
Civil War, 26, 29, 36, 37, 58–73
Claiborne, William Charles Cole,
   47, 98
Clark family, exogamy in, 106
Claus, George, 176
Coco family, 118
Comeau, 183
Comeau, Adolphe, 174
Comeau, Charles Duclize, 116,
   174
Commandants, 46
Confederate Conscription Act, 63
Conrad, Glenn R., 75
Conway, Thomas, 136
Cormier, L. A., 62
Cormier, L. E., 62
Côte Gelée (present-day Broussard,
   La.), 55, 116, 117, 119, 121, 173–
   75, 183, 184
Credeur family, exogamy in, 106
Creighton, J. R., 183
Creighton, John, 183
Creole ponies, 17, 30, 65, 67
Creoles: definition of, 4; relations
   with Acadians, 4, 8–10, 13, 38,
   44, 45, 50, 56, 59, 92, 94, 95, 97,
   99, 105–06, 108–09, 120, 128,
   151, 169
Crosby, J. Schuyler, 69
Cypress Island region, 118, 120,
   121, 130

Daigle, Pierre, 73
Daniels, R. L., 104, 136
Davis, Jefferson, 71
DeBlanc, Alcibiades, 137, 138, 145,
   146
DeClouet, Alexandre, 49, 60
Dejean, Felix, 125
Delegos, Pierre A., 6
Democratic Party, 49–55, 57, 59, 94,
   99, 134, 135, 138–42, 147, 148
Dennett, Daniel, 82
Derosier, Charles, 127
DeRudio, Charles C., 147
Dezauche, M., 132–33
Domengeaux, Louis, 174
Domengeaux family, 39
Domingue family, exogamy in, 106
Donaldsonville, La., 99, 170
Donaldsonville Artillery Battery, 62
Doucet, Pierre Z., 119, 174
Douglas, Stephen A., 59, 60
Dubois family, exogamy in, 106
Dubourg, Louis-Guillaume-Valentin,
   36
Dugas, Joachim, 183
Dugat, Jules, 118, 174
Dugat, Rosemond, 174
Duperier, Alfred, 26
Dupré, Lucius J., 60
Dupuy, Adolphe, 54, 57
Dupuy, Hélène, 73
Dupuy, V. J., 57
Durand, 139

East Baton Rouge Parish, 6, 180,
   182
Eastin, Hazard, 174
Eclaireurs Indépendants du Bayou
   Mallet, 126
Eighteenth Louisiana Infantry, 64,
   67, 71, 72
Enforcement Acts of 1870 and 1871,
   142
Estaville, Lawrence, 137

Eunice, La., 151
Evangeline Parish, 110, 111, 151

Faquetaique area, 57, 123, 173
Farm Securities Administration, 75
Faul family, exogamy in, 106
Fausse Pointe area, 49, 119, 173
First Louisiana Cavalry (Union), 73
Floods, 78, 79
Fontenot, Paul, 130
Foreman, Asa, 174
Fort Pitt, 92
Fort Sumter, 61
Fortier, Alcée, 21, 29, 32
Forty-second Ohio Infantry, 69
Fournet, V. A., 64, 65
Fourth Louisiana Cavalry Regiment, 70, 71, 126
Franchebois, Napoleon, 127
François family, exogamy in, 106
Franklin, La., 70, 137
Franklin (La.) *Planters' Banner*, 122, 137
Franklin, William B., 68, 69, 126
Free Persons of Color, 55, 123–25, 128, 131, 176–78
Freedmen's Bureau, 136, 140
French immigrants ("Foreign French"), 38, 95, 105, 110, 169
Fusionist ticket, 142

Galaxy Magazine, 100
Gardner, Emma Kitchell, 96
Gaudet, J. K., 60
Georgetown University, 96
German Coast, 46, 48
Godeau, Don Louis, 126
Grand Coteau, La., 33, 51, 170
Grande Pointe area, 15, 121, 173
Grant, Ulysses S., 141, 143, 144, 147
Gray, Henry, 67
Great Texas Overland Expedition, 66
Green, Thomas, 66

Grivot, Maurice, 122
Gros Chevreuil area, 57, 123
Gudbeer, August, 117, 177
Guerillas, 73
Guidry *dit* Canada, Olivier, 119, 121–22, 177
Guidry, Alexandre, 16
Guidry, Alexis O., 53
Guidry, D., 116, 174
Guidry, Edmond, 70
Guidry, Eloi, 116, 174
Guidry, Geneus, 122
Guidry, Joseph V., 174
Guidry, Joseph, 174
Guidry, Lessin, 174
Guidry, T. P., 125
Guidry, Treville, 174
Guidry family, exogamy in, 105
Guilbeau, P. D., 183
Guilbeaux, Edmond, 118, 174
Guilbeaux, Lucien, 174
Guilbeaux, Placide, 119, 175
Guillory, Martin, 126, 127

Haiti, 124
Hamilton, Alexander, 48
Harding, George C., 63, 64
Harris, Georga A., 98
Haydel family, 152
Hayes, Bosman, 126
Herpin, Aladin, 177
Herpin, Dolzin, 177
Herpin, Valsin, 177
Herpin family, exogamy in, 106
Hébert, Amant, 97
Hébert, C. O., 57
Hébert, Charles, 183
Hébert, Desire, 175
Hébert, Dosité, 183
Hébert, Isaac, 47
Hébert, Louis, 62, 97, 98
Hébert, Paul Octave, 53, 59
Hébert, Pierre, 73
Hébert, Valéry, 97

Himel family, 152
Hoffman, Wickman, 69
Houma, La., 170
Huin, Tiburse, 119, 177
Hulin family, 39
Hyatt, W. W., 67
Hymel family, 39

Iberia Parish, 146, 180–82
Iberville Parish, 6–8, 13, 14, 48, 55, 57, 61, 81, 87, 131, 142, 155–56, 158–68, 180–82
Irwin, Richard, 68
Isle des Cannes, 183

Jackson, Andrew, 49
Jacquemoud family, exogamy in, 106
Jan, Ange-Marie-Felix, 33
Jay Cooke & Co., 86
Jayhawkers, 66, 71, 72, 76, 124–28, 131, 132
Jeanerette, La., 29, 173
Jeansonne, Terence, 125
Jefferson Parish, 107, 172
Johnson family, exogamy in, 106
Johnson, Isaac, 51
Judice, Alcée, 175
Judice, Desire, 175

Kellogg, William Pitt, 143–46
Kidder family, exogamy in, 106
Knights of the White Camelia, 136–41
Ku Klux Klan, 136, 137

La Pointe. *See* Breaux Bridge
Lac Simonet, 173
Lachausée, Raphael, 116, 175
Lacouture, Jean, 177
Lafayette Parish, 6–9, 11, 13–16, 41, 49, 52, 53, 55, 60, 69, 80, 92, 116, 117, 119–21, 131, 136–38, 140, 141, 144, 145, 155, 158–68, 173, 180–84

Lafourche District, 5, 47
Lafourche Parish, 5–7, 12, 13, 23, 28, 48–50, 52, 53, 57, 82, 132, 133, 155, 158–68, 180–82
Lagrange, Emilien, 56, 120–22
Lamphier, C. Michael, 90, 91
Landry, Aristide, 50
Landry, Camille, 57
Landry, Catoir, 128, 129
Landry, Charles, 128
Landry, Desire, 119, 175
Landry, Emile, 177
Landry, J. O., 62
Landry, Joseph, 47, 48
Landry, Norbert, 183
Landry, Philippe, 72
Landry, Trasimond, 53, 54, 57
Latiolais, Alexandre, 119, 175
Laussat, Pierre-Clement, 46
Lauve, Justice, 129
Lawton, J. B., 41
LeBlanc, Andre, 50
LeBlanc, Dudley J., 3
Lebleu de Comarsac, 175
Lieberson, Stanley, 91
Lincoln, Abraham, 60, 61
Litwack, Leon, 133
Livingston Parish, 107
Lockett, Samuel, 110
Loreauville, La., 15
Louisiana Bureau of Immigration, 85
Louisiana Purchase, 92, 98
Louisiana, forced heirship laws of, 11, 16
Louisiana, state constitution of 1812, 51, 97
Louisiana, state constitution of 1845, 52, 53, 57
Louisiana Supreme Court, 36, 152
Louviere family, exogamy in, 106
Lynchings, 56, 130

Maggy, Capt., 175
Marie the Pole, 177

Marksville, La., 173
Martel, B. A., 126
Martin, Andre Valerien, 118, 175
Martin, Charles Z., 119
Maryland, 5
Mason, F. H., 69
Maux, Aurelien, 177
Maux, Dosithée, 177
McDonald, Forrest, 84
McEnery, John, 142–45
McWhiney, Grady, 84
Megret, Antoine D., 35–36
Melançon, Edmond L., 60
Menn, Karl Joseph, 7
Mermentau River, 17
Mexico, 124
Miller family, exogamy in, 106
Mire, La., 56
Mississippi River, 4–9, 11, 48, 76, 78, 82
Montell, William Lynwood, 149
Moore, Thomas O., 60
Morell, H. C., 125
Morrell, W. C., 70
Morris, Raymond N., 90, 91
Mouton, A. E., 49, 175
Mouton, Alc., 175
Mouton, Alexandre, 15, 38, 49, 51, 52, 54, 57, 59, 60, 62, 72, 94, 96, 118, 119, 121–23, 175
Mouton, Charles Homer, 53, 54, 57, 138, 145
Mouton, Charles Z., 175
Mouton, Ignace, 118, 175
Mourton, J. E., 183
Mouton, Jean, 96
Mouton, Jean-Jacques Alexandre Alfred, 56, 62–64, 71, 72, 96, 97, 119, 121, 175
Mouton, William, 98, 138
Mouton family, exogamy in, 105
Murr, Auguste, 118, 175

New Brunswick, 91
New England, 48

New Iberia, La., 33, 170
New Orleans, La., 6, 17, 36, 46, 63, 79, 86, 87, 107, 108, 110, 117, 139, 140, 145–48
New York, N.Y., 23, 86, 87
Nicholls, Francis T., 147, 148
Nineteenth Army Corps, 68
Northern Pacific Railroad, 86
Nunez, Numa, 175

Olmsted, Frederick Law, 23, 84, 103
Opelousas, La., 63, 124, 125, 127, 133, 134, 139, 140, 144, 170
Opelousas (La.) *Courier*, 56, 57, 122–24, 127, 130, 133
Opelousas, La., district, 11, 92, 110
Ord, Edward, 67
Orleans Parish, 172
Our Lady of the Sacred Heart Catholic Church, 33

Packard, Stephen B., 147
Paillet, 139
Paincourtville, La., 128, 129
Panic of 1873, 83, 86
Parks, La., 15
Patin, C. T., 183
Patin, Dupré, 175
Payne, James A., 76, 135
Penn, D. B., 142
Perry, Robert, 70
Petite Anse, 15
Peyretti, Lawrence, 34
Pierre Part, La., 12, 14, 109
Pitre family, exogamy in, 106
Plaquemine Brulée area, 51, 57, 123, 124, 126, 127, 130. *See also* Church Point
Plaquemine Iberville South, 80, 97
Plaquemine Ridge, 125
Plaquemine, La., 152, 170
Plaquemines Parish, 107, 108, 172
Poché, Felix Pierre, 72
Poe, Edgar Allan, 101
Pointe Coupée Parish, 107, 108, 172

Pont Breaux. *See* Breaux Bridge
Pont Perry, 173
Prairie Mamou, 125
Prairie Robert, 173
Pratt, John G., 63
Prévost, Paul, 175
Primo, Euclide, 177
Primo, Hervilien, 177
Primo family, 177
Pugh, W. W., 28
Pulaski, Tenn., 136

Quatrevingt family, 39, 152
Quebec, Canada, 91
Quebecois, 90–91

Ramasserie, 22
Red River, 70, 78
Reed, Thomas, 178
Renaissance Louisianaise, 132
Republican Party, 130, 135, 136,
    138–43, 146
Rhoads, Albert, 100, 103
Rice, Oscar A., 140
Richmond, Va., 73
Rigues, John, 119, 175
Robichaud, Jean, 33
Romero, Bernard, 178
Romero, Pierre, 119
Rouly, Maximin, 178
Rousseau, Zelia, 96
Royville, La., 183

Saint Bernard Catholic Church,
    33
Saint Bernard Parish, 107
Saint Charles Catholic Church, 33
Saint Charles Parish, 39, 46, 107,
    108, 172
Saint James Parish, 6, 12, 13, 48, 50,
    60, 72, 82, 92, 99, 109, 142, 155–
    56, 158–68, 172, 180–82
Saint John the Baptist Catholic
    Church, 34

Saint John the Baptist Parish, 39, 46,
    107, 108, 172
Saint John the Evangelist Catholic
    Church, 33–37
Saint Joseph Catholic Church, 93,
    94
Saint Julien, Aurelien, 175
Saint Julien, J. G., 183
Saint Julien, Paul-Leon, 175
Saint Landry Parish, 7, 11, 13–17,
    23, 41, 49–53, 56, 60, 66, 69, 70,
    82, 92, 99, 109, 110, 117–19,
    121–23, 126–28, 130, 133, 134,
    136–39, 141, 144, 155, 158–68,
    172, 180–82
Saint Landry Progress, 139
Saint Martin de Tours Catholic
    Church, 33
Saint Martin Parish, 6, 13–16, 41,
    49, 51, 53, 54, 60, 73, 92, 99, 109,
    117–19, 130, 136–38, 141, 142,
    145, 146, 155, 158–68, 172, 180–
    82
Saint Martinville, La., 33, 36, 49,
    119, 121, 137, 145, 146, 170,
    173
Saint Mary Magdalen Catholic
    Church, 30, 33
Saint Mary Parish, 6, 7, 12–15, 92,
    129, 138, 140, 155, 158–68, 180–
    82
Saint Peter's Catholic Church, 33
Saint-Domingue refugees, 93
San Francisco, Calif., 115, 117
Santa-Maria de la Plata, 178
Saunier, Sylvin, 127
Savoie, Louis, 175
Savoie, Théodule, 128
Savoy, François, 125
Schermerhorn, Richard Alonzo, 89–
    90
Schuyler, Philip, 48
Scotland, 48
Scott, La., 56, 110, 122
Scribner's magazine, 136

Seventy-fifth Regiment (U.S.), 133
Seymour, Horatio, 141
Seymour Knights, 138, 140
Sibley, H. H., 65
Simon, Edouard, 96
Sindics, 45
Sitterson, J. Carlyle, 85
Sixth Louisiana Infantry, 62
Sixth Militia Regiment, 47
Slavery, 4, 5, 7, 10, 15, 17, 54, 55, 57, 60, 61, 73, 75, 77, 131, 133
Slavery: slave regulations, 55; slave revolts, 55
Society of Mutual Protection, 116, 118
Society of the Ladies of Benevolence, 34
Spanish Lake, 63
Sparks, W. H., 150
Stanton, Capt., 175
Stone, Charles P., 67, 126
Sunset, La., 110
Swamps, 14

Tax Resisting Association, 144
Taylor, Joe Gray, 75, 82, 143, 144
Taylor, Richard, 64–66, 70, 124, 126
Terrebonne Parish, 6, 11–13, 21, 49, 50, 52, 53, 57, 82, 142, 155, 158–68, 172, 180–82
Texas, 93, 101, 117, 120, 150
Theall family, exogamy in, 106
Theriot, A., 94
Theriot, Euzelieu, 128, 129
Theriot, Hypolite, 129
Theriot, Nichols, 129
Thibodaux, Henry Schuyler, 48
Thibodaux, La., 83, 99, 152, 170
Thibodaux (La.) *Sentinel*, 83, 128
Thibodeaux, Elise, 68
Thibodeaux, Narcisse, 69
Tixier, Victor, 95
Traiteurs, 31–32

Tunnell, Ted, 140
Turner, Nat, 54
Twenty-eighth Louisiana Infantry, 62
Twenty-ninth Wisconsin Volunteer Infantry Regiment, 68

United States Military Academy (West Point), 56, 96, 97, 121
United States Senate, 51

Veillon, James, 127
Venable family, exogamy in, 106
Vermilion Parish, 6, 13, 15–18, 41, 49, 53, 60, 82, 84, 92, 95, 109, 117–19, 121, 125, 136–38, 140, 141, 155, 158–68, 173, 180–82
Vermilion River, 7, 9, 15, 16, 66, 68, 110
Vermilionville (present-day Lafayette, La.), 33–36, 57, 67, 69, 72, 82, 107, 116, 118, 120, 121, 123, 146, 152, 170, 173, 183
Verret family, 39, 152
Vicksburg, Miss., 72
Vienna, Austria, 86
Vigilantes, 55–57, 63, 113–24, 130, 136–44, 173, 175–79
Villeré, Jacques, 48
Virginia, 92
Vital, Aristide, 178
Voorhies, Alfred, 175

Wagner, Dr., 120
Walker, L. P., 62
War of 1812, 6
Ward, Clarence, 80
Warmoth, Henry Clay, 141, 142
Washington, D. C., 147, 170
Washington, La., 57, 123, 127
Waud, A. R., 101–03
Weitzel, Godefrey, 64
West Baton Rouge Parish, 6–8, 13, 34, 48, 49, 55, 57, 81, 99, 155–56, 158–68, 172, 180–82

Whig Party, 49–50, 52, 53, 99
Whipple, Henry P., 68
White League, 136, 144–48, 183, 184
Wickliffe, Robert C., 56, 57, 119, 122, 123

Williams, John, 178
World War II, 75

Yellow Jacket Battalion, 64–67
Young, Joseph B., 127
Young, Madison, 125